Winning in Court
on the
Law of Facts

Winning in
Court on the
Law of

FACTS

William Farnum White

Prentice-Hall, Inc.
Englewood Cliffs, N. J.

Prentice-Hall International, Inc., *London*
Prentice-Hall of Australia, Pty. Ltd., *Sydney*
Prentice-Hall of Canada, Ltd., *Toronto*
Prentice-Hall of India Private Ltd., *New Delhi*
Prentice-Hall of Japan, Inc., *Tokyo*

LIBRARY OF CONGRESS
CATALOG CARD NUMBER: 74–37403

This publication is designed to provide accurate and authoritative information with regard to the subject matter covered. It is sold with the understanding that the publisher is not engaged in rendering legal, accounting, or other professional advice. If legal advice or other expert assistance is required, the services of a competent professional person should be sought.

—From a Declaration of Principles jointly adopted by a Committee of the American Bar Association and a Committee of Publishers and Associations.

PRINTED IN THE UNITED STATES OF AMERICA
ISBN—0-13-960856-7
B&P

Dedicated to

my patient and able partners of
White, Sutherland, Brownstein & Parks,
Portland, Oregon

Acknowledgements

Special thanks for valuable suggestions and comments are due to Hon. Kenneth J. O'Connell, Chief Justice of the Supreme Court of the State of Oregon, who read the chapters on circumstantial evidence, and to Hon. Gus J. Solomon, Senior Judge of the United States District Court for the District of Oregon, who reviewed the chapter on making meaningful findings of fact.

It was the author's participation in SCRIBES, national organization of writers on legal subjects, that got him going on this effort and the work and competence of his secretary, Mrs. Jane Zinda, which not only kept him going, but also enabled him to write and practice law at the same time. Son Craig handled the tedious job of checking citations. Again, my thanks.

Foreword

Prefaces of late are but panegyrics. However, *Winning in Court on the Law of Facts* needs no encomium. Its accurate and concise summing up of those principles of law which serve to test the sufficiency of proof speaks for itself. Its subject necessarily is precedency, and its target the Bar and the Judges who, respectively, germinate and develop the precedents of the law. The author is well and favorably known through his thirty-six years of active trial practice in the state and federal courts located in California and Oregon. His success at the trial bar is higher praise for his work than anything which is said here.

The author says that he was inspired to write *Winning in Court on the Law of Facts* by Chief Justice Burger's address at the A.B.A. Convention Prayer Breakfast in St. Louis in 1969. It was there that the Chief Justice said, *inter alia,* that "in the trial courts the facts are often 'the whole ball game'." Nothing has more truth and, in saying so with such persuasion, the Chief Justice influenced the writing of a book profoundly needed by lawyers, judges and administrative agencies.

Before undertaking my assignment to the United States District Court for the Northern District of California (San Francisco), I decided to do some "refreshing" on trial techniques. I turned to the State Trial Judges Book written by a distinguished group of judges in 1969. But it devoted only twenty-one lines of its four hundred and five pages to a consideration of Findings of Fact and Conclusions of Law. An excerpt read: "Nothing tests the soundness of a judge's decision so much as the process of preparing his own findings and conclusions in the case." And, I add what every judge knows—that nothing is more correct. Having learned nothing from the Judges

7

Book, I requested the library to send me any books available on findings of fact, conclusions of law, the sufficiency of evidence, etc. They reported that there were no works in print, other than on jury instructions. Over half of the cases I heard were non-jury ones, and I was obliged to prepare findings of fact and conclusions of law. While counsel very obligingly filed suggested ones, I found them insufficient. To understand the enormity of the task involved in drafting findings of fact and conclusions of law in protracted anti-trust cases, one has to do it himself. *Winning in Court on the Law of Facts* would have been most helpful to me. While Mr. Justice Holmes found that "judges may ascertain them [facts] in any way which satisfied their conscience," The Common Law, 151, my experience on the trial court teaches me to the contrary: indeed, even on Circuit I found lawyers combing the record with a fine tooth comb in search of errors in the factual statements of my opinion. However on the Supreme Court the Holmes rule of conscience might be apropos. Perhaps the finality of that Court's decisions may well occasion this.

Fact finding is not a mathematical exercise, but in the law many things must be learned as facts. As Mr. Justice Cardozo used to say: "They are the coin we must have . . . to pay our way." The Growth of the Law, 98.

The dozen chapters of *Winning in Court on the Law of Facts* cover every facet of the problem, including Judicial Review of Findings of Administrative Agencies and Appellate Review of Findings of Trial Courts as well. For the trial lawyer it should save valuable time and insure against error; for the judge it should prove a valuable tool in evaluating the sufficiency of proof and in the drafting of findings; and for the law student who is engaged in a clinical court program, it is a good "How to do it" book.

In my view *Winning in Court on the Law of Facts* furnishes not only a bibliography of precedents on the elements of proof necessary in a given case, but sparks the imagination in locating error which might lead to reversal on appeal. This is not to say, however, that it is the complete answer. While the rule of past cases can teach, can provide answers, can offer hope of reversal, it is not the Magi. For this, each lawyer only through hard work shall win the laurels or else wear the thistles.

——*Tom C. Clark*
Associate Justice of the
United States Supreme Court, Retired

How This Book Can
Help You Win in Court

In any trial it is most difficult to wrestle with facts—they are such stubborn things. To help in such a task this book invents a new topic of the law which the author calls the "Law of Facts." This topic includes, among others, those principles of law which the courts have developed: (1) to test sufficiency of evidence for jury consideration; (2) for making valid and meaningful findings of facts; and (3) for reversing judgment upon appeal because the court below made a clearly erroneous finding of fact.

For the first time this book puts into a single package the principles and case law dealing with sufficiency of evidence and findings of fact. Although the book is directed to trial and appellate practice before federal courts, the principles and cases set forth for the most part should be equally persuasive in state courts. The best way to help a busy trial lawyer is to hand to him a case in point. With that in mind this book cites about a thousand cases. The cases either illustrate a principle or are factually digested for ready reference.

The Best Remedy on the Facts Can Easily Be Selected

Set forth in Chapter 1 are the facts essential for almost every kind of civil case which can be brought in the federal courts. By browsing through this chapter you will be reminded of remedies you have perhaps forgotten. Knowing the basic facts of your client's case, you can select the most appropriate remedy for him with some assurance he will be able to prove his case when he gets to court.

For example, suppose an eighty-year-old widow comes to your

office and spins a tale of woe. She has been defrauded of securities and real estate by a clever "con" man and his gang who have fled to several other states. You see difficulty in your client proving all facts essential to common law fraud. However, as you peruse Chapter 1 you find an easier-to-prove civil remedy for fraud implied from Section 10b of the Securities and Exchange Act of 1934. You further find that the involvement of real estate with the securities does not destroy the remedy if all were involved in a single fraudulent scheme. You now have a remedy fitting like a glove because service of process can be had across state lines—you can bring the gang as defendants into one courtroom. You can even couple with the main action one to set aside the fraudulent transfer of the real property.

Handling Cases Thin on Their Facts

As a trial attorney you will sooner or later have a case which is thin on its facts. At that time you will be keenly interested in reading the four chapters dealing with circumstantial evidence. Suppose that next week you must try a wrongful death case for a young widow who lost her husband in a head-on collision between two trucks. There were no witnesses to the collision since both drivers were killed. You must prove the defendant's truck was on the wrong side of the road at time of impact. All you have as evidence is the debris of the collision on the highway. Can you get the widow's case to the jury? You will find in Chapter 5 (dealing with the "more probable than not" rule) a case, much like your case, wherein a widow and four children got their case to the jury and from the jury a substantial verdict.

When you undertake your first case involving conspiracy or a fraudulent scheme, you will want to read Chapter 4 and learn how the quality of collective impact can make circumstances and events (which, in themselves, are of little moment) become winningly significant when collectively considered. You will find in the chapter cases illustrating sufficient as well as insufficient proof of conspiracy.

Chapter 6 is a part of the wonderland of inference drawing. It treats implied consent and implied-in-fact contracts. You can find cases which show circumstances from which courts have permitted juries to find implied consent and even implied-in-fact understandings between persons. Under what circumstances can an employee recover compensation for giving a useful business idea to his boss when the subject of compensation was never discussed? What about the implied-in-fact indemnity contract which the United States Supreme Court fashioned in admiralty as between shipowner and stevedore? In what situation does a court find an implied covenant to a written contract between two parties? You can find quick answers to these and other questions in Chapter 6.

How to Prepare Good Findings of Fact

When you win an involved case and the court orders you to prepare findings of fact, you are likely to approach the task with considerable trepidation. Your concern can be overcome by reading Chapter 2 on setting forth judicially-determined questions of fact and Chapter 9 on the making of valid and meaningful findings of fact. For example, you wonder if the scope of a corporate agent's authority is a matter of fact or law. Chapter 2 will tell you it is a matter of fact. By including this matter in your findings of fact, you may have won the case on appeal, since such a finding will not be easily set aside by the appellate court. Being the most vital step to judgment, findings of fact must be carefully done. A trial lawyer wanting to hang onto his hard won judgment and the trial judge wanting to keep from getting reversed on appeal could do well to read Chapter 9 and find what appellate courts have said about good and poor findings of fact.

Administrative agencies in the federal bureaucracy spew orders and regulations throughout the land which greatly affect people and industry. Since the very heart of administrative action is that of fact finding, Chapter 10 is devoted to the judicial review of findings of administrative agencies. When your client wishes you to lead an attack in court upon an administrative order or regulation, you can benefit by reading Chapter 10 and learning in what court to go to seek judicial review, the narrow scope of such review, and whether your client has standing to sue. The chapter also includes cases wherein courts have set aside findings of administrative agencies.

Facts on Appeal—Also the Seventh Amendment

You can't win them all. Suppose you try a ship collision case which turns on pure fact. Because you have prepared and presented your case well, you are amazed when the court finds your ship at fault and the other ship free of fault. At once your client asks you whether he should appeal the case and if so what his chances are of winning on appeal. You know that on appeal your client will collide immediately with the rule that the appellate court will not disturb findings of fact unless clearly erroneous. By turning to Chapter 11 you will find most, if not all, of the cases in which federal appellate courts have reversed judgment because they concluded that findings of fact were clearly erroneous. What better way can you estimate your client's chances on appeal?

One of these days you will experience the disappointment of having a substantial verdict in your client's favor taken away by an appellate court because it could not find the evidence to support the verdict, which the jury did in rendering the verdict. This will be the time you will keenly re-read Chapter 12. It treats the little-remembered Seventh Amendment to the United States Constitution which forbids a court from re-examining facts found by a jury. You will see all of the cases wherein the Supreme Court has enforced the Seventh Amendment. Perhaps you will gain new hope as you prepare a petition for a writ of certiorari to the United States Supreme Court.

If this book does nothing more than make you aware of the importance of being able to distinguish between a finding of fact and a conclusion of law, it will have served you well.

——Bill White

Table of Contents

Foreword   7

How This Book Can Help You Win in Court   9

The Best Remedy on the Facts
   Can Easily Be Selected — 9
Handling Cases Thin on Their Facts — 10
How to Prepare Good Findings of Fact — 11
Facts on Appeal—Also the Seventh Amendment — 11

1 Essential Findings of Facts for Most Cases   21

2 Judicially Determined Questions of Fact   37

Few Questions of Fact Reserved for
   Court and Not Jury — 39
Cases—General — 40
Business Transaction Cases — 41
Contract Cases — 42
Divorce Cases — 44
Insurance Policy Cases — 44

2   Judicially Determined Questions of Fact . . . . **continued**

Negligence Cases — 45
Malicious Prosecution and Slander Cases — 48
Principal and Agent Cases — 48
Real Property Cases — 49
Tax Cases — 49

3   Challenging the Sufficiency of Evidence **51**

Tools for the Job — 51
Rule 50 of the Federal Rules of
*   Civil Procedure — 52*
The Directed Verdict — 53
Judgment Notwithstanding Verdict — 57
The Measuring Stick — 60
The Historical Struggle to Get "Substantial
*   Evidence" as the Measuring Stick — 60*
The Current Struggle to Keep "Substantial
*   Evidence" as the Measuring Stick — 63*

Pertinent Law Review Articles on
*   Challenging the Sufficiency of Evidence — 68*

4   Circumstantial Evidence—Quality of Collective Impact . .   **71**

Illustration of Circumstantial Evidence
*   and Its Strength — 71*
Collective Impact — 72
The Fraudulent Scheme and Conspiracy — 74
Insufficient Evidence to Prove Conspiracy — 75
Sufficiency of Evidence to Prove Conspiracy
*   Illustrated — 76*
A Practical Tip: Have Rulings on Motion to
*   Strike Reserved — 79*

Pertinent Law Review Articles on Conspiracy — 80

**5   Circumstantial Evidence—"More Probable
      Than Not"—"Res Ipsa Loquitur"** **83**

 The "More Probable Than Not" Rule — 84
 *Not Everything Put to Jury Under
  "More Probable Than Not" — 86*
 The "Res Ipsa Loquitur" Doctrine — 89
 The Unusual Which Suggests Negligence — 90
 Probability That Defendant Had Control of Event — 91
 *Policy Considerations for Applying
  "Res Ipsa Loquitur" — 93*
 Single Vehicle Inexplicably Leaving Highway — 95
 *Pyramiding of Inference upon Inference
  Not Necessarily Fatal — 95*

 *Pertinent Law Review Articles on
  Circumstantial Evidence — 96*

**6   Circumstantial Evidence—Implied Consent—
      Implied-in-Fact Contracts** **97**

 Implied Consent — 97
 Implied-in-Fact Contracts — 99
 An Agreement to Later Agree—Not a Contract — 99
 Furnishing Things or Services — 100
 Furnishing Ideas for the Boss — 102
 Implied Covenants to Express Contracts — 103
 The Maritime Implied-in-Fact Indemnity Contract — 105

 Pertinent Law Review Articles on Implied Contracts — 108

**7   Filling in the Chinks—Presumptions—
      Judicial Notice** **109**

 "Inferences" and "Presumptions" Distinguished — 109
 *How State-Created Presumptions Work
  in the Federal Courts — 112*

7   Filling in the Chinks—Presumptions— Judicial Notice . . . . **continued**

Rebuttable Presumptions Useful in Completing Facts for a Case — 113
Conclusive Presumptions Are Really Rules of Substantive Law — 120
Constitutionality of Presumptions: Conclusive Presumptions in Particular — 121
Judicial Notice Can Be Taken of Facts of Common Knowledge — 122
Facts of Which Federal Courts Have Taken Judicial Notice — 123

Pertinent Law Review Articles on Presumptions and Judicial Notice — 126

8   Where Evidence Has Been Found Insufficient **129**

Double Talk—Is the Testimony Like It Sounds? — 129
Not Enough to Prove Negligence — 130
Not Enough to Prove Causation — 134
Not Enough to Prove Damages — 135
Not Enough to Prove Insurance Policy or Contract Cases — 135
Not Enough to Prove Tax Cases — 137
Not Enough to Prove Cases Concerning Business Transactions — 137
Not Enough to Prove NLRB Unfair Labor Charges — 138
Not Enough to Prove Anti-Trust Cases — 139
Not Enough to Prove in Miscellaneous Cases — 139

9   Make Meaningful Findings of Fact **141**

Findings of Fact—the Most Vital Step to Judgment — 141
Practice: Rule 52 of Federal Rules of Civil Procedure — 142

9   Make Meaningful Findings of Fact . . . . **continued**

Leave Some Meat on the Conclusionary Bone — 144

General, Special, Ultimate and
"Stepping Stone" Findings — 145

Quality of Findings Vary with Different
Proofs and Cases — 147

Court-Fashioned versus Attorney-Fashioned
Findings of Fact — 148

Settling Findings—First Too Little—
Then Too Much — 150

What Happens When Findings of
Fact Are Inadequate? — 152

What Are Not Findings of Fact? — 155

Nothing Can Be Done After Notice of
Appeal Is Filed — 156

Pertinent Law Review Articles on
Making Meaningful Findings of Fact — 156

10   Judicial Review of Findings of Administrative Agencies . .   **157**

Right of Review—"Standing to Sue" — 158

Certain Agency Actions Are Not Subject to Review — 159

Actions Reviewable—Ripeness for Review — 160

Scope of Judicial Review Is Very Limited — 161

Setting Aside Agency Action As Being
Arbitrary or Capricious — 162

Setting Aside Agency Action for Abuse of Discretion — 164

Setting Aside Agency Action for
Inadequate Findings of Fact — 164

Setting Aside Agency Action for
Lack of Substantial Evidence — 166

Further Reasons for Setting Aside Agency Action — 167

How and Where to Go to Get Judicial Review — 169

Pertinent Law Review Articles on
Judicial Review of Findings of
Administrative Agencies — 172

**11   Appellate Review of Findings of Fact—
       The "Unless Clearly Erroneous" Rule** **175**

> *Rule 52(a) Brings Law, Equity and
>   Admiralty Under Same Tent — 176*
> *Supreme Court Limits Itself in
>   Applying "Clearly Erroneous" — 178*
> *"Ultimate" Findings Appear Excepted
>   from Rigor of Rule 52(a) — 179*
> *Kind of Evidence Presented May
>   Relax Court's Application of Rule 52(a) — 181*
> *Protective Findings Against Reversal
>   Because Findings Are Clearly Erroneous — 184*
> *"Mechanical" Rules Employed by Appellate Courts
>   in Reviewing Findings of Fact — 185*
> *Findings of Fact Which Federal Courts Have
>   Found to Be Clearly Erroneous — 187*
> *In Admiralty Cases — 187*
> *In Anti-Trust—Business—Labor and
>   Patent Cases — 189*
> *In Contract and Insurance Policy Cases — 191*
> *In All Cases As to Damages, Amount or Value — 192*
> *In Negligence Cases — 194*
> *In Tax Cases — 194*
> *In Miscellaneous Cases — 196*
>
> *Pertinent Law Review Articles on
>   Appellate Review of Findings of Fact — 197*

**12   The Seventh Amendment—
       A Constitutional "No-No"** **199**

> *In Seventeenth Century The People
>   Feared Losing the Right to Jury Trial — 199*
> *In What Cases Is the Right to
>   Trial by Jury Preserved? — 200*
> *"Any Court of the United States" Means Just That — 204*
> *". . . According to the Rules of the Common Law"*

**12 The Seventh Amendment—
A Constitutional "No-No"** .... **continued**

Means the Law of England in 1791 — 205
Practices Within Ambit of the Seventh Amendment — 206
*Trial Court Review of the Excessive Verdict or
Inadequate Award — 207*
*Appellate Court Review of the Excessive Verdict
or Inadequate Award — 209*
*How the Supreme Court Has Enforced the
Seventh Amendment — 212*
*Cases Reversed by Supreme Court Because
Lower Court Reexamined Verdicts — 213*
*Denial of Certiorari with Dissent Because
of Seventh Amendment — 215*
*Cases Where Supreme Court Found
No Seventh Amendment Violation — 215*

*Pertinent Law Review Articles on
the Seventh Amendment — 216*

Index **217**

Essential Findings of   1
Facts for Most Cases

This is an idea chapter, a browse-through chapter and one of the most useful in the book. It lists most, if not all, civil actions which can be brought in the federal courts with the facts of each which are necessary to be found by court or jury in order for your client to win. Why federal actions? Because federal decisions in diversity actions cover the broad spectrum of the common law and in addition there have arisen over recent years additional civil remedies which have sprung expressly or impliedly from federal statutes.

Most of us lawyers have often jumped too quickly to the selection of a legal remedy for our clients. We listen to our client's statement of the facts, being impressed with the strong features, and either over-looking or hoping to get around at a later date the adverse portion of his factual package. We sometimes select a general type of action which first comes to mind and plunge into battle, not considering that there might be a newer and more fitting remedy. It is much better to fit the remedy to your client's facts at the very beginning than to select the remedy and hope, as more facts become known, your client can prove the action you have chosen for him to secure his needed relief. You will find in this chapter civil actions about which you have forgotten, and some of which you have perhaps never known. Did you know that your client can be sued for damages resulting from personal injury or death (up to $5,000) if he knows about, and is able, but refuses or neglects to break up a conspiracy aimed at denying the injured person or decedent his civil rights?[1]

By fitting your client's facts to those essential to prove various

---

[1] Civil Rights Act, 42 USC # 1986

causes of action you can preliminarily spot weaknesses as well as make timely elections, and a wise selection of remedy. Your client claims that the franchise agreement he had recently paid $50,000 for was induced by fraudulent misrepresentations of the franchisor. If your client can give prompt notice and offer to return everything of value received, he can effect rescission of the agreement and then, in suing for return of his $50,000, he needs only to prove that he relied upon a material misrepresentation of fact without having to prove that the franchisor intended to deceive. However, if your client cannot give timely notice, you had better not select rescission as his remedy.

Jurisdictionally speaking, the federal court has some pitfalls as well as some advantages as compared with state courts. Jurisdiction of the United States District Court depends either upon diverse citizenship of plaintiff and defendant with amount in controversy exceeding $10,000, or that the action be founded upon a Constitutional provision, federal statute or a federal subject such as admiralty. In a federal based case you can fight over as little as one dollar should principle dictate.[2] In the diversity case the federal court applies the law of the appropriate state. One pitfall in the diversity case lies in not remembering that not only a corporation's citizenship, i.e. state of incorporation, but also its *principal* place of business must be diverse to the citizenship of the opposing party.

Advantages also exist in the federal system. In certain cases, court process can be served across state lines. Did you know that if you wish to pay the expense, you can, with court consent, subpoena as a witness an American citizen residing in a foreign country?[3] You also have a broad discovery procedure in the federal court which might not exist in your state court. Then again, certain federal statutes provide for the court to award reasonable attorney fees to your client if he is successful. When found to exist, the matters of "federal" jurisdiction, right to serve process across state lines, and the right to reasonable attorney fees will be mentioned in the actions listed. Where jurisdiction depends upon diversity of citizenship, such will be assumed and not mentioned.

Only one *caveat*: If you don't fire your law clerk should he fail to "Shepardize" every case to assure its currency, and if you yourself

---

[2] Hewlett v Barge Bertie (4 Cir., 1969) 418 F2d 654
[3] 28 U.S.C. Sec. 1783

do not delve deeper into the law than the cases cited in this chapter, you do not deserve to win any case.

Accounting, prove: (1) implied or express agreement—privity,[4] or (2) a fiduciary relationship between plaintiff and defendant;[5] (3) breach or failure to account for entrusted money or property; (4) transaction so complicated that plaintiff has no adequate remedy at law.[6]

Account, open, and current or mutual, prove: (1) Express or implied agreement of money due or to become due upon an unfinished series of transactions (not series of independent bills).[7]

Account stated, prove: (1) An express or implied contract as to amount due on a past transaction.[8]

Adverse possession (or right by prescription) prove: (1) plaintiff occupied (or used) defendant's land for State required period of time and throughout period possession was (1) actual, (2) visible, (3) exclusive, (4) hostile, and (5) that plaintiff paid the taxes (where required by state law).[9]

Assumpsit, prove: (1) defendant obligated to pay money to plaintiff either on express contract or a contract implied in law (quasi) to prevent unjust enrichment by reason of breach of contract.[10]

Anti-trust, per se violation, price fixing, prove: (1) combination or agreement between supplier and retail outlets to fix or control retail price of product; (2) damages; (3) attorney fees; (4) process crossing state lines; (5) federal jurisdiction.[11]

Anti-trust, per se violation, boycotts, prove: (1) combination or agreement among defendants in competing trade not to sell to or buy from plaintiff; (2) damages; (3) attorney fees, (4) process crossing state lines, (5) federal jurisdiction.[12]

---

[4] Moran v Rosender (Vir. Is., 1965) 240 F. Supp. 740, 742

[5] Chabot v Empire Trust Co., (SDNY, 1960) 189 F. Supp. 666

[6] Dairy Queen, Inc. v Wood, (1962) 369 U.S. 469

[7] Isthmian Steamship Co. v United States, (SDNY, 1957) 191 F. Supp. 335

[8] James Wood General Trading Establishment v Coe, (SDNY, 1961) 191 F. Supp. 330, 334 (reversed on other grounds in 297 F2d 651)

[9] Pan American Petroleum Corp. v Candelaria (10 Cir., 1968) 403 F2d 351, 355

[10] Archawski v Hanioti, (1956) 350 U.S. 532, 534

[11] Simpson v Union Oil Co., (1964) 377 U.S. 13, 17

[12] Radiant Burners, Inc. v Peoples Gas, Light & Coke Co. (1961) 364 U.S. 656

Anti-trust, per se violation, division of markets and territory, prove: (1) Combination or agreement among defendant competitors or supplier and customers to divide up territory and customers among themselves; (2) damages; (3) attorney fees; (4) process across state lines; (5) federal jurisdiction.[13]

Anti-trust, per se violation, tying arrangements, prove: (1) Defendant supplier imposing upon customer as condition of selling one product to buy and sell another product; (2) damages; (3) attorney fees, (4) process across state lines; (5) federal jurisdiction.[14]

Anti-trust, per se violation, monopoly, prove: (1) master agreement between distributor and retailer or concerted conduct which has effect to monopolize trade in defendants to exclusion of plaintiff; (2) damages; (3) attorney fees; (4) process across state lines; (5) federal jurisdiction.[15]

Anti-trust, per se violation, use of patents to coerce, prove: (1) defendant used its basic patent to compel a licensee as a condition of use to agree to transfer all patent rights of licensee in future to defendant; (2) damages; (3) attorney fees; (4) process across state lines; (5) federal jurisdiction.[16]

Bills and notes, prove: (1) note executed and delivered by defendant; (2) plaintiff holder in due course,[17] (3) if any conditions precedent in instrument they were performed or excused; (4) note due and payable; (5) amount due, interest, attorney fees; (6) (if possible and to avoid defenses within privity of defendant) that plaintiff received the note in good faith, for value and without notice of any infirmity in instrument.[18]

Broker or agent of non-disclosed or partially disclosed principal, prove: (1) plaintiff entered into contract with broker defendant who failed to disclose identity of his principal prior to execution of contract; (2) breach of contract; (3) damages against broker as principal.[19]

---

[13] Timken Roller Bearing Co. v United States, (1951) 341 U.S. 593, 599

[14] United States v Loew's, Inc. (1962) 371 U.S. 38, 44–45

[15] United States v Griffith, (1948) 334 U.S. 100, 105–106

[16] United States v General Electric Co. (1926) 272 U.S. 476; 80 F. Supp. 989, 1006

[17] Hull v Brandywine Fibre Products Co., (Del., 1954) 121 F. Supp. 108

[18] Equipment Acceptance Corp. v Arwood Car Mfg. Co., (6 Cir. 1941) 117 F2d 442

[19] Propstra v Dyer, (2 Cir., 1951) 189 F2d 810

Civil rights, for damages, prove: (1) defendant while acting under color state ordinance, regulation, custom, usage or statute; (2) subjected or caused plaintiff to be subjected within the United States to the deprivation of rights or immunities or privileges secured to him by the Constitution and laws of the United States; (3) resulting damages.[20]

Civil rights, conspiracy to deny for damages, prove: (1) defendants conspired; (2) purpose to impede or hinder due course of justice in state; (3) intent to deny plaintiff equal protection of law; (4) acts done under color of state law; (5) plaintiff injured in his person or property or was deprived of exercising right or privilege of United States citizenship.[21]

Civil rights, refusal to aid or prevent violation for damages, prove: (1) elements of conspiracy under 42 USC #1985; (2) defendant had knowledge of wrong conspired to be done or about to be committed; (3) had power to prevent or aid in preventing; (4) neglected or refused to so do; (5) wrong thereafter done; (6) damages for plaintiff's personal injuries or if killed, damages to widow or next of kin, not exceeding $5,000.[22]

Civil rights, peonage, for damages, prove: (1) plaintiff required to serve or labor under laws or usages of a state which have been declared null and void by 42 USC #1994; (2) resulting damages.[23]

Civil rights, for injunction and attorney fees, prove: (1) defendant violated Civil Rights Act, 42 USC #2000; (2) defendant discriminated or segregated against plaintiff or his class on basis of race, color, religion or national origin in public places such as inns, motels, hotels, cafeterias, soda fountains, retail stores, gasoline stations, theatres, sports arenas; (3) which serve interstate travelers or uses products moved in interstate commerce; (4) amount for reasonable attorney fees.[24]

Contract, reformation, prove: (1) Mutual mistake of fact on part of both plaintiff and defendant parties to contract.[25]

Contract, abandonment, prove: (1) Contract; (2) that both

---

[20] 42 USC #1983; De Witt v Pail, (9 Cir., 1966) 366 F2d 682

[21] 42 USC #1985 (3); Hoffman v Haiden, (9 Cir., 1959) 268 F2d 280, 292

[22] 42 USC #1986

[23] Bryant v Donnell, (Tenn., 1965) 239 F. Supp. 681

[24] Newman v Piggie, (1968) 390 U.S. 400

[25] Levy v Dossin's Food Products, (Mich., 1947) 72 F. Supp. 855

parties to contract either expressly or by their unequivocal conduct evidenced mutual intent to abandon an existing contract.[26]

Contract, breach, prove: (1) Contract; (2) plaintiff performed all conditions precedent or facts excusing;[27] (3) a demand upon defendant to perform only if contract or implied circumstances might require;[28] (4) breach of contract by defendant; (5) reasonable amount of damages suffered by plaintiff foreseeably caused by defendant's breach.

Contract, rescission for breach, prove: (1) contract; (2) defendant made a substantial breach which went to the root of the contract (not merely a collateral breach);[29] (3) plaintiff with reasonable promptness notified defendant of his election to rescind contract and at same time tendered to defendant everything of value which plaintiff received under contract for everything of value which defendant received;[30] (4) amount of damages reasonably require to restore plaintiff to his status quo prior to contract.[31]

Contract, rescission, induced by fraud, prove: (1) Contract; (2) plaintiff performed conditions precedent or facts showing waiver;[32] (3) plaintiff, upon discovery of misrepresentations which induced contract, promptly notified defendant of election to rescind and at same time offered to return to defendant everything of value which he received in exchange for everything of value which defendant received;[33] (4) defendant made misrepresentation of material facts to plaintiff upon which plaintiff had a right to and did rely as inducing execution of contract;[34] (5) amount of damages necessary to restore plaintiff to his status quo prior to contract.[35]

Contract, specific performance, prove: (1) A contract which is not contrary to public policy,[36] whose terms are not uncertain or am-

---

[26] Armour & Co. v Celic, (2 Cir. 1961) 294 F2d 432

[27] Friedman v Decatur Corp., (DC, 1943) 135 F2d 812

[28] Independent Distillers of Kentucky (In re), (Ky., 1940) 34 F. Supp. 708

[29] Arrow Petroleum Co. v Johnston, (7 Cir., 1947) 162 F2d 269, cert. denied 332 U.S. 817

[30] Acme Process Co. v United States, (Ct. Cl., 1965) 347 F2d 509

[31] Acme Process Co. v United States, (Ct. Cl., 1965) 347 F2d 509

[32] Cummings v Universal Pictures Co., (Calif., 1944) 62 F. Supp. 611

[33] Western Cas. & Surety Co. v Herman (8 Cir., 1963) 318 F2d 50 1 ALR3d 1184

[34] Miller v Protrka, (Or., 1951) 238 P2d 753

[35] Acme Process Co. v United States, (Ct. Cl., 1965) 347 F2d 509

[36] Ford v Oregon Electric Ry. Co. (Or., 1911) 117 P. 809

biguous,[37] the specific performance of which is not impossible or difficult,[38] or not calling for the performance of personal services,[39] and preferably but not necessarily a contract involving land[40] or standing timber to be cut,[41] or crops from specified land,[42] or containing a covenant not to compete;[43] (2) plaintiff has performed all that the contract requires or facts showing waiver by defendant;[44] (3) defendant has breached contract and refuses to perform; (4) plaintiff has neither a speedy nor adequate remedy at law and specific performance is required.

Damages, destruction or loss of property, prove: (1) difference between market value before and after damage to property; (2) or when total loss market value at time of loss, or (3) reasonable cost of repairing damage if property worth repairing.[45, 46]

Damages, breach of contract, prove: (1) loss of net and not gross profits except where operating expenses are fixed when gross profits might be measured,[47] or (2) difference in value where breach causes damage to property;[48] or (3) benefit of bargain, i.e. making plaintiff whole as if contract had been performed instead of breached;[49] (4) generally income taxes not considered in measuring damages.[50]

Damages, punitive, prove: (1) Defendant's conduct was wanton and malicious; (2) wealth of defendant.[51]

Damages, wrongful death, pecuniary loss, prove: (1) life expectancy of decedent; (2) probable future earnings of decedent had he lived; (3) what share of future earnings widow and children would have received; (4) present worth of what widow and children would

---

[37] Alexander v Alexander, (Or., 1936) 58 P2d 1265

[38] McDonough v Southern Oregon Mining Co., (Or., 1945) 159 P2d 829

[39] Phez Co. v Salem Fruit Union (Or., 1922) 201 P 222, 205 P 970

[40] Temple Enterprises v Combs, (Or., 1940) 100 P2d 613, 128 ALR 856

[41] Paullus v Yarbrough, (Or., 1959) 347 P2d 620

[42] Livesley v Johnston, (Or., 1904) 76 P 946

[43] McCallum v Asbury, (Or., 1964) 393 P2d 774

[44] Balla v Ireland, (Or., 1948) 196 P2d 445

[45] United States v State of Md. for Use of Meyer, (DC Cir., 1963) 322 F2d 1009 (reversed other grounds in 382 U.S. 158)

[46] Hewlett v Barge Bertie (4 Cir., 1969) 418 F2d 654

[47] Distillers Distributing Corp. v. J. C. Millett Co., (9 Cir., 1963) 310 F2d 162

[48] Gleason v Title Guarantee Co. (5 Cir., 1962) 300 F2d 813

[49] New Amsterdam Cas. Co. v Mitchell, (5 Cir., 1954) 325 F2d 474

[50] Hanover Shoe, Inc. v United Shoe Machinery Corp., (Pa., 1965) 245 F. Supp. 258 (reversed other grounds in 392 U.S. 481)

[51] Hannigan v Sears, Roebuck & Co., (7 Cir., 1969) 410 F2d 285

have received; (5) loss, if any, from employment oriented retirement benefits; (6) instruction, moral training and education superintendence which children could have expected to receive from decedent had he lived; (7) federal rule is that decedent's income taxes, or social security benefits, are not considered unless decedent is in high earnings bracket at time of death.[52]

Declaratory judgment, prove: (1) actual controversy existing between plaintiff and defendant desirable of reasonably quick declaration of rights as between them.[53]

Ejectment, prove: (1) plaintiff has possessory title—right to enter land occupied by others.[54]

Estopple, in pais, prove this defense by showing: (1) opposing party by words or conduct led defendant to believe certain facts were true and of which he did not otherwise know and in so relying defendant changed his position to his loss and detriment.[55]

False imprisonment, prove: (1) plaintiff restrained of his liberty under the probable imminence of force without any legal cause or justification; (2) damages.[56]

Food, Drug and Cosmetic Act, misbranding product, prove: Defendant's product (such as a surgical nail) was misbranded in violation of 21 USC #352; (2) that misbranding was a proximate cause of damage; (3) damages. Civil liability implied from violation of Food, Drug & Cosmetic Act, 21 USC #352.[57]

Fraud, common law, prove: (1) Defendant made a false material statement of fact to plaintiff; (2) knowing and believing it to be false; (3) intending that plaintiff rely and act upon same; (4) plaintiff not knowing of falsity relying thereon; and (5) suffering damages as result thereof.[58]

Fraud, in purchase or sale of securities, prove: (1) that directly or indirectly connected with a transaction the mails or an instru-

---

[52] Michigan Central R. Co. v Vreeland, (1913) 227 U.S. 59; United States v Hayashi, (9 Cir., 1960) 282 F2d 599; Petition of Marina Mercante Nicaraguense (2 Cir., 1966) 364 F2d 118

[53] 28 USC #2201

[54] Shapiro v Christopher, (DC Cir., 1952) 195 F2d 785

[55] Central Bank & Trust Co. v General Finance Corp. (5 Cir., 1961) 297 F2d 126

[56] Nesmith v Alford, (5 Cir., 1963) 318 F2d 110

[57] Orthopedic Equipment Co. v Eutsler, (4 Cir., 1960) 276 F2d 455, 460

[58] Parker Precision Products Co. v Metropolitan Life Ins. Co., (3 Cir., 1969) 407 F2d 1070

mentality of interstate commerce was used; (2) that a security as broadly defined in the Securities and Exchange Act of 1934[59] was involved; (3) that defendants violated Rule 10B-5[60] of the Securities and Exchange Commission which reads:

> It shall be unlawful for any person, directly or indirectly, by the use of any means or instrumentality of interstate commerce, or the mails, or of any facility of any national securities exchange,
>
> (a) To employ any device, scheme, or artifice to defraud.
>
> (b) To make any untrue statement of a material fact or to omit to state a material fact necessary in order to make the statements made, in the light of the circumstances under which they were made, not misleading, or
>
> (c) To engage in any act, practice, or course of business which operates or would operate as a fraud or deceit upon any person,
>
> . . . in connection with the purchase or sale of any security

(4) damages and (5) if desirable, cancelation and voiding of legal instruments under Section 29 of the Act; (6) process crossing state lines; (7) federal jurisdiction.

Note: The definition of a "security" is unusually broad. Use of mails or an instrumentality of interstate commerce need only be indirect, i.e. an innocent bank clearing a check or even a stockbroker accounting to its home office across a state line.[61] Since the implied civil action under Section 10(b) of the Securities and Exchange Act of 1934 and Rule 10(b)-5 applies generally to both buyer and seller other more restrictive civil remedies will only be mentioned.

Under Securities Act of 1933: (1) misstatements or omissions in a securities registration statement, Section 11;[62] (2) violation of registration or prospectus regulations, Section 12(1).[63] (3) fraud in prospectus or oral statement, Section 12(2).[64]

Under Securities and Exchange Act of 1934: (1) Damage arising from manipulation of registered securities, Section 9(e);[65] (2)

---

[59] 15 USC Sec. 78 c(10)

[60] SEC Rule 10b-5

[61] Fratt v Robinson (9 Cir., 1953) 203 F2d 627, 37 ALR2d 636; William F. White, Swindlers and the Securities Acts (Feb., 1959) ABAJ, Vol. 45, No. 2; Alan R Bromberg, Securities Law—Fraud, SEC Rule 10b-5, McGraw-Hill (1969)

[62] 15 USC p 77K

[63] 15 USC p 77L

[64] 15 USC p 77L

[65] 15 USC p 78i

short swing trades of insiders, Section 16(b);[66] (3) false statements in documents filed with Securities and Exchange Commission or a national stock exchange, Section 18.[67]

Fraudulent transfer, prove: (1) Plaintiff a creditor to debtor who transferred property (if existing creditor at time of transfer only constructive fraud need be proved; if a subsequent creditor actual fraud need be proved); (2) defendant a grantee of property transferred from debtor or defendant grantee of grantee, if holding property; only debtor need be a defendant if he has retained interest in property transferred; (2) specific transfer identifying property; (3) if plaintiff is an existing creditor—that debtor is insolvent and property transferred was all that debtor had left and effect of transfer was to defraud plaintiff;[68] if plaintiff a subsequent creditor that debtor transferred property with intent to hinder, delay or defraud his creditors and that defendant grantee took with knowledge of debtor's fraudulent intent.[69]

Note: Fed. Rule 18 (b) F.R.C.P. permits a plaintiff to state a claim for money against a defendant and at same time a claim to set aside a transfer by defendant as being fraudulent to plaintiff without first having obtained a money judgment against defendant.

Insurance policy, public liability, prove: Plaintiff was the insured; (2) terms of policy; (3) plaintiff complied with all conditions precedent, i.e. filing proof of loss, notice, etc., or that the defendant waived them; (4) plaintiff's loss fixed by either judgment or agreement with defendant insurer; (5) loss within terms of policy.[70]

Insurance policy, life insurance, prove: (1) Plaintiff is beneficiary; (2) policy terms and in effect; (3) death of insured while policy in effect.[71]

Interpleader, prove: (1) plaintiff has money or property worth $500 or more or has issued a note, bond, certificate or policy of insurance valued at $500 or more; (2) two or more persons of diverse citizenship claim or may claim the money or property; (3) plaintiff has deposited such money or property into the registry of the District Court or given bond payable to the clerk of the court to abide by

---

[66] 15 USC p 78p
[67] 15 USC p 78R
[68] Orr v Bauer (Or., 1937) 67 P2d 770
[69] Allen v Dodge (Or., 1921) 202 P. 717
[70] State Farm Mutual Auto Ins. Co. v Brewer, (9 Cir., 1968) 406 F2d 610
[71] Dick v New York Life Ins. Co. (1959) 359 U.S. 437

decree of court; (3) plaintiff has a real risk of vexatious and conflicting claims to property.[72] *Note:* Upon interpleader Court can enjoin other actions against plaintiff and issue process across state lines, 28 USC #2361.

Injury to railroad employee (F.E.L.A.) prove: (1) plaintiff injured or killed while employed by railroad in interstate commerce; (2) injury or death resulted in whole or in part from negligence of defendant railroad; (3) damages.[73] *Note:* Contributory negligence is not a bar but only goes to mitigation of damages; right to jury trial; jurisdiction federally based but concurrent with state courts.

Injury to seaman, unseaworthiness, prove: (1) plaintiff a seaman (crew member, longshoreman, etc.); (2) defendant shipowner failed to furnish and maintain his vessel and appurtenances in a reasonably fit condition for their intended use, (3) that such failure contributed in whole or in part to plaintiff's injuries; (4) damages; (5) jurisdiction may, but need not, be federally based on admiralty side of court.[74]

Injury to seaman, negligence, prove: (1) plaintiff is the master or a member of the crew of a vessel; (2) plaintiff's injuries are due in whole or in part to the negligence of his employer—the vessel owner; (3) damages; (4) jurisdiction may, but need not be federally based on admiralty side of court.[75]

Injury to member of crew of vessel, maintenance and cure, prove: (1) Plaintiff a member of a crew of a vessel; (2) irrespective of fault of anyone (except intoxication or deliberate injury by plaintiff himself) plaintiff became injured or ill while in service of the vessel (may be shore leave in foreign port); (3) reasonable amount of his keep (room and board) per day while ashore getting well; (4) until found fit for duty or maximum cure attained; (5) reasonable attorney fee in cases where vessel owner deliberately refuses or delays payment. *Note:* U.S. Public Health Service furnishes medical treatment (cure) free of charge to merchant seamen. No maintenance allowed while in hospital. Courts usually follow union agreement as to amount of daily maintenance, i.e. $8.00 per day.[76]

Death of seaman resulting from unseaworthiness, prove: (1)

---

[72] 28 USC #1335; Knoll v Socony Mobil Oil Co. (10 Cir., 1966) 369 F2d 425
[73] 45 USC #51
[74] Mitchell v Trawler Racer, Inc., (1960) 362 U.S. 539
[75] Jones Act, 46 USC #688, F.E.L.A. 45 USC #51, 53
[76] Vaughan v Atkinson (1962) 369 U.S. 527

Plaintiff appointed legal representative of decedent's estate suing on behalf of dependents; (2) decedent at time of death performing work traditionally done by seamen as, for example, either serving as a member of the crew of a ship or loading or unloading a ship as do longshoremen; (3) that a vessel or her equipment were unseaworthy in that equipment was not reasonably fit for its intended use, (sometimes performing work of ship in an unsafe manner constitutes unseaworthiness); (4) that the unseaworthiness contributed in whole or in part to decedent's death; (5) damages as measured under standard for wrongful death in F.E.L.A. 45 U.S.C. Sec. 51 et seq. which was applied to seamen by the Jones Act, 46 U.S.C. Sec. 688 pecuniary loss suffered by dependents. *Note:* Until *Moragne v States Marine Lines,* (1970) 398 U.S. 375 the seaman's dependents suing for wrongful death had to depend upon either the Jones Act, Death on the High Seas Act 46 U.S.C. Sec. 761 et seq., or a State wrongful death statute and occasionally they "fell between the chairs." Now, *Moragne,* supra, gives a wrongful death remedy in addition to the mentioned statutes. The new remedy is applicable to any seaman on any kind of vessel in any navigable waters. The Supreme Court has not as yet spelled out the measure of damages, but suggests that perhaps the measure under F.E.L.A. is proper.

Death on high seas by wrongful act, prove: (1) Decedent met his death by wrongful act, neglect, or default occurring on the high seas (or in airplane over the high seas) beyond a marine league from shore of United States; (2) plaintiff is the personal representative of dependent relatives; (3) defendant is the vessel owner or person who would have been liable if death had not ensued; (4) damages measured by fair and just compensation for the pecuniary loss sustained by the persons for whose benefit the action is brought.[77] *Note:* If wrongful death action provided by laws of a foreign country such action thereon may be maintained on the admiralty side of the District Court. If a seaman dies on a vessel on the high seas, his action for wrongful death is based upon the Jones Act, 46 USC #688.

Labor, recover unpaid wages below minimum, prove: (1) plaintiff employee filed in court written consent for action; (2) plaintiff employee engaged in work pertaining to interstate commerce; (3) amount of unpaid wages below wage and overtime standards pre-

---

[77] Death on the High Seas Act, 46 USC #761, 762

scribed by Fair Labor Standards Act, 49 USC #206 and 207; (4) an additional amount equal to unpaid wages as liquidated damages; (5) reasonable attorney fee; (6) federally based jurisdiction.[78]

Labor, unpaid minimum wages as ordered by NLRB, air pilot, prove (1) Plaintiff engaged in type of employment for which NLRB established a minimum wage; (2) amount unpaid; (3) remedy implied from 49 USC #496(b)(2).[79]

Labor, damages against union for breach of contract, prove: (1) Defendant a labor union or association; (2) defendant party to a collective bargaining agreement in which it agreed not to strike; (3) breach; (4) damages; (5) plaintiff employer a party to or for whom the contract was to benefit.[80]

Railroad, rebates, discrimination or unlawful charges, prove: (1) defendant railroad directly or indirectly by any special rate, rebate, drawback or other device charged or received from any person greater or less compensation for service rendered than it charges others for like services in violation of 49 USC #2; (2) full amount of damages suffered by plaintiff; (3) reasonable attorney fees to be taxed as costs. *Note:* Federal jurisdiction, but plaintiff must elect to proceed either in District Court or before Interstate Commerce Commission; not both.[81]

Railroad, enjoining violation of Commission order, prove: (1) Plaintiff injured by railroad continuing to violate order of Interstate Commerce Commission; (2) defendant railroad violating order; (3) need federal injunction mandatory or otherwise against railroad to enforce compliance.[82]

United States, non-tort claim, prove: (1) Plaintiff has valid claim for recovery of any tax, penalty or excess erroneously, illegally or wrongfully assessed or collected under internal revenue laws, or (2) any other civil action or claim founded upon the Constitution, any Act of Congress or any regulation of an executive department, or upon any express or implied contract; (3) if claim does not exceed

---

[78] 29 USC #216, Allen v Atlantic Realty Co., (5 Cir., 1967) 384 F2d 527

[79] 49 USC #496(b)(2); Laughlin v Riddle Aviation Co., (5 Cir., 1953) 205 F2d 948

[80] 29 USC p 160; Local 127, United Shoe Workers; AFL-CIO v Brooks Shoe Mfg. Co., (3 Cir., 1962) 298 F2d 277

[81] 49 USC #8, 9

[82] 49 USC #16(12); Brogan v Pennsylvania R. Co., (Ill., 1962) 211 F. Supp. 881

$10,000 jurisdiction may be laid either in District Court or Court of Claims; if more than $10,000, only in Court of Claims.[83]

United States, tort claim, prove: (1) Plaintiff suffered personal injury, death or property damage; (2) caused by the negligent or wrongful act or omission of any employee of the Government while acting within the scope of his office or employment, under circumstances where the United States, if a private person, would be liable to plaintiff under the (state) law of the place where the act or omission occurred. (*Note:* District Court sitting without jury has exclusive jurisdiction.)[84]

Vessel, statutory maritime lien against, prove: (1) Plaintiff furnished repairs, supplies, towage, use of dry dock or marine railway, or any other necessaries to any vessel upon order of her owner or person authorized by owner; (2) vessel is in jurisdiction of court and is arrested; (3) amount of unpaid claims.[85]

Vessel, non-statutory maritime lien against, prove: (1) Plaintiff as member of crew of vessel or a longshoreman working on vessel, or a seaman injured tortiously upon vessel, or owner of cargo already placed aboard vessel and has a claim for unpaid wages or damage. Or, that plaintiff is a salvor of the vessel or owner of another vessel in collision with the offending vessel and has a claim; (2) the vessel is within the territorial jurisdiction of the Court and is arrested and held. *Note:* Salvage, crew's wages and tort claims have precedence over other maritime liens including that of a preferred ship mortgage.[86]

Vessel, loss or damage to cargo, prove: (1) Plaintiff is holder of bill of lading and entitled to possession of goods entrusted to carrier; (2) cargo was delivered to the vessel in good condition; (3) cargo either not re-delivered or if re-delivered was found in damaged condition; (4) damage. *Note:* Duties and rights of water carriers are set forth in Carriage of Goods by Sea Act.[87]

Vessel, marine collision, prove: (1) Plaintiff vessel navigated in accordance with the applicable nautical rules of the road and was not otherwise negligent; (2) defendant violated one or more of the nautical rules of the road or was otherwise negligent; (3) such faults caused

---

[83] 28 USC #1346(a)

[84] 28 USC #1346(b)

[85] 46 USC #971

[86] Logue Stevedoring Corp. v The Dalzellance, (2 Cir., 1952) 198 F2d 369; Canadian Aviator, Ltd. v United States, (1945) 324 U.S. 215

[87] Carriage of Goods by Sea, Od, 46 USC 1300 et seq.

or contributed to the collision; (4) damages. *Note:* where both vessels are at fault the total damages whether to one or both of the vessels are apportioned equally between the two vessels.[88]

Vessel, limitation of liability, prove: (1) That which occurred aboard the vessel to otherwise make her owner liable for loss or destruction of property, damage or injury by collision or for any loss, damage or forfeiture was *without the privity or knowledge* of such owner. *Note:* Limiting liability is more complicated than stated, and there are certain exceptions affecting large passenger carrying vessels. However, the Act basically applies to all vessels of any size. Limitation of liability is to value of vessel after collision (if sunk, nothing). Petition to limit must be filed within six months from notice of any claim.[89]

Vessel, indemnity by owner against stevedore, prove: (1) A longshoreman (or other harbour worker) employed by defendant stevedore company has sued vessel owner for damages resulting from injury received aboard the vessel due to her unseaworthiness; (2) the claimed unseaworthiness was brought into play or created by negligence of defendant stevedore (or other longshoremen working vessel in employ of stevedore); (3) vessel owner as defendant in longshoreman's action tenders defense to stevedore and tender is denied; (4) plaintiff longshoreman recovers from defendant shipowner by judgment or reasonable settlement; (5) in action against stevedore (either in longshoreman's case or separately) the liability visited upon plaintiff shipowner was brought about by the unworkmanlike stevedore service performed by defendant stevedore; (6) costs of defending the seaman's action including reasonable attorney fees and amount of judgment and costs obtained by longshoreman against vessel owner.[90]

Vessel, maritime contract, prove: (1) Plaintiff is party with defendant to a maritime contract; almost any contract related to water commerce or vessel (except contract to build vessel), i.e. bill of lading, charter party; (2) defendant breached contract; (3) damages resulting from breach. *Note:* Advantage is that if a maritime contract, the amount in controversy need not exceed $10,000, or diversity of citizenship be established.[91]

---

[88] Illinois-Union Star, (9 Cir., 1967) 378 F2d 356
[89] 46 USC #183
[90] Ryan Stevedoring Co. v Pan-Atlantic S.S. Corp. (1956) 350 U.S. 124
[91] Archawski v Hanioti, (1956) 350 U.S. 532, 534

Water carrier, violation of Interstate Commerce Act, prove: (1) defendant is a water carrier subject to regulation of Interstate Commerce Commission; (2) defendant violated a provision of the Act; (3) plaintiff's full damages sustained by reason of violation; (4) reasonable attorney fees.[92]

---

[92] 49 USC p 908(b)

Judicially Determined   2
Questions of Fact

A key to success in winning any case in court is to recognize before commencement of the trial precisely what the issues of fact will be and what the issues of law will be. This is often easier said than done.

As a rule, the court decides questions of law while the jury decides questions of fact. If the question should be one of mixed law and fact, the jury will decide the question upon a specific instruction of the court as to the law to be applied.[1] If you have a type of case that you feel can only be won before a jury, by all means ponder well whether the critical question upon which the case is likely to turn is one of fact or one of law. Do this before you take the case into your office and do not wait until you are near the conclusion of the trial with opposing counsel persuasively arguing for a directed verdict.

Recognizing questions of fact is likewise important in cases where a court and not a jury becomes the fact finder. Neither the court nor the prevailing attorney can fashion meaningful findings of fact unless the findings essential to the case are fully understood. Inadequate findings can sometimes spell defeat in a case otherwise entitled to stand up under appeal.

Trial questions have been classified as those involving fact or law or a mixture of fact and law. Generally, a question of fact involves the finding of an ultimate fact from the evidence presented while a question of law involves determining the legal effect to be given to the ultimate fact as found.[2] A mixed question of fact and law is one in-

[1] McCrowell v Southern Ry Co. (NC, 1942) 20 SE2d 352, 357

[2] Hoover v Allen, (SDNY, 1965) 241 F. Supp. 213, 235; (holding out to public); a question of law is always raised in deciding whether evidence is "substan-

volving the formulation of a legal standard and at the same time arriving at an ultimate fact to be measured by the legal standard.[3] As will be seen later, courts of various jurisdictions differ not only as to what are questions of fact and law, but also what are questions of fact and mixed questions of fact and law. A good example is that of the Court of Appeals for the Second Circuit treating negligence as a question of mixed fact and law[3] while the Court of Appeals for the Ninth Circuit steadfastly treats negligence as a question of fact.[4] As long as the trial court will put a mixed question of fact and law to the jury subject to its instruction on the law phase of the question, you will get your client's case to the jury. The difference between the mixed question and the fact question will only be felt on appeal where the appellate court will review the mixed question free of the "unless clearly erroneous" rule while not the fact question.

We are here concerned with *questions* of fact. Is there an issue of fact arising from either conflicting evidence or conflicting reasonable inferences to be drawn from undisputed fact? Until the question has been created, the matter of something being law or fact is of little concern.

In the process of distinguishing between questions of law and questions of fact you have two situations where a question of law is apt to appear. The first is from the very nature of the question itself. Does the question pose the effect to be given to certain facts? For example, is the court confronted with only construing a written contract to determine if it is breached, or is the court concerned with determining if certain conversations and letters created a contract? In the first instance, the court has a question of law to resolve, while in the second, a question of fact. The second situation arises from the quality and force of the evidentiary facts. Where certain facts overwhelmingly point in only one direction, what might otherwise be a question of fact resolves itself into a question of law. Whether a dye works is a nuisance by reason of its emission of noise and smoke rests upon the degree of noise and smoke emitted. Ordinarily, what comprises a nuisance is a question of fact. However, prove that the dye works emits unusually excessive smoke and noise as compared with neighboring industry, or the dye works manager is indifferent to injuring those about him, and the usual question of fact can become one

---

tial" or "sufficient" to deny motions for directed verdicts or for judgments n.o.v., *Merlo v Public Service Co. of Northern Illinois,* (Ill. 1943) 45 NE2d 665
   [3] Mamiye Bros. v Barber S.S. Co., (2 Cir., 1966) 360 F2d 774
   [4] United States v Fotopulos, (9 Cir., 1950) 180 F2d 631

of law because the conclusion of fact points unequivocally to the single ultimate fact of nuisance.[5] This idea is also prevalent in the circumstantial evidence case. If undisputed facts justify with reason more than one reasonable inference, including the one needed to make a case, the question is one of fact for the jury. If, however, only one reasonable inference can be drawn from the undisputed facts, the question becomes one of law for the court.[6] Thus we see that common sense plays a much greater role in the common law than most people imagine.

Few Questions of Fact Reserved for Court and Not Jury

It should be pointed out that certain questions of fact for various reasons are resolved by the court as questions of law. Among the few of these arbitrary exceptions are: (1) Law of a foreign jurisdiction proven as a fact but determined by the court;[7] (2) Lack of probable cause in action for malicious prosecution or false arrest;[8] (3) The spontaneity and timing of a defendant's declaration against interest to admit the declaration into evidence under *res gestae*.[9] (4) Credit to be given against judgment for plaintiff where plaintiff received money from a co-tortfeasor[10] or medical and compensation benefits received by plaintiff from defendant in a longshoremen's case.[11]

If the busy trial lawyer or the harried trial judge is to be helped in his problem of resolving which questions are fact and which are law he is best served with a case in hand. The remainder of this chapter will set forth cases wherein courts have determined certain questions to be questions of fact. Differing views will be noted. By finding here a judicially determined question of fact in point with the question with which you are concerned, you will at least have a case to help you resolve your problem. Should you not find a case in point, you may conclude that probably your question is one of law or possibly it has either not been decided, or if decided, not been included in this chapter.

---

[5] Loftin v McGregor, (Fla. 1943) 14 So2d 574

[6] Eckhardt v Industrial Accident Commission, (Wis. 1943) 7 NW2d 841, 842

[7] Leary v Gledhill, (NJ, 1951) 84 A2d 725; Anno: 23 ALR2d 1437

[8] *Pallett v Tompkins*, (Wn. 1941) 118 P2d 190, 192

[9] Harrison v Baker, (Ala., 1954) 71 So2d 284; MacDonald v Appleyard, (NH, 1947) 53 A2d 434; Anno: 56 ALR2d 374

[10] State Farm Mut. Auto Ins. Co. v Bourne, (5 Cir., 1955) 220 F2d 921 (for court); Husky Ref. Co. v Barnes, (9 Cir., 1941) 119 F2d 715, 134 ALR 1221 (for jury); Anno: 94 ALR2d 36

[11] Jack Weaver v American Mail Lines, (9 Cir., 1969) 408 F2d 674

Cases—General

A question of fact exists as to:

Abandonment of property, *De Bardeleben Coal Co. v Cox,* (Ala., 1917) 76 So 409 (vessel); *Tilman v Melton,* (Mo., 1942) 165 SW 2d 684, 687 (school property).

Adverse possession of land, *Rambo v United States,* (Ga., 1941) 2 FRD 200, 201; *Sullivan v Huber,* (Minn., 1941) 297 NW 33, 34; *Smith v Tremaine,* (Or., 1960) 350 P2d 180, 82 ALR2d 1.

Age, *Artukovich v Astendorf,* (Cal., 1942) 125 P2d 16, 19.

Cause, *R. J. Reynolds Tobacco Co. v Newby,* (9 Cir., 1944) 145 F2d 768.

Conspiracy, *Gary Theatre Co. v Columbia Pictures Corp.,* (7 Cir., 1941) 120 F2d 891, 894.

Contempt, *Ex Parte Hadley,* (Calif., 1943) 135 P2d 381, 383.

Custom and Usage, *Electrical Research Products v Gross,* (9 Cir., 1941) 120 F2d 301, 305.

Damages, amount and kind, *City of Miami v Thigpen,* (Fla., 1943) 11 So2d 300, 301.

Dedication to the public, *City of Easton v Koch,* (Pa., 1943) 31 A2d 747, 751; *Sawicki v Connecticut Railway & Lighting Co.,* (Conn., 1943) 30 A2d 556, 558.

Delivery of deed, *Oberholtz v Oberholtz,* (Oh., 1947) 74 NE2d 574, 577.

Duress, its existence being fact and of what it consists being law, *Walk-A-Show v Stanton,* (Md., 1943) 35 A2d 121, 122.

Good faith, *Hood v Meininger,* (Pa., 1954) 105 A2d 126, 44 ALR2d 1106 (Owner being satisfied with contractor's work).

Identity, *Woodfine v Maier,* (Or., 1959) 338 P2d 681, 81 ALR2d 857; *Re Hayden,* (Kan., 1953) 254 P2d 813, 36 ALR2d 1278; *Whittemore v Lockheed Aircraft Corp.,* (Cal. 1944) 151 P2d 670.

Intent of a person, fraudulent or otherwise, *Luikart v Bosse,* (Neb., 1942) 5 NW2d 128, 132; *People v De Marcello,* (NY, 1941) 31 NYS2d 608, 610.

Invention, *Gordon v Conlon Corp.* (Ill., 1941) 42 F. Supp. 962, 963.

Justification, *State v Burk* (Wn., 1921) 195 P 16, 21 ALR 193; (killing animal to protect property); *State v Rathbone,* (Mont., 1940) 100 P2d 86.

Mental capacity, *Page v Prudential Life Ins. Co.,* (Wn., 1942) 120 P2d 527, 531.

Nuisance, *Hume v Laurel Hill,* (Cal. 1905) 142 F 552; *State v Turner,* (SC, 1942) 18 SE2d 372, 375.

Permanent injury, *United Verde Extension Mining Co. v Littlejohn,* (9 Cir., 1922) 279 F 223.

Residence and citizenship, *United States v Beda,* (2 Cir., 1941) 118 F2d 458, 459; *State ex rel Crosland v Board of Education,* (Minn., 1904) 97 NW 885; Anno: 56 ALR2d 372 (Residence of student for purposes of tuition).

Reasonableness, *Suits v Glover,* (Ala., 1954) 71 So2d 49, 43 ALR2d 465; *Calway v Williamson,* (Conn., 1944) 36 A2d 377 (teacher spanking pupil).

Undue influence, *Love v Harris,* (Ind., 1957) 143 NE2d 450, 454; *Erg v Erg,* (Or., 1942) 131 P2d 198, 201.

Unfair competition, *Krem-Ko Co. v R. G. Miller & Sons,* (2 Cir., 1934) 68 F2d 872, 874; *Wood v Peffer,* (Cal., 1942) 130 P2d 220, 225; but found to be a mixed question in: *James Heddon's Sons v Millsite Steel & Wire Works,* (6 Cir., 1942) 128 F2d 6, 13.

Voluntary payment, *Wachovea Bank & Title Co. v Miller,* (NC, 1922) 115 SE 161.

Waiver and estopple, *Jersey Discount Co. v Aetna Ins. Co.,* (NJ, 1942) 25 A2d 506, 507.

Will, execution, In *Re Goldsworthy's Estate,* (Cal., 1942) 129 P2d 949, 951.

Business Transaction Cases

A question of fact exists as to whether:

A corporation has liquidated, C. M. Menzies, Inc., 34 B.T.A. 163.

A partnership existing, *Nahmod v Nelson*, (Fla., 1941) 3 So2d 162, 164.

Discovery of minerals, *Dallas v Fitzsimmons*, (Colo., 1958) 323 P2d 274, 66 ALR2d 551.

Holder in due course by transferee of commercial paper originating as a security transaction by affiliate of transferee, *Brown v Farmer & Ochs Co.*, (6 Cir., 1954) 209 F2d 703.

Oral statements of seller amount to an express warranty of goods sold, *Hercules Powder Co. v Rich* (8 Cir., 1924) 3 F2d 12, 67 ALR1d 619; *Shippen v Bowen*, (1887) 122 U.S. 575.

Use of purchased article by buyer for time sufficient to constitute waiver of right to rescind sale, *Achilli v Alongi*, (Ill., 1952) 104 NE2d 645; but question of law when ice box kept for eight months before rescission, *C. V. Hill & Co. v Parker* (Tex., 1940) 145 SW2d 330; Anno: 41 ALR2d 1195.

Shipper ratified carrier's delivery of cargo though misdelivered, *Lake Shore & MSR Co. v W. H. McIntyre* (Ind., 1915) 108 NE 978.

Person not named in application for registration of securities is in control of applicant's business, *Archer v Securities and Exchange Commission*, (8 Cir., 1943) 133 F2d 795, 799.

Contract Cases

A question of fact exists as to whether:
A contract was made, *Hickey v Glass*, (Ky., 1941) 149 SW2d 535, 536.

Ascertainment of the terms of a contract as distinguished from construction of the terms, *John A. Frye Shoe Co. v Williams*, (Mass., 1942) 46 NE2d 1, 7.

Novation of an existing contract, *Credit Bureau Adjust. Dept. v Cox Bros.*, (Or., 1956) 295 P2d 1107, 61 ALR2d 750.

An implied warranty to perform a workmanlike service was breached by a stevedore. *Delanguville v Simonsen*, (5 Cir., 1971) 437 F2d 597.

Resolving the ambiguity in a contract provision upon extrinsic evidence admitted for that purpose is a question of fact but first deciding if contract is ambiguous is question of law, *Neff v Mutual Life Ins. Co. of New York,* (Calif., 1941) 119 P2d 404, 407.

Bill of Sale intended as a chattel mortgage, *State v Snyder* (Idaho, 1951) 233 P2d 802, 33 ALR2d 358; *Prentiss Tool & Supply Co. v Schmirmer,* (NY, 1892) 32 NE 849.

Oral promise of president of corporation to pay for goods sold to corporation as original promise not barred by statute of frauds, *Goldsmith v Erwin,* (4 Cir., 1950) 183 F2d 432, 20 ALR2d 240.

Buyer is bound by printed conditions on unsigned confirmation order sent by seller or broker, *Land Oberaesterreich v Gude,* (2 Cir., 1940) 109 F2d 635; *A. M. Kidder & Co. v Turner,* (Fla., 1958) 106 S2d 905, 71 ALR2d 1083.

Parties to contract are in *pari delicto, Ryan v Motor Credit Co.,* (NJ, 1941) 23 A2d 607, 620.

Facts existing at time of making contract support declaration that actual damage cannot be practically ascertained in order to justify provision for liquidated damages, *Associated Press v Emmett,* (Calif., 1942) 45 F. Supp. 907, 917.

Going on active duty with U.S. Navy created conflict of interest to frustrate a party's obligation under contract to solicit Government business, *Havens v Rochester Ropes, Inc.,* (NY 1942) 39 NYS2d 444, 447.

Amount of work performed and materials furnished by general contractor in performance of contract, *Happel v United States* (Mo., 1959) 176 F. Supp. 787, 788.

Where servant negligently causes injury and servant relationship is denied written contract supposedly containing all rights and duties of parties will not prevent ascertainment of servant's relationship, *Mid-Continent Petroleum Corp. v Vicars,* (Ind. 1943) 46 NE2d 253, 256.

Failure of contractor to meet specifications of contract, *General Steel Products Corp. v United States,* (NY, 1941) 36 F. Supp. 498, 501.

Reasonable time provided in contract for thing to be done, *Lyon v Goss,* (Calif., 1942) 123 P2d 11, 19; but question of law in *Franklin Paint Co. v Flaherty,* (Me., 1943) 24 A2d 651, 652.

Whether work done by contractor was required by contract, *Hiebert v United States,* (Alaska, 1964) 235 F. Supp. 466, 467.

Failure to read contract as preventing reformation of contract for mutual mistake of fact, *Medford v Kimmey,* (Tex., 1927) 298 SW 140. Anno: 81 ALR2d 7, 41.

Owner selling property for less than price listed with broker as breach of broker's contract, *Thompson v Foster,* (NC, 1954) 82 SE2d 109, 46 ALR2d 843; *Nardelli v T. C. Triplett Bldg. Co.,* (Ariz., 1931) 298 P 402.

Divorce Cases

A question of fact exists as to:

What constitutes extreme cruelty, *Dion v Dion,* (Conn., 1941) 23 A2d 314, 315.

Physical violence of one spouse versus provocation of other, *Popescu v Popescu,* (Calif., 1941) 115 P2d 208, 211.

Plaintiff entitled to alimony, *Barber v Barber,* (NH, 1943) 30 A2d 278.

Changed conditions and best interest of child, *Cheesbrough v Jensen,* (Idaho, 1941) 109 P2d 889.

Insurance Policy Cases

A question of fact exists as to whether:

An insured was accidentally killed while provoking a fight, *Peoples Loan & Invest. Co. v Travelers Ins. Co.,* (8 Cir. 1945) 151 F2d 437; *Shields v Prudential Ins. Co.,* (NJ, 1951) 79 A2d 297, 26 ALR2d 392.

Death by other than use of intoxicating liquor, *Flannagan v Provident Life & Acc. Ins. Co.,* (4 Cir., 1927) 22 F2d 136.

Death except as result of internal disease, i.e. arteriosclerosis, *Svenson v Mutual L. Ins. Co.,* (8 Cir., 1937) 87 F2d 441; but can easily become question of law, *Britton v Prudential Ins. Co.,* (Tenn., 1959) 330 SW2d 326, 82 ALR2d 605.

Damage resulting from fire and not excepted explosion where both occur, *Merrimack Mut. F. Ins. Co. v Lanasa,* (Va., 1961) 118 SE2d 450, 82 ALR2d 1118.

Lightning causing damage, *Clouse v St. Paul Fire & Marine Ins.* (Neb. 1950) 40 NW2d 820, 15 ALR2d 1008.

Answers to questions in application being false and also being material, *Anastasio v Metropolitan Life Ins. Co.,* (Pa. 1942) 27 A2d 510, 512; *Guardian Life Ins. Co. v Barry,* (Ind., 1941) 32 NE2d 599, 607.

Good health on date of policy, *National Life & Acc. Ins. Co. v Green,* (Miss., 1941) 3 So2d 812, 813.

Bias or prejudice of appraiser appointed under policy, *Mizrahi v Nat. Ben Franklin Fire Ins. Co.* (NY, 1942) 37NYS2d 698, 700.

What amounts to total disability, *Erreca v Western States Life Ins. Co.,* (Calif., 1942) 121 P2d 689, 696.

Cooperation of insured under policy agreement, *Lindsay v Gulf Ins. Co.,* (La., 1942) 7 So2d 757, 760.

Negligence Cases

Negligence and its proximate cause of injury are questions of fact for jury and only become questions of law for court when reasonable men would not differ on evidence when considered in its most favorable light, *Oklahoma Natural Gas Co. v McKee,* (10 Cir., 1941) 121 F2d 583, 585.

A question of fact exists as to whether:

Negligence is gross or ordinary, *Copp v Van Hise,* (9 Cir., 1941) 119 F2d 691, 695.

Two or more persons are joint wrongdoers, *Hudson v Weiland,* (Fla., 1942) 8 SO2d 37, 38.

Forgetfulness of a known danger constitutes want of ordinary care, *Iden v Zeeman Clothing Co.,* (Calif., 1942) 122 P2d 626, 627.

Superseding cause was sufficient to prevent negligence from being a substantial factor of injury, *Colligan v Reilly,* (Conn., 1942) 26 A2d 231, 233.

Contributory negligence and its proximate cause of injury, *McWane v Hetherton,* (Calif., 1942) 125 P2d 8, 86.

Willfully or wantonly inflicting injury, *Robins v Pitcairn,* (7 Cir., 1942) 124 F2d 734, 736.

Foreseeability of conduct causing injury, *Lomano v Ideal Towel Supply Co.,* (NJ, 1947) 51 A2d 888 (Leaving keys in car started by stranger; *Ferroggiaro v Bowline,* (Calif., 1957) 315 P2d 446, 64 ALR2d 1355 (knocking down traffic signal, the lack of which caused subsequent collision); question of law: *Richards v Stanley,* (Calif., 1954) 271 P2d 23; Anno: 51 ALR2d 633 d 652.

Existence of real peril to invoke emergency rule, *Zickrick v Strathern,* (Minn., 1941) 1 NW2d 134, 136.

Speed of vehicle, *Hopkins v Pacific Electric R. Co.,* (Calif., 1941) 118 P2d 872, 875.

Failure to yield right of way, *Hodges v McCullom,* (Calif. 1941) 117 P2d 44, 46.

Prior knowledge of defect in stair as constituting contributory negligence, *Oles v Dubinsky,* (Mass., 1918) 121 NE 405; Anno: 26 ALR2d 468; or of guy wire hazard on property, *Virginia Public Service Co. v Carter,* (Va., 1937) 190 SE 155.

Pedestrian contributorily negligent for failure to walk on statutory proper side of highway, *Smith v Orangetown* (NY, 1944) 57 F. Supp. 52, affirmed in (2 Cir., 1945) 150 F2d 782; *Mursky v Brody,* (NJ, 1935) 181 A 273; Anno: 4 ALR2d 1258.

Passing vehicle crowding another vehicle off road, *Zurfluh v Lewis County* (Wn., 1939) 91 P2d 1002; Anno: 48 ALR2d 232.

Negligence of power company in not grounding wires through which lightning entered house, *Alabama Power Co. v Bryant,* (Ala. 1933) 146 So. 602; Anno: 25 ALR2d 722, 742.

At time of accident one is engaged in activities connected with the military, *Nowotny v Turner,* (NC, 1962) 203 F. Supp. 802; *Wilcox v United States,* (NY, 1953) 117 F. Supp. 119.

Ownership of vehicle involved in accident, *Louisville Taxicab & T. Co. v Johnson,* (Ky., 1949) 224 SW2d 639, 27 ALR2d 158.

Payment of hospital bills by municipality to injured employee as waiver to necessity of file written claim for injury, *Beaumant v Silas,* (Texas, 1947) 200 SW2d 690; Anno: 65 ALR2d 1279, 1305.

Admission of a defendant to a tort while away from scene and of which he had no personal knowledge, *Casey v Burns,* (Ill., 1955) 129 NE2d 440, 54 ALR2d 1060.

Negligent failure of landlord to repair light fixture as cause of injury, *Seldin v Nixon Realty Corp.,* (NY, 1934) 275 NYS 438; Anno: 86 ALR 841.

Drowning of seaman caused by employer's negligence, *Schultz v Penn. R. Co.,* (1956) 350 U.S. 523.

Negligently permitting fire to spread as cause of damage, *Osborn v Whittier,* (Calif., 1951) 230 P2d 132; *Boynton v Fox Denver Theatres,* (Colo., 1950) 214 P2d 793, 24 ALR2d 235.

Negligent medical treatment necessitated by defendant's negligence as cause of injury, *Spivey v Atteberry,* (Okla., 1951) 238 P2d 814, 27 ALR2d 1259.

Psychoneurotic injury caused by airplane automobile collision, *Hoff v United States,* (10 Cir., 1959) 268 F2d 646.

Contractor's negligence in construction as cause of injury to person after structure has been turned over to owner, *Hale v Depaoli,* (Calif., 1948) 201 P2d 1, 13 ALR2d 183.

Trustee's negligence in failure to sell bank stock, *Hatfield v First National Bank of Danville,* (Ill, 1942) 46 NE2d 94, 99.

Condition in public street as being dangerous, *Barker v City of Los Angeles,* (Calif., 1943) 135 P2d 573.

Dangerous street condition existing sufficiently long for constructive notice, *George v City of Los Angeles,* (Calif., 1942) 124 P2d 872, 875.

Motion of train sufficiently unusual as to constitute negligence, *United States v De Back,* (9 Cir., 1941) 118 F2d 208, 210.

Sufficiency of slipperyness of floor to constitute negligence, *Nicola v Pacific Gas & Electric Co.,* (Calif., 1942) 123 P2d 529, 531.

Airplane pilot abandoning radio beam to fly on average compass course as negligence, *Johnson v Western Air Express Corp.,* (Calif., 1941) 114 P2d 688, 696.

Failure to discover faulty land description as inexcusable neglect to bar reformation of deed, *Hanlon v Western Loan & Building Co.,* (Calif., 1941) 116 P2d 465, 475.

Malicious Prosecution and Slander Cases

A question of fact exists as to whether:

Defendant's malice is in excess of qualified privilege in libel or slander action, *People Life Ins. Co. v Talley,* (Va., 1936) 186 SE 42; *Russell v Penn Mut. Life Ins. Co.,* (Pa., 1935) 179 A 798. Anno: 55 ALR2d 828.

Delay in bringing arrested person before a committing magistrate as being unreasonable, *Rounds v Bucher,* (Mont. 1960) 349 P2d 1026, 98 ALR2d 962; but question of law if facts not in dispute, *Anderson v Foster,* (Idaho, 1953) 252 P2d 199.

Probable cause for detaining store customer erroneously believed to be a shoplifter, *Isaiah v Great A & P Tea Co.,* (Ohio, 1959) 174 NE2d 128, 86 ALR2d 430.

Principal and Agent Cases

A question of fact exists as to whether:

Who of several is employer of an injured employee (longshoreman) treated as question of fact ("It is, perhaps, a little of each"— fact and law) *Mastro's Case,* (9 Cir., 1969) 419 F2d 143.

Existence, scope and extent of an agent's authority, *United States v Romitti,* (9 Cir., 1966) 363 F2d 662; *Leonard v North Dakota Co-op Wool Marketing Ass'n.* (ND, 1942) 6 NW2d 576, 578.

Milk route driver an independent contractor or agent of milk distributor, *Gomillion v Forsythe,* (SC, 1950) 62 SE2d 297, 53 ALR2d 169.

Employee in scope of employment while driving employer's car *R. J. Reynolds Tobacco Co. v Newby,* (9 Cir., 1944) 145 F2d 768, 54 ALR2d 13, 74.

Employee's wife driving automobile furnished employee by his employer as agent of employer for imposing liability upon employer, *Leonard v North Dakota Co-op Wool Marketing Ass'n.* (ND, 1942) 6 NW2d 576, 578; however, where defendant is engaged in an automobile driveaway business by arranging delivery of automobiles from Detroit to distant points and one such automobile became involved in accident in California with injured plaintiff obtaining in California a judgment against defendant on theory the driver was agent, the Michigan Supreme Court would not consider the agency question as one of fact so as to preclude it from reviewing the case *Johnson v Haley,* (Mich., 1959) 98 NW2d 55, 558.

Real Property Cases

A Question of fact exists as to:

Boiler on premises in control of landlord or tenant for purpose of lease agreement to repair, *Cohen v Reif,* (Ky., 1928) 4 SW2d 388.

Landlord's conduct estopping him from claiming tenant did not give timely notice to renew lease, *Khourie Bros. v Jonakin,* (Ky., 1927) 300 SW 612, Anno: 51 ALR2d 1404.

Acceptance of deed by grantee, *Henneberry v Henneberry,* (Calif., 1958) 330 P2d 250; but question of law if no dispute on facts, *Henry v Heggie,* (NC, 1913) 79 SE 982; Anno: 74 ALR2d 1005.

Repudiation of landlord's title by widow of tenant, *Watson v Hardin,* (Ark., 1910) 132 SW 1002.

Deed given as mortgage under oral trust agreement and its repudiation, *Emmons v Jones,* (Texas, 1923) 246 SW 1052; Anno: 54 ALR 74.

Broker procured buyer which owner sold directly to at low price, *Hartzog v Dean,* (Ark., 1949) 223 SW2d 820; Anno: 46 ALR2d 883.

Tax Cases

A question of fact exists as to whether:

Taxpayer is holding property primarily for sale to customers, *Real Estate Mortg. & G. Co. v District of Columbia,* (DC Cir., 1944) 141 F2d 361; *Rubino v Commissioner,* (9 Cir., 1951) 186 F2d 304; but has been treated as mixed question, *Reynolds v Commissioner,* (1 Cir., 1946) 155 F2d 620.

Purposes for which expenditures were made, *Peerless Stages v Commissioner,* (9 Cir., 1942) 125 F2d 869, 871.

Unified control of corporations so as to make a single employing unit, *Washington Oil Corp. of Texas v State,* (Tex., 1941) 159 SW2d 517, 522.

Gain or loss in exchange of property, *United States v State Street Trust Co.,* (1 Cir., 1942) 124 F2d 948, 951.

True value of property, *American Steel & Wire Co. v Board of Revision of Cuyahoga County,* (Ohio, 1942) 40 NE2d 426, 427.

Redemption of stock as taxable dividend, *Hirsch v Commissioner,* (9 Cir., 1941) 124 F2d 24, 28.

Accumulations beyond reasonable needs, *J. M. Perry & Co. v Commissioner,* (9 Cir., 1941) 120 F2d 123, 125.

Reasonableness of salary paid corporate secretary, *Sportwear Hosiery Mills v Commissioner,* (3 Cir., 1942) 129 F2d 376, 378.

Location of chief office of corporation, *City of Newark v State Board of Tax Appeals,* (NJ, 1942) 23 A2d 789.

Whether stock has become worthless during tax year, *Dunbar v Commissioner,* (7 Cir., 1941) 119 F2d 367, 369.

Gift made in contemplation of death, *People v Scarborough,* (Ill., 1942) 44 NE2d 845, 847.

Challenging the
Sufficiency of Evidence

3

Until you have proven by competent evidence every fact essential to your case you cannot get it to the jury, let alone win a favorable verdict. Often where only circumstantial evidence is available the getting into the ball park is much more difficult than winning the ball game. Is your evidence sufficient for jury consideration? That is always a threshold question for the trial judge, a question which at times can become excruciatingly difficult to decide. In meeting this threshold issue it is important to know when and how to challenge the evidence as well as to understand the standard of law which the trial judge will use in measuring evidence for size. In this chapter we point out to you the tools for the job and the measuring stick within the rules and practice of the federal courts. It should be expected that these procedural methods vary in the respective state jurisdictions but basically the tools and measuring sticks remain comparable if not the same.

Tools for the Job

Sufficiency of evidence is usually challenged by a motion for a directed verdict after both plaintiff and defendant have presented their respective evidence,[1] although the motion can be made after plaintiff's opening statement[2] or upon the close of plaintiff's case in chief.[3] A second challenge to sufficiency of the evidence can be made

[1] Rule 50(a)

[2] Gundersheimer's, Inc. v Bakery Union (DC., 1941) 119 F2d 205; Oscanyon v Arms. Co. (1880) 103 U.S. 261

[3] Bayamon, Thom, McAn, Inc. v Miranda (1 Cir., 1969) 409 F2d 968

after a jury has returned its verdict providing a motion was properly made for a directed verdict prior to the case being submitted to the jury. This post-verdict challenge is accomplished by a motion for judgment notwithstanding the verdict, otherwise known as motion for judgment *non obstante veredicto* or a motion for judgment n.o.v.

Rule 50 of the Federal Rules of Civil Procedure

Rule 50 of the Federal Rules of Civil Procedure as amended in 1963 presents a clear cut procedure for challenging sufficiency of evidence in the federal courts. It reads:

(a) *Motion for Directed Verdict: When Made; Effect.* A party who moves for a directed verdict at the close of the evidence offered by an opponent may offer evidence in the event that the motion is not granted, without having reserved the right so to do and to the same extent as if the motion had not been made. A motion for a directed verdict which is not granted is not a waiver of trial by jury even though all parties to the action have moved for directed verdicts. A motion for a directed verdict shall state the specific grounds therefor. The order of the court granting a motion for a directed verdict is effective without any assent of the jury.

(b) *Motion for Judgment Notwithstanding the Verdict.* Whenever a motion for a directed verdict made at the close of all the evidence is denied or for any reason is not granted, the court is deemed to have submitted the action to the jury subject to a later determination of the legal questions raised by the motion. Not later than 10 days after entry of judgment, a party who has moved for a directed verdict may move to have the verdict and any judgment entered thereon set aside and to have judgment entered in accordance with his motion for a directed verdict. A motion for a new trial may be joined with this motion, or a new trial may be prayed for in the alternative. If a verdict was returned the court may allow the judgment to stand or may reopen the judgment and either order a new trial or direct the entry of judgment as if the requested verdict had been directed. If no verdict was returned the court may direct the entry of judgment as if the requested verdict had been directed or may order a new trial.

(c) *Same: Conditional Rulings on Grant of Motion.* (1) If

the motion for judgment notwithstanding the verdict, provided for in subdivision (b) of this rule, is granted, the court shall also rule on the motion for a new trial, if any, by determining whether it should be granted if the judgment is thereafter vacated or reversed, and shall specify the grounds for granting or denying the motion for the new trial. If the motion for a new trial is thus conditionally granted, the order thereon does not affect the finality of the judgment. In case the motion for a new trial has been conditionally granted and the judgment is reversed on appeal, the new trial shall proceed unless the appellate court has otherwise ordered. In case the motion for a new trial has been conditionally denied, the appellee on appeal may assert error in that denial; and if the judgment is reversed on appeal, subsequent proceedings shall be in accordance with the order of the appellate court.

(2) The party whose verdict has been set aside on motion for judgment notwithstanding the verdict may serve a motion for a new trial pursuant to Rule 59 not later than 10 days after entry of the judgment notwithstanding the verdict.

(d) *Same: Denial of Motion.* If the motion for judgment notwithstanding the verdict is denied, the party who prevailed on that motion may, as appellee, assert grounds entitling him to a new trial in the event the appellate court concludes that the trial court erred in denying the motion for judgment notwithstanding the verdict. If the appellate court reverses the judgment, nothing in this rule precludes it from determining that the appellee is entitled to a new trial, or from directing the trial court to determine whether a new trial shall be granted. As amended Jan. 21, 1963, eff. July 1, 1963

The Directed Verdict

Since the directed verdict is a carry over from the common law, Rule 50 is constitutional and does not deprive a person of his right to trial by jury[4] and does not violate the Seventh Amendment which forbids a court to re-examine facts found by a jury.[5]

The charm of Rule 50, as amended in 1963, lies in its elimination of waiver traps which existed at common law and which can yet be found in some state jurisdictions. No longer must a party make an express reservation for right to present evidence for jury consideration

---

[4] Helene Curtis Industries, Inc. v Pruitt, (5 Cir., 1967) 385 F2d 841

[5] Drinan v A. J. Lindemann & Hoverson Co., (Wis., 1956) 141 F. Supp. 73, affirmed in (7 Cir., 1956) 238 F2d 72

should motion for a directed verdict be denied.[6] No longer is the fact-issue removed from jury consideration where all parties move for a directed verdict in favor of themselves.[7] No longer need the trial judge in granting a motion for a directed verdict go through the hypocrisy of having a juror sign a form for a verdict which the jury never rendered.[8]

The one important thing to remember when moving for a directed verdict is to state the specific grounds upon which the motion is based. This requirement is to apprise the court and other counsel precisely where you contend the evidence is deficient. If the deficiency is an oversight or otherwise can be cured, the trial court in its discretion will usually permit the cure to be accomplished.

It is only in the unusual type of case where after pretrial discovery you believe the opponent cannot produce adequate evidence that you should move for a directed verdict after an opening statement and before evidence is presented. In the right case it can save much trial time. If as in *Reynolds v Penn. R.R. Co.*, (7 Cir., 1959) 267 F2d 231 the Plaintiff cannot state facts which he intends to prove sufficiently to show that the defendant did not provide plaintiff with a safe place to work a motion for directed verdict for defendant is in order. However, just as federal courts hesitate to grant summary judgments under Rule 56 so are they hesitant to direct verdicts upon opening statements. This undoubtedly is because of a firm belief that a litigant should have a full day in court and also perhaps that the evidence as actually presented may turn out to be stronger than the attorney's opening statement indicates.

Of course, a motion for a directed verdict can also be made at close of plaintiff's case in chief. Motions to dismiss or for involuntary non-suit when made in a federal court will be treated as a motion for a directed verdict.[9] For these reasons it becomes important to know the effect of the granting of such motion at an intermediate stage of the trial. Is the plaintiff foreclosed from re-filing his action? At common law the non-suiting of a plaintiff did not foreclose him from filing another action and trying again.[10] Under present federal prac-

---

[6] Sampliner v Motion Picture Patents Co., (1920) 254 U.S. 233

[7] North Amerc. Acc. Ins. Co. v Anderson, (10 Cir., 1938) 100 F2d 452; ANNO: Directed Verdict Motions-Waiver 68 ALR2d 300

[8] 28 USCA Rule 50(a)

[9] Meyonberg v Penn. R.R. Co., (3 Cir., 1947) 165 F2d 50; Taylor v Cirino, (6 Cir., 1963) 321 F2d 279

[10] Central Transp. Co. v Pullman's Car Co., (1891) 139 US 24, 39

tice, in light of Rule 50(a) on directed verdicts and Rule 41(b) on involuntary dismissals, the grant of a directed verdict at any stage of the trial will become a decision on the merits and preclude a re-filing of a new action *unless* the court for good reason chooses to dismiss the action without prejudice. In *Safeway Stores v Fannon,* (9 Cir., 1962) 308 F2d 94 the trial judge upon motion for a directed verdict granted the motion and dismissed the case *without prejudice* to the plaintiff. The Court of Appeals for the Ninth Circuit, after pointing out that Rule 41(b) usually contemplated dismissals with prejudice, held in that case the trial court abused its discretion in dismissing the case without prejudice upon granting motion for a directed verdict. It might have been otherwise had plaintiff, at time of opposing the motion for a directed verdict, indicated plaintiff's ability to find evidence to cure the deficiency in proof or it appeared that plaintiff's attorney had somehow "butchered" his client's case.

One should hesitate, except in the clearest of cases, to move for a directed verdict before the end of all proof. In *Williams v Slade,* (5 Cir., 1970) 431 F2d 605 the injured person was a passenger in automobile A which had collision with automobile B. Plaintiff sued both driver of A and B claiming both were negligent in the intersection collision. When the plaintiff rested, her host, driver of A, moved for a directed verdict based upon the testimony that the green traffic light was in her favor. Motion was granted. Driver of car B in his defense thereafter testified that the green intersection light was in his favor. With A already out of the case, the jury considered only the case against B with the result a defense verdict was returned to exonerate B. Thereupon, plaintiff appealed the granting of directed verdict to A and got a reversal and new trial on the basis that there was an issue of fact as to A's contributory negligence which should have gone to the jury. However, what is significant in this case is that the appellate court granted a new trial for the plaintiff against both A and B, holding that both A and B could have each contributed to the accident and it would be unfair to plaintiff to have A only as her target on the second trial. What about the "double jeopardy" of B who had already been exonerated by the jury in the first trial?

While ordinarily a motion for a directed verdict is granted to a moving party not having the burden of proof, do not overlook the possibility that a party such as a plaintiff carrying the burden of proof can move for and be granted a directed verdict. Of course, for a party who has the onus of proof, the evidence must be so one-sided in his favor as to be overwhelming.[11] In *Hanley v Hedler,* (3 Cir., 1967) 380 F2d 986, plaintiff in an automobile collision case proceeded upon *res ipsa loquitur* theory which in New Jersey is only a permissible inference not justifying a motion for a directed verdict. However, the defendant's proof unequivocally showed that the cause of collision was failure of brakes of defendant's vehicle which had previously been negligently repaired by defendant's son. That changed the ball game. The Court of Appeals held that the trial court erred in not granting plaintiff's motion for a directed verdict. The case was remanded for trial on the damage issue only. When a moving vehicle hits a properly located stationary object such as a scaffold and injures a workman on the scaffold, don't be surprised if the court grants the plaintiff a directed verdict on liability and submits only the issue of damages to the jury. *Baumann v Maloney Concrete Co.* (D.C., 1967) 278 F. Supp. 463. Where plaintiff sues his employer as a Jones Act seaman for injuries received while working on a special purpose harbor craft it is usually a question of fact as to whether or not he is a seaman. However, where the evidence is not in dispute it can be a touch and go question as to whether plaintiff is entitled to a directed verdict on that point. *Soucie v Trautwein Brothers,* (Calif., 1969) 79 Cal. Rptr 671.

Finally, it must be borne in mind that a motion for a directed verdict properly goes to challenging all of the evidence and not just a part of it. If, for example, the plaintiff fails to prove one of several allegations of negligence or a defendant fails to prove one of his affirmative defenses, neither of which entitles the other party to a verdict, the proper tool to be employed is a motion to strike the particular allegation or a motion to withdraw the specific issue from the jury, or, possibly, requesting a peremptory instruction to the jury on such partial but specific unproven issue or contention.[12]

Just because you may have earlier moved for a summary judgment on basis of no genuine issue of fact for jury determination is no reason why you should not later move for a directed verdict if the evidence still appears to you to be insufficient.[13] While a trial court might hesitate early in the litigation to grant a summary judgment it could very well during the trial decide otherwise. One should not be prejudiced in making successive attacks on sufficiency of evidence. On

---

[11] Grey v First National Bank, (5 Cir., 1968) 393 F2d 371
[12] Rochester Civic Theatre, Inc. v Ramsay, (Minn., 1966) 368 F2d 748
[13] Robbins v Milner Enterprises, Inc. (5 Cir., 1960) 278 F2d 492

that subject the trial court throughout the case should always be free to change its mind. The burden of persuasion is heavy on him who moves for a directed verdict. However, it is only by moving for a directed verdict that one can focus the trial court's attention upon the deficiency of proof. It has been considered good practice for a trial court, when granting a motion for a directed verdict, to give its reasons and point to where the proof is deficient.[14]

Judgment Notwithstanding Verdict

Only when a party has moved for a directed verdict at the close of all of the evidence and such motion is either denied or otherwise not granted can the party make his second challenge to the sufficiency of the evidence by a motion for judgment notwithstanding the verdict. This important condition precedent is not satisfied if some other defendant moved for a directed verdict and the defendant moving for judgment notwithstanding had not also done so.[15] Even if defendant had moved for a directed verdict upon plaintiff's opening statement or upon the close of plaintiff's case in chief he still must do so again upon close of all evidence in the case if he is to qualify for right to move for judgment notwithstanding the verdict.[16] An exception to this rule is when after an earlier motion for a directed verdict has been denied, the trial judge orally indicates that the later motion will not be necessary to preserve the mover's rights.[17] Once the motion for directed verdict is made at close of the evidence whether or not the court rules on the motion or reserves ruling the court's subsequent submission of the case to the jury is deemed to be subject to the legal questions raised by the motion for the directed verdict. However, it has been held that the court cannot enter a verdict on his own contrary to that of the jury without a motion being made for judgment notwithstanding the verdict.[18]

A motion made during trial to strike evidence or pleadings is not a sufficient equivalent to a motion for a directed verdict which is required to be made in order to later make a motion for judgment

---

[14] Morse v Moretti, (DC., Cir., 1968) 403 F2d 564

[15] Deakyne v Commissioner of Lewes (Del., 1968) 44 F.R.D. 425

[16] Bayomon Thom, McAn, Inc. v Miranda, (1 Cir., 1969) 409 F2d 968

[17] Jack Cole Co. v Hudson, (5 Cir., 1969) 409 F2d 188

[18] Compton v United States, (8 Cir., 1967) 377 F2d 408

notwithstanding verdict.[19] However, it has been held that a written requested instruction for a directed verdict is a sufficient equivalent to the motion for a directed verdict to entitle the party requesting such an instruction to move for judgment notwithstanding verdict.[20] Reliance should not be made on a requested instruction as being a substitute for a motion for a directed verdict as Rule 50 requires a motion for a directed verdict to specify grounds upon which it is based. It does not seem likely that a requested peremptory instruction will contain specific grounds for the direction of the verdict.

As will be next discussed the measure of evidence for its sufficiency is governed in the federal courts by federal law although in a diversity case the elements comprising the cause of action is one of substantive law based upon the law of the particular state.[21] The same measuring stick is applied to motion for a directed verdict as well as to a motion for judgment notwithstanding the verdict.[22] In event the jury becomes "hung" and is dismissed without having returned a verdict, there is no constitutional reason why the court cannot enter a verdict in accordance with a previously made motion for a directed verdict.[23] However, should a mistrial or "hung jury" occur after a motion for directed verdict has been made and denied, the trial court cannot set the case for retrial until 10 days have elapsed within which the party who moved for the directed verdict has had right to exercise his right to move for a judgment notwithstanding the verdict. *Grace Lines, Inc. v Motley,* (2 Cir., 1971) 439 F2d 1028. Rule 50 permits the trial court to either reserve ruling on motion for a directed verdict or to deny it and reconsider the question when and if a motion for judgment notwithstanding the verdict is made. If the question is close or there is doubt about deciding the motion for a directed verdict, it is good practice for the trial court to reserve ruling on the motion for a directed verdict and submit the case to the jury.[24] If the case is weak on facts it is very likely that the jury will return a verdict consistent with that sought upon the motion for the directed verdict, making

---

[19] Jefferson Realty of South Dade Inc., v Fidelity & Deposit Co. of Md., (5 Cir., 1969) 410 F2d 847

[20] Roberts v Pierce, (5 Cir., 1968) 398 F2d 954. To the contrary: Dudding v Thorpe (W. D. Pa., 1969) 47 F. R. D. 565; Budge Manufacturing Co. v United States (3 Cir., 1960) 280 F2d 414

[21] Boeing Company v Shipman (5 Cir., 1969) 411 F2d 365; Shaw v U.S. Fidelity & Guaranty Co., (3 Cir., 1938) 101 F2d 92

[22] Glazer v Glazer, (5 Cir., 1967) 374 F2d 390

[23] O'Brien v Tholl, (2 Cir., 1960) 283 F2d 741

[24] Morse v Moretti, (DC Cir., 1968) 403 F2d 564

unnecessary a ruling on the motion. If otherwise, the jury will have decided the damage issue, and if upon appeal the court's direction of the verdict is reversed, a proper judgment can be entered without necessity for a second trial.

The most marked innovation of Rule 50 is its relating of motion for a new trial alternatively and conditionally with the motion for judgment notwithstanding the verdict. It gives both the trial and appellate courts freedom to order a new trial if in the interest of justice such appears to be the proper move. You will observe in subsection (b) of Rule 50 a party who has moved for a directed verdict may within ten days after *entry* of judgment on the verdict as returned move not only for judgment notwithstanding the verdict (and judgment thereon) but also join therewith a motion in the alternative for a new trial should the motion for judgment notwithstanding the verdict be denied. With the case in such a posture the trial court has the freedom to act four different ways.[25] It may:

(1) Order the verdict and judgment already entered to stand;
(2) Vacate the judgment as entered and order judgment notwithstanding the verdict;
(3) Vacate the judgment as entered and order a new trial;
(4) Vacate the judgment as entered and dismiss the action without prejudice.

Rule 50 by its subsection (c) provides for conditional rulings in event the motion for judgment notwithstanding the verdict is granted while subsection (d) provides for conditional rulings in event the motion for judgment notwithstanding the verdict is denied. On appeal all parties acting timely can argue for and against these conditional rulings and thus within due process of law permit the appellate court to affirm or reverse rulings and conditional rulings of the trial court as justice may dictate. Between a careful reading of Rule 50 and the Supreme Court's pronouncement upon the working and purpose of Rule 50 in *Neely v Martin K. Elby Construction Co.*, (1967) 386 U.S. 317 you can figure how best to proceed in your specific case both on post-judgment motions and on appeal therefrom. The trial court cannot frustrate this conditional appellate review for the reason that subsection (b) of Rule 50 requires it to rule one way or the other on the motion for new trial with its reasons if it should grant the motion for judgment notwithstanding the verdict.

---

[25] Cone v West Virginia Pulp & Paper Co., (1947) 330 U.S. 213, 215

Aside from Rule 50 the courts in unusual situations have not hesitated to enter or re-enter judgments n.o.v. In *Conerly v Flower,* (8 Cir., 1969) 410 F2d 941 the jury returned a $40,000 personal injury verdict against a defendant. Because the defendant's attorney represented that defendant's insurance coverage was only $20,000, plaintiff agreed to entry of judgment for the smaller amount. Seven months later plaintiff discovered that the insurance coverage had been mis-represented. Upon this disclosure the District Court re-entered judgment for the full $40,000 verdict.

The Measuring Stick

To measure anything one needs a measuring stick. This is true in measuring evidence for its sufficiency. It is helpful to understand that the rule of law which the trial judge will apply in measuring evidence for sufficiency is but a part and parcel of the long struggle over the power of the court to exercise its supervisory role over jury verdicts. Both court and jury are continuously vying for what each regards its fair share of the action. Our measuring stick is also measuring this viability of the common law.

The Historical Struggle to Get "Substantial Evidence" as the Measuring Stick

The notion that common law justice required a jury of an accused's peers to decide facts was born in England during the period of the Norman Inquisition.[26] At that time jurors were selected for their personal knowledge of the facts of the case and not, as today, for their lack of knowledge of either the case or the parties involved. In ancient England the trial judge supervised the jury verdict through a coercive practice called "attaint."[27] If the judge did not like the verdict which the jury returned, he would dismiss the jury and call another one. If the second jury found that the first jury's verdict was false, the judge would then accept the second verdict and thereupon throw all of the

---

[26] Smith, Young B., "The Power of the Judge to Direct a Verdict," Col. L. R. Vol. 13, p. 111 (1924)

[27] Thayer, Evidence, 137–140; Scott, Fundamentals of Procedure in Actions at Law, p. 90.

jurors of the first jury into jail or otherwise severely punish them. Such was the medieval practice of "attaint." Fortunately, in 1670 "attaint" came to a screeching halt as an aftermath to the historic trial of William Penn and William Mead tried by their peers on a charge of participating in an unlawful assembly. When the first jury acquitted these defendants, and the second jury found the first verdict to have been false, the judge jailed all of the jurors of the first jury. Upon one of the first writs of *habeas corpus* the Court of Common Pleas struck down the practice of attaint and freed the incarcerated jurors.[28]

Finally, when it came about that juries were to decide cases upon evidence presented in court and not upon what they might have known or heard about the case, litigants began demurring to the evidence to keep the case from going to the jury. To demur, the moving party had to admit the facts as proved by his opponent and let the judge decide as a matter of law whether or not the facts were sufficient upon which to base a judgment. The demurrer to the evidence as then practiced was not too popular as its rules were not very sporting. If the demurring party did not succeed, he was precluded from introducing further evidence on his part, and the case either went to the jury on the opponent's evidence, or judgment was entered against the moving party.[29]

Once the coercive practice of "attaint" and the unfair demurrer to evidence had run its course, the idea developed that judges were to decide law and jurors were to decide facts. This idea prevails today. The hiatus existed in the problem of how and to what extent was the court to supervise the verdict of the jury. Over-supervision would result in the court and not the jury ultimately deciding fact and no supervision would deny a litigant due process of law as anyone could present any kind of evidence to a jury with it deciding a case on sympathy, whim or speculation. To solve this problem of court supervision over the jury verdict, the Supreme Court of the United States in 1856 first put forth what can be generally termed the "scintilla" rule. In *Richardson v City of Boston,* (1856) 19 Howard 263 it reversed a judgment based upon a directed verdict holding that as long as there was *some* evidence to support the averment the case was for the jury. Only when there was no evidence could a court direct a verdict. However, sixteen years later in 1872 the Supreme Court of the United States rejected the "scintilla" rule and replaced it with the

---

[28] Bushel's Case, (1670) C. J. Vaughan, 124 Eng. Reprints 1006
[29] Wood v Gunston, (1655) Style J., 82 Eng. Reprints 867; Stephens v White, (Va., 1796) 2 Wash. 203

"substantial evidence" rule in *Improvement Co. v Munson,* (1872)
14 Wall. 442. It did this following England's abandonment of the
"scintilla" rule.[30] The Supreme Court defined its "substantial evidence"
rule as follows, p. 448:

> Nor are judges any longer required to submit a question to a
> jury merely because some evidence has been introduced by the
> party having the burden of proof, unless the evidence be of such
> a character that it would warrant the jury in finding a verdict in
> favor of that party . . . .
>
> Formerly it was held that if there was what is called a *scintilla*
> of evidence in support of a case the judge was bound to leave it
> to the jury, but recent decisions of high authority have estab-
> lished a more reasonable rule; that in every case, before the
> evidence is left to the jury, there is a preliminary question for
> the judge, not whether there is literally no evidence, but whether
> there is any upon which a jury can properly proceed to find a
> verdict for the party producing it, upon whom the *onus* of proof
> is imposed.

We will shortly consider the "substantial evidence" rule in light
of present day cases, but before doing so it is important to keep in
mind that the standard is more liberal when the trial court is faced
with deciding to set aside a verdict and grant a new trial as distinguished from either directing a verdict or granting a motion after the
verdict for a judgment notwithstanding the verdict (judgment n.o.v.).
Early in our jurisprudence the practice was developed of granting a
non-suit to a plaintiff who had failed to prove his case. A non-suit was
less drastic than a directed verdict because the plaintiff could refile and
try his case again if not time barred.[31]

With the setting aside of a verdict and granting a new trial being
less drastic than the "sudden death" of a directed verdict, it came
about early[32] and is presently the law[33] that a trial judge in his discretion may set aside the verdict of a jury and grant a new trial if he
considers the verdict to be against the *weight* of all the evidence in the

---

[30] Toomey v London Ry. Co., (1857) 3 C.B. (n.s.) 146, 140 Eng. Reprints
694

[31] Castle v Bullard, (1859) 23 How. 172; Johnson v Elwood, (1874) 56
N.Y. 614

[32] Jones v Spencer, (1898) 77 L.T.R. 536; Stuart v Simpson, (N.Y., 1828)
1 Wend. 376, 379; Bouchot v Cochrane Chemical Co., (D.C. 1901) 110 Fed. 919,
922; Mt. Adams Railway Co. v Lowery, (6 Cir., 1896) 74 Fed. 463

[33] Cone v West Virginia Pulp & Paper Co., (1947) 330 U.S. 212, 215, 216

case.[34] It must be clearly remembered that on motion for a directed verdict only the evidence most favorable to the opponent (usually his own) is measured for sufficiency while on a motion to set aside a verdict and grant a new trial all of the evidence, much of which may be conflicting, is *weighed* to determine whether the verdict rendered is against the *weight* of the evidence. Because weighing evidence is really nothing but appraising evidence as the jury is supposed to do, the verdict should be very repulsive to the facts and justice to warrant a trial court setting it aside and granting a new trial. Appellate courts will usually clip the wings of the trial court should it be otherwise.[35]

The Current Struggle to Keep "Substantial Evidence" as the Measuring Stick

"Substantial evidence" as the rule for measuring evidence sailed blissfully along at the level of the Supreme Court of the United States until it was shattered, in *Rogers v Missouri Pacific Railroad Co.,* (1956) 352 U.S. 500 and three other companion cases;[36] all involving the Federal Employers' Liability Act ("FELA") and the Jones Act.[37] Not only did the justices differ as to whether the "scintilla" or "substantial evidence" rule was being applied to measure the evidence in each specific case, but they also differed over the policy of prolifically granting writs of certiorari in this class of case and not in

---

[34] Parsons v Bedford, Breedlove & Robeson, (1830) 3 Pet. 433, 7 L. Ed. 732; Marsh v Illinois Central R. Co., (5 Cir. 1949) 175 F2d 498, 499, 500; McKinley v Skids A/S Arizona (E. D. Pa., 1968) 286 F. Supp. 691

[35] Brush v Constable, (1916) 166 App. Div. 543, 152 N.Y. Supp. 20: However, the trial court's role in ruling on motion for new trial should be more than to serve as a conduit between the jury and the clerk's office for entry of a judgment. *Compton v Overseas Corp.,* (2 Cir., 1970) 425 F2d 1130.

[36] Considered with *Rogers, supra* No. 28 were: Herdman v Pennsylvania R. Co., (1957) 352 U.S. 518, No. 46; Webb v Illinois Central R. Co., (1957) 352 U.S. 512, No. 42; and Ferguson v Moore-McCormack Lines, (1957) 352 U.S. 521, No. 59

[37] To the uninitiated the Federal Employers Liability Act ("FELA") 45 U.S.C. ##51–60 is an Act of Congress giving right to all employees of a railroad to sue the railroad for injuries while on the job *caused in whole or in part* by the negligence of the railroad. Employee is entitled to a trial by jury. Contributory negligence is not a bar to recovery, but only is considered in diminishing the award in proportion to percentage-wise fault of the employer and employee. The Jones Act, 46 U.S.C. #688 is an Act of Congress adopting FELA and giving the seaman who is member of a crew of a vessel the same right against the vessel owner for the latter's negligence as the employee of a railroad. Unseaworthiness is an absolute liability imposed upon a shipowner by the general maritime law to maintain his ship in a seaworthy condition and renders him liable to a seaman for injury caused by an unseaworthy vessel or its appurtenances. Contributory negligence of seaman goes to mitigation in an unseaworthiness case as under the Jones Act and FELA

others.[38] Our immediate concern is that in *Rogers, supra* and its companions the Supreme Court did not announce any change from "substantial evidence" to "scintilla," but just applied "scintilla." The Supreme Court correctly observed that calling its appraisal of evidence "substantial" or "scintilla" was of no aid in solving the problem of determining sufficiency of the evidence.[39] What is sufficient or insufficient is at best a factual judgment or an attitude of the Supreme Court. However, generally naming the standard being applied, whether "scintilla," "substantial," or any other expression of degree is useful to describe the measuring stick to be used by the courts below. Left unanswered and for the bar and bench to wonder about was: Whether the Supreme Court's obvious relaxed view of sufficiency of evidence was to be restricted to FELA and Jones Act cases and whether, if so restricted, it was to be further restricted to the "causation" element of the FELA case because of the comparative negligence feature of that Congressional Act. What the Supreme Court appeared to do to the "substantial evidence" rule is succinctly expressed in the dissenting opinion of Mr. Justice Harlan: 352 U.S. 563:

> For my part, to overturn the judgments below simply involves second-guessing the Missouri Supreme Court, the Court of Appeals for the Seventh Circuit, and the Court of Appeals for the Second Circuit, on questions of fact on which they brought to bear judgments neither capricious nor unreasonable and on which they made a "fair assessment of a record."
>
> I dissent also for another reason. No scientific or precise yardstick can be devised to test the sufficiency of the evidence in a negligence case. The problem has always been one of judgment, to be applied in view of the purposes of the statute. It has, however, been common ground that a verdict must be based on evidence—not on a scintilla of evidence but evidence sufficient to enable a *reasoning* man to infer both negligence and causation by *reasoning from the evidence. Moore v Chesapeake & O. R. Co.,* 340 U.S. 573. And it has always been the function of the court to see to it that jury verdicts stay within that boundary, that they be

---

[38] Mr. Justice Frankfurter was consistently voting against granting certiorari to re-appraise evidence in these cases and dissenting on basis that writ was improvidently granted. In note at 352 U.S. 510 are listed 17 cases reversed because a jury question was found and three were not found and affirmed. Also, see Appendix by Mr. Justice Douglas in Wilkerson v McCarthy, 336 U.S. 53, 71. Mr. Justice Frankfurter made his own Appendix of decisions relating to sufficiency of evidence in his dissent in Ferguson v Moore-McCormack Lines (1956) 352 U.S. 521 at 548

[39] Galloway v United States, (1943) 319 U.S. 372, 395

arrived at by reason and not by will or sheer speculation. Neither the Seventh Amendment nor the Federal Employers' Liability Act lifted that duty from the courts. However, in judging these cases, the Court appears to me to have departed from these long-established standards, for, as I read these opinions, the implication seems to be that the question, at least as to the element of causation, is not whether the evidence is sufficient to convince a reasoning man, but whether there is any scintilla of evidence at all to justify the jury verdicts. I cannot agree with such a standard, for I consider it a departure from a wise rule of law, not justified either by the provision of the FELA making employers liable for injuries resulting "in whole or in part" from their negligence, or by anything else in the Act or its history, which evinces no purpose to depart in these respects from common-law rules.

For these reasons I think the judgments in Nos. 28, 42, and 59, as well as that in No. 46, should be affirmed.

It appears that after *Rogers, supra* the trend of the Supreme Court continued to be the granting of certiorari and reversing *per curiam* many FELA and Jones Act cases where both United States and state trial and appellate courts took cases away from juries for lack of sufficient evidence. This is seen two years later in Mr. Justice Harlan's dissent in *Senkler v Missouri Pacific Railroad,* (1958) 356 U.S. 326 at 332:

> This case is a further step in a course of decisions through which the Court has rapidly converted the Federal Employers Liability Act, 35 Stat. 65 as amended, 45 U.S.C. ##51–60 (and the Jones Act which incorporates the FELA, 41 Stat. 1007, 46 U.S.C. #688), into what amounts to a workman's compensation statute.
>
> This process recently gained marked momentum with *Rogers v Missouri Pacific R. Co.,* 352 U.S. 500, 524, 559, decided at the 1956 Term where the Court in effect established a "scintilla" rule in these cases for judging the sufficiency of the evidence on the issue of "causation." In subsequent decisions that rule has been extended, *sub silentio* to cover also the issue of negligence."[40]

---

[40] Webb v Illinois Central R. Co. 352 U.S. 512; Ferguson v Moore-McCormack Lines, Inc., 352 U.S. 521; Shaw v Atlantic Coast Line R. Co., 353 U.S. 920; Futrelle v Atlantic Coast Line R. Co., 353 U.S. 920; Deen v Gulf, Colorado & S. F. R. Co., 353 U.S. 925! Thomson v Texas & P. R. Co., 353 U.S. 926; Ringhiser v Chesapeake & O. R. Co., 354 U.S. 901; McBride v Toledo Terminal R. Co., 354 U.S. 517; Gibson v Thompson, 355 U.S. 18; Stinson v Atlantic Coast Line R. Co., 355 U.S. 62; Honeycutt v Wabash R. Co., 355 U.S. 424; Ferguson v St. Louis-San Francisco R. Co., 356 U.S. 41; Butler v Whiteman 356 U.S. 271

As important as it is to the bench and bar[41] the Supreme Court as late as 1972 has not let it be known whether its decisions respecting the measuring of evidence for sufficiency in FELA and Jones Act cases are to apply to common law cases tried before a jury. Belief that the Supreme Court's purpose is to relax the measuring stick for FELA and Jones Act cases and not other cases is fortified in its frequent expression of its "broad humanitarian" policy to see that the railroad worker and seaman gets his trial by jury come what may.[42]

However, in 1969 the Court of Appeals for the Fifth Circuit took a giant step toward crystalizing the principle that "substantial evidence," if not the measuring stick in FELA cases was to remain the measuring stick for all other common law actions tried to a jury. Earlier in 1967 the Court of Appeals for the Fifth Circuit had held in *Planters Manufacturing Co. v Protection Mut. Ins. Co.,* (5 Cir., 1967) 380 F2d 869 certiorari denied 389 U.S. 930, that Federal courts must apply the same standards employed in FELA cases to diversity cases in determining sufficiency of evidence. Next came *Boeing Company v Shipman,* (5 Cir., 1968) 389 F2d 507 wherein a panel of the same Court followed the *Planter* case. In that case an employee of Boeing Company in Alabama was injured while painting in a poorly ventilated room and sued Boeing Company for not providing him a safe place to work. The District Court had jurisdiction by diversity of citizenship. The jury awarded the employee $25,000. The District Court denied Boeing Company's motion for directed verdict and motion for judgment n.o.v. The Court of Appeals affirmed. Upon petition the Court of Appeals for the Fifth Circuit granted rehearing *en banc*[43] because of the importance of formulating a proper standard in federal court to test the sufficiency of the evidence for submission of cases to the jury. On rehearing, an array of able legal talent appeared *amicus curiae* along with the parties. The United States Court of Appeals for the Fifth Circuit in *Boeing Company v Shipman,* (5 Cir., 1969) 411 F2d 365, sitting *en banc* with Circuit Judge Ainsworth writing a scholarly opinion for the Court and Circuit Judge Rives writing an equally scholarly but even longer opinion in dissent, held on April 7, 1969:

---

[41] 2B Barron and Holtzoff, Federal Practice and Procedure, #1075, pp. 401, 404 (Wright ed. 1961)

[42] *Seas Shipping Co. v Sieracki* (1946) 328 U.S. 85 at 94–95

[43] Before John R. Brown, Chief Judge, and Rives, Wisdom, Gewin, Bell, Thornberry, Coleman, Goldberg, Ainsworth, Godbold, Dyer, Simpson and Morgan, Circuit Judges, En Banc.

(1) In diversity cases federal rather than state law applied to determine sufficiency of the evidence;[44]

(2) statutory actions under FELA significantly differ from common law actions in terms of standard of proof and as a consequence the "scintilla" test of sufficiency of evidence employed in FELA cases was not to be applied in the common law jury action; overruling *Planter,* supra and

(3) that henceforth in the Fifth Circuit in common law actions where jurisdiction is based on diversity of citizenship a "substantial evidence" rule as formulated by the Court would apply to measuring evidence for its sufficiency. The Court then announced the rule to be, p. 374:

> On motions for directed verdict and for judgment notwithstanding the verdict the Court should consider all of the evidence—not just that evidence which supports the non-mover's case—but in the light and with all reasonable inferences most favorable to the party opposed to the motion. If the facts and inferences point so strongly and overwhelmingly in favor of one party that the Court believes that reasonable men could not arrive at a contrary verdict, granting of the motions is proper. On the other hand, if there is substantial evidence opposed to the motions, that is, evidence of such quality and weight that reasonable and fair-minded men in the exercise of impartial judgment might reach different conclusions, the motions should be denied, and the case submitted to the jury. A mere scintilla of evidence is insufficient to present a question for the jury. The motions for directed verdict and judgment n.o.v. should not be decided by which side has the better of the case, nor should they be granted only when there is a complete absence of probative facts to support a jury verdict. There must be a conflict in substantial evidence to create a jury question. However, it is the function of the jury as the traditional finder of the facts, and not the Court, to weigh conflicting evidence and inferences, and determine the credibility of witnesses.

Since the Court affirmed the employee's judgment in the Court below when his evidence was measured by the newly pronounced measuring stick, petition for certiorari to the Supreme Court has not occurred.

---

[44] The State of Alabama has adopted the "scintilla" rule in measuring evidence for sufficiency. *Huff v Vulcan Life & Accident Insurance Co.,* (1968) 281 Ala. 615, 206, So2d 861

The opinion and dissenting opinion in 411 F2d 365 has probably considered all of the cases and writings on the subject.

Subsequent decisions have referred to the new rule as the "Boeing Company" rule.[45] It appears to be nothing more than the "substantial evidence" rule with more definition. It is a fair conclusion that only a "scintilla" of evidence is needed to get a FELA or Jones Act case to the jury, but that the "substantial evidence" rule which has prevailed in the federal system since 1872 will continue to be the measuring stick for jury trials in all diversity cases. It will be interesting to see what other Circuits and the Supreme Court think about the new rule which the Court of Appeals for the Fifth Circuit named: "THE SUBSTANTIAL EVIDENCE OR REASONABLE MAN TEST."

Pertinent Law Review Articles on
Challenging the Sufficiency of Evidence

"Sufficiency of Evidence to Take Federal Diversity Case to Jury: The Two Decisions in Boeing versus Shipman," Lyman H. Harris, and Editorial Supplement Surveying State Standards, *Defense Law Journal,* Vol. 19, p. 265 and 278 (1970)

"Evidence—Sufficiency for Directed Verdict—Can a Judge Hold a Candle to Twelve Reasonable Men?" Robert Tarnoff, *De Paul Law Review,* Vol. 18, p. 322 (1968)

"Motions Testing the Sufficiency of Evidence," Philip A. Trautman, *Washington Law Review,* Vol. 42, p. 787 (1967)

"Multiple Sufficiency Tests in Federal Courts: The Scope of Lavender," *Utah Law Review,* Vol. 1970, No. 1, p. 155 (1970)

"Directed Verdicts and the Right of Trial by Jury in Federal Courts," John E. Bagalay, Jr., *Texas Law Review,* Vol. 42, p. 1053 (1964)

"Motion to Set Aside the Verdict: Evidence Deficiencies," Gregory U. Evans, *William and Mary Law Review,* Vol. 6, p. 216 (1965)

"Torts—Motion for Directed Verdict Against Co-Defendants Solely on the Issue of Liability Improperly Denied," *Syracuse Law Review,* Vol. 14, p. 705 (1963)

---

[45] *Pemberton v Pan American World Airways, Inc.,* (5 Cir., 1970) 423 F2d 426

"A Century Old Problem: Federal or State Law as Determinative of a Directed Verdict in a Federal Court," S. D. Roberts Moore, *University of Richmond Law Review,* Vol. 4, p. 282 (1970)

"Standard for a Directed Verdict in Diversity Cases," Kathianne Knaup, *St. Louis University Law Journal,* Vol. 14, p. 349 (1970)

"Post-Verdict Motions under Rule 50; Protecting the Verdict Winner," *Minnesota Law Review,* Vol. 53, p. 358 (1968)

Circumstantial   4
Evidence—Quality of
Collective Impact

Whether because of the infamous Dreyfus case in France a century ago or what, a large segment of the public has the misconception that circumstantial evidence is weak and inferior to direct evidence. How often have you heard friends remark: "If I ever sit on a jury, I'll never convict upon circumstantial evidence."? Although we are here concerned with sufficiency of evidence to get to the jury, it is appropriate to point out that in trying a circumstantial evidence case you had better, early in the trial, explain to the jury exactly what circumstantial evidence is and dispel any notions that it is inferior to direct evidence.

There is no mystery about circumstantial evidence which is sometimes called "indirect evidence."[1] It really is nothing but establishing a base for inference drawing. It is the proving by direct evidence a fact or set of facts from which another fact, usually an ultimate fact, can reasonably be inferred. In civil cases juries have understood what circumstantial evidence is through the following bank robbery illustration which has sometimes been effectively used upon opening statement.

Illustration of Circumstantial Evidence and Its Strength

Let us suppose the FBI arrests a suspect an hour after a bank has been robbed in the lobby of a nearby hotel while he is hurriedly checking out. Marked money from the teller's cage of the earlier

---

[1] Oregon Revised Statutes, 41.080

robbed bank is found in his possession. Those sets of facts comprise circumstantial evidence from which the jury might, but need not, determine that the arrested suspect is probably the person who robbed the bank. What has happened is that the jury has been asked to make a reasonable deduction of an ultimate fact from circumstantial facts directly established.

Suppose in the same bank robbery case an eye witness is produced who identifies the suspect as being the person who produced a gun at the teller's cage in the bank, and was seen fleeing the bank. That, of course, would be direct evidence. Which is the most compelling? Either can be. Certainly, the circumstantial evidence would be more compelling if the eye witness to the robbery was a little old lady without her glasses, or if with her glasses only saw the suspect fleetingly in poor light and from a poor position. Honest witnesses can often be wrong in either not observing accurately or not describing accurately what they observed. As far as it goes, the marked money on the suspect in the hotel shortly after the robbery is damning circumstantial evidence against the suspect. However, that might not necessarily be true.

Suppose the suspect was arrested a month later in a bar room with the marked money in his possession, but under circumstances where he could very well have received it as change from the bartender. The circumstantial evidence now becomes pretty weak and the little old lady with or without her eye glasses might be the very one upon whom to rely. A trial judge from training and experience understands how either direct or indirect evidence can be the most compelling, but often the jury cannot until it is clearly explained and illustrated.

There is nothing more fascinating than trying a circumstantial evidence case if, of course, you have a good one. Until fully understood, the average juror might have a prejudice against circumstantial evidence. On the other hand, once a jury knows what you are talking about, it will have as much relish as you in drawing upon circumstances to figure out "who did it." We are, after all, little "Perry Mason's" at heart. Jurors are no exception.

Collective Impact

Imagine, if you will, that in jumping to a factual conclusion you use a springboard. The springboard is the circumstantial evidence. The soundness of your conclusion depends upon the soundness of the spring in your springboard. There is a quality that runs as a common thread through all kinds of circumstantial evidence. This quality is that a number of circumstances, each having little in themselves to justify the drawing of a desired inference, can, when taken together, generate a most compelling inference. Let us call this common thread the quality of "collective impact." While "collective impact" is by no means restricted to cases involving fraudulent schemes or conspiracy it is most evident in these kind of cases.

The Supreme Court of the United States first recognized the validity of "collective impact" in *The Slavers* (*Reindeer*) (1864) 69 U.S. 383. In that case the bark *Reindeer* had been condemned and sold for having been built in New York with intent of her American owner to employ her in the slave trade contrary to law. The owner was protesting that the evidence was not sufficient to prove the violation. The vessel was built in New York with the professed purpose of making her first voyage to Falmouth, England. Indeed, she cleared New York with customs papers showing her bound for England and with a manifest showing normal cargo aboard including "boxes of hardware." However, she put in at Havana, Cuba and remained there for about six months before leaving that port under charter to a foreigner. Bad weather caused her to put into Newport, Rhode Island where she was seized and condemned.

What went wrong? Circumstantial evidence caught up with the *Reindeer* and her owner. The hardware cargo, while not necessarily so, was of the kind used in the slave trade. Her papers showed Falmouth, England as port of destination, but an entry in her deck log showed her as having encountered navigational difficulties at a longitude and latitude in which she could only have found herself if bound for West Africa and not Falmouth, England. An investigation in Havana revealed that her American owner had gone to Cuba and had tried to sell the vessel to the foreigner under terms which made the charter have all the ear-marks of sham. Furthermore, there was a "sea letter" out of Cuba found aboard the *Reindeer* which was only to be opened and shown to Cuban authorities in event they boarded her at sea. The "sea letter" named a West African port as her destination. The Supreme Court in 1864 had little difficulty finding the true intended use of the vessel and the true operator. As to the circumstantial evidence, the Court stated (p. 401):

> Circumstances altogether inconclusive, if separately considered, may, by their number and joint operation, especially when

corroborated by moral coincidences, be sufficient to constitute conclusive proof.

The Fraudulent Scheme and Conspiracy

While the concept of the fraudulent scheme is not foreign to the common law,[2] its development of recent has mostly occurred in the federal courts which have taken jurisdiction under mail and securities fraud statutes. The idea of the fraudulent scheme is to let the swindlers concoct any kind of a chain of deceptive events they desire and then to denounce them, providing they are sufficient to point to a fraudulent purpose.[3]

Aside and apart from the fraudulent scheme, which need only to involve one person, is civil or criminal conspiracy. A conspiracy is shown upon proof that two or more persons acting under agreement, tacit or otherwise, combine to commit an unlawful act, or if a lawful act, to employ unlawful means.[4] It is sufficient if the agreement is only a mutual mental action coupled with intent to commit injury.[5] Since most schemes and conspiracies must by their nature remain clandestine, they almost always are required to be established by circumstantial evidence. That is where "collective impact" comes into the picture to make a little of everything and really not much of anything develop like a thunder cloud to sometimes strike an inference as compelling as a bolt of lightning.

In proving a conspiracy case the circumstantial evidence has as its inferential target the proving that each of the defendants had at least some knowledge, explicit or implied, of the principal purpose of the conspiracy and did some act on their part to infer participation.[6] Sufficient and insufficient circumstantial evidence of conspiracy is illustrated in *Miller v United States,* (9 Cir., 1967) 382 F2d 583 where on appeal the male defendant, Miller, was convicted of conspiracy to transport heroin across the Mexican border while the woman defendant, Joseph, was acquitted. Miller was twice seen at the home

---

2 Stewart v Wright (1904) 130 Fed. 905

3 Nassan v United States, (4 Cir., 1942) 126 F2d 613; Deaver v United States, (DC Cir., 1946) 155 F2d 740; Durland v United States, (1896) 161 U.S. 306

4 Ragsdale v Watson (W.D. Ark., 1962) 201 F. Supp. 495 Edward v James Stewart & Co., (DC Cir., 1947) 160 F2d 935

5 Neff v World Pub. Co., (8 Cir., 1965) 349 F2d 235

6 Chavez v United States, (9 Cir., 1967) 382 F2d 583

of a known narcotics peddler in Mexico; his car was used to transport the narcotics across the border. A co-conspirator testified that delivery of the narcotics to Miller for the border crossing was to be made along the highway to the border. Such evidence was sufficient to put Miller's case to the jury and convict him. On the other hand, the woman Joseph was acquitted for insufficiency of the evidence to connect her to the conspiracy. At most the evidence showed that the Joseph woman took Miller in her car to Mexico where she for the first time visited the home of the known narcotics peddler. A co-conspirator testified that her car was to be used to deliver the narcotics to Miller along the highway. She was an occupant in her own car which was seen stopping along the highway. This evidence was held insufficient to establish knowledge on the part of the Joseph woman. Mere association with an established co-conspirator or even sharing the same office with him may raise a strong suspicion of knowledge and intent but such alone is not sufficient as it is not the only reasonable inference capable of being drawn from mere fact of association.[7] The same is true where a defendant visits a house containing jewelry stolen the night before and buys some of it. The circumstance is not sufficient to prove the defendant at the time of purchase knew the jewelry was stolen.[8]

Insufficient Evidence to Prove Conspiracy

Where the arch-conspirator stays on his employer's payroll to sell excursion cruises, but works during the time for a competitor, the competitor availing himself of the arch-conspirator's services, and in effect stealing the employer's business, cannot be liable as a conspirator where it appears that he did not know that the arch-conspirator had not quit his former employer and believed that he had.[9] Likewise, when a general contractor pays money directly to a sub-contractor instead of to a bank as he had been instructed, this act cannot make the general contractor a conspirator against an alleged joint venturer of the sub-contractor when the general contractor had no knowledge of the existence of the joint venture.[10]

In NLRB unfair labor practices cases, an employer cannot be

---

[7] Hoffman v Herdman's Ltd., (SDNY, 1966) 41 F. R. D. 275
[8] United States v Ford, (7 Cir., 1963) 324 F2d 950, 952
[9] Tolchester Lines, Inc. v Dowd, (SDNY, 1960) 253 F. Supp. 643
[10] Bushman Const. Co. v Conner, (10 Cir., 1965) 351 F2d 681

charged with conspiring with an employee-forelady to discriminate against a union where the forelady, unknown to the employer, engages in anti-union activities.[11] Nor, does proof that the employer dominated the grievance procedure set up in a collective bargaining agreement be sufficient to infer that he also dominated an employee association subsequently created.[12]

Circumstantial evidence still remains insufficient to tie a defendant into a conspiracy where at best it is equivocal, that is to say, inferring proper conduct equally as much as improper conduct. An employer cannot be made a conspirator in a discriminatory labor practice case where he had a legal right to discharge an employee and so acted.[13] The same is true of a company who rehires a lesser number of employees after a labor dispute for privileged jobs in accordance with the settlement agreement, but it is claimed the company was acting in bad faith. Its actions of limited re-employment were as much dictated by business efficiency and limited need as it was bad faith.[14]

When it comes to conspiring to violate anti-trust laws in a price fixing case, the fact finder cannot speculate as to the existence of a conspiracy. While there is a delicate factual line, price-fixing is not established by only proof of (1) parallel price activity or (2) unilateral dealing without proof of intent to monopolize (3) or any facts from which conspiracy cannot be inferred.[15] It has also been held that a corporation and its employees or its officers and directors cannot comprise "two or more persons" necessary to get a conspiracy off the ground.[16] As can be seen, knowledge and scienter must somehow be inferred from the circumstantial evidence to prove either conspiracy or a fraudulent scheme.

Sufficiency of Evidence to Prove Conspiracy Illustrated

Having seen what has been held insufficient to prove conspiracy let us get back to the quality of "collective impact" as defined in the

---

[11] Cuppies Mfg. Co. v NLRB (8 Cir., 1939) 106 F2d 100

[12] NLRB v Standard Oil Co., (10 Cir., 1942) 124 F2d 895

[13] NLRB v Kaye, (7 Cir., 1959) 272 F2d 112

[14] AFL-CIO v United Aircraft Corp., (Conn., 1969) 299 F. Supp. 877

[15] Fiumara v Texaco Inc., (ED Pa., 1962) 204 F. Supp. 544

[16] Zelinger v Uvalde Rock Asphalt Co., (10 Cir., 1963) 316 F2d 47; Tobman v Cottage Woodcraft Shop (SD Calif., 1961) 194 F. Supp. 83

1864 case of *The Slavers* (*Reindeer*), supra, and look at a more recent successful application of this notion. While there are many fraudulent scheme-conspiracy cases in the books,[17] perhaps the best for us to consider is that of *Errion v Connell* (9 Cir., 1956) 236 F2d 447, because three of the seven conspirators appealed claiming insufficient evidence to link them to the fraud and the Court of Appeals specified exactly what evidence tied each to the conspiracy. Errion was the arch-conspirator. He fraudulently imposed upon Mrs. Connell, an eighty-year-old widow of Seattle, Washington to sell him $124,000 of securities and real property in exchange for 125 acres of near worthless tideland represented by him to be valuable oyster beds. The other conspirators came into the dealing later by accepting title to real property, closing transactions, handling money, acting as fronts and in lulling Mrs. Connell into not discovering earlier the deception practiced upon her. As to sufficiency of the evidence, the Court of Appeals stated (p. 456):

Sufficiency of the Evidence

The findings of fraud are not clearly erroneous. The trial judge was most emphatic in his statements as to what degree of proof was required as to each and every appellant, and he clearly stated what were the circumstances and transactions which supported a finding of a fraudulent part played by each appellant.

The trial judge regarded, and properly, that all the appellants were engaged in *one single fraudulent scheme.*

As to Violet Kellerstraus: She was a sister of Mr. Errion and lived in an adjoining apartment with him. She had a joint bank account with Mr. Errion, and in other particulars was in a close relationship with him. She took title to one of Mrs. Connell's homes in Seattle in her own name and when the home was sold she converted the proceeds into cashier's checks and deposited them to Holdorf's account and her joint account with Mr. Errion. Her testimony on the stand was fantastic and unbelievable, and the judge commented at the conclusion of the trial on her attitude and response. We therefore conclude, as did the trial judge, that she couldn't have undertaken the sale of Mrs. Connell's home in Seattle, secured the funds, signed the documentary papers, distributed the funds received, and have done the secre-

---

[17] Hooper v Mountain States Security Corp., (5 Cir. 1960) 282 F2d 195; Ellis v Carter, (9 Cir., 1961) 291 F2d 270; Barnard v United States, (9 Cir., 1965) 342 F2d 309

tarial work for Errion without having knowledge of the scheme, and without knowingly cooperating in perpetuating the fraud.

As to Amy Errion: Amy Errion, the wife of Mr. Errion, performed certain acts which, in other circumstances might appear innocent. But in the circumstances and facts of this case it is clear that she knowingly participated in the fraudulent scheme. She sold the stocks secured from Mrs. Connell. She was present when conversations took place with Mrs. Connell. She took what the judge described as a "lulling trip" with Mrs. Connell to Southern California, in order to prevent Mrs. Connell from ascertaining the true facts. Mrs. Errion later secured some $122 from Merrill, Lynch, Fenner and Beane, which she deposited to her own account. The evidence supports a finding of participation in the scheme.

As to C. W. Williamson: Mr. Williamson entered into the scheme later. His own statements clearly show that he either had an express, or a tacit, agreement with the other appellants as to the fraudulent scheme. His actions clearly show that he was merely projected into the plan in order to act as a conduit to "feed" Mrs. Connell funds in order to further lull her into a sense of security. The funds were not his own, but were from sources over which Mr. Errion had control. The so-called "Indenture of Lease" required him to start production of oysters on the land but he admitted that he did not. Clearly, he was implicated in the scheme.

From the above, it can be seen that not only were the isolated transactions of Mrs. Errion, Violet Kellerstrauss and C. W. Williamson put into juxtaposition to prove a single scheme, but the character of the transactions inferred knowledge on part of each and all.

For another example, an attorney who incorporates a company which borrows money and draws corporate resolutions and borrowing documents, leaving out the name of a person who really is organizing the corporation and securing the borrowed money is clearly possessed of the privity essential to a conspirator.[18] In an anti-trust price fixing case, while unilateral dealing in itself is not incriminating, it can become so where a favored retail customer raises his retail prices against his own interest without having been given a corresponding raise by his wholesaler.[19]

---

[18] United States v Luxenberg, (6 Cir., 1967) 374 F2d 241, 250

[19] Sanitary Milk Producers v Bergjans Farm Dairy Co., (ED., Mo., 1965) 241 F. Supp. 476 Affirmed in 368 F2d 679

Furthermore, once a fraudulent scheme or conspiracy has been established, the evidence necessary to link a particular defendant to the conspiracy may be slight to constitute the necessary substantiality. As the Court held in *Isaacs v United States,* (8 Cir., 1962) 301 F2d 706 at 725:

> Once there is satisfactory proof that a conspiracy has been formed, the question of a particular defendant's connection with it may be a matter of whether the stick fits so naturally into position in the fagot as to convince that it is part of it.

Another area in the common law where "collective impact" is recognized is in the actions brought to set aside fraudulent transfers of property. In this type of case "badges of fraud" are as infinite in number and form as are the resources and versatility of human artifice.[20] When these "badges of fraud" are sufficiently numerous to create suspicion that the transaction lacks bonafideness, the burden of going forward usually shifts to the defendant-grantee to satisfactorily explain that he took the property for a valuable consideration and without notice.[21] Again, circumstantial evidence gathers a collective momentum in order to prove fraud.

A Practice Tip: Have Rulings on Motion to Strike Reserved

If you are about to try your first conspiracy case, do not expect to find too much in the books on how to do it. Just do it. If you are putting in a case against six conspiring defendants, you will perhaps have as many attorneys as defendants against you. Every time you put a witness on the stand to testify to a transaction involving one defendant, those attorneys representing the other defendants will object to the testimony and move to strike it until you have first established the conspiratorial agreement connecting their respective client-defendant. At this point you concede that the evidence should be stricken unless it connects the other defendants, but ask the trial judge to admit the evidence subject to later renewal of motions to strike at end of your case as to those defendants not proven to be connected with the conspiracy. The trial judge, if experienced, will

---

[20] Shealy v Edwards, (1883) 75 Ala. 411
[21] Evans v Trude, (Or., 1952) 240 P2d 940

probably handle the procedure as you ask. At the conclusion of your case you will find virtually all of your proof subject to a motion to strike. If, however, your proof packs a collective impact sufficient to infer a fraudulent scheme or a conspiracy, the trial judge will deny renewed motions to strike and hold that the evidence taken as a whole proves the tacit agreement to conspire on part of all defendants. How else can one better pull himself up by his own bootstraps?

Pertinent Law Review Articles on Conspiracy

"The Logic of Conspiracy—United States v Spock," 416 F2d 165, *Wisconsin Law Review,* Vol. 1970, p. 191. (1970)

"United States v Palermo: Multiple Conspiracy and the Right to Examine a Separate Jury," *Northwestern University Law Review,* Vol. 65, p. 134 (1970)

"Evidence—Hearsay—Co-Conspirators Exception," Newal Squyres Jr., *Texas Tech University Law Review,* Vol. 2, p. 121 (1970)

"A Psycho—Analytic Peeks at Conspiracy," Al Katz, *Buffalo Law Review,* Vol. 20, p. 239 (1970)

"Conspiracy and the First Amendment," *Yale Law Journal,* Vol. 79, p. 872 (1970)

"Complicity in a Conspiracy as an Approach to Conspiratorial Liability," Cameron R. Williams, *UCLA Law Review,* Vol. 16, p. 155 (1968)

"Distribution and the Sherman Act—The Effects of General Motors, Schwinn and Sealy," Larry L. Williams, *Duke Law Journal,* Vol. 1967, p. 732 (1967)

"Conspiracy to Defraud," T. B. Hadden, *Cambridge Law Journal,* Vol. 1966, p. 248 (1966)

"Intra-Enterprise Conspiracy under Section 1 of the Sherman Act," George W. Stengel, *Mississippi Law Journal,* Vol. 35, p. 5 (1963)

"Some Legal Aspects of Industrial Espionage," I. Louis Wolk, *Practical Lawyer,* Vol. 9, p. 87 (1963)

"Two Trees or One?—The Problem of Intra-Enterprise Conspiracy," Richard V. Barndt, *Montana Law Review,* Vol. 23, p. 158 (1962)

"Conspiracy—Evidentiary Value of Conscious Parallelism," Michael J. Doyle, *Marquette Law Review,* Vol. 45, p. 633 (1962)

"The Doctrine of Criminal Conspiracy and Its Modern Application to Labor," Morris D. Forkosch, *Texas Law Review,* Vol. 40, p. 303 (1962)

Circumstantial Evidence— 5
"More Probable Than Not"—"Res Ipsa Loquitur"

Just as "collective impact" is a quality common to all types of circumstantial evidence cases, so is the "more probable than not" rule.[1] Just as "collective impact" is mostly evident in fraudulent schemes and conspiracy cases, so is "more probable than not" mostly evident in negligence cases. For these reasons we consider "more probable than not" in the negligence cases where the rule has been most frequently articulated.

As we have seen under the *Boeing Company* rule[2] there must be a conflict in substantial evidence to put a case to the jury. If the inference to be drawn from circumstantial evidence is so overwhelming as to only point in one direction, a directed verdict should be granted.[3] However, when the evidence is such that fairminded men may draw different inferences therefrom and *reasonably* disagree as to what the verdict should be, then the case must go to the jury.[4] However, to avoid the speculation situation, the key ingredient is men

---

[1] "More probable than not" was applied to measure sufficiency of evidence to establish a contract in *Kaufman v Fisher,* (Or., 1962) 371 P 2d 948. The evidence revealed an indefinite and incomplete conversation between a passenger and driver the night before they went on a fatal drive in a jeep. From such evidence the jury was allowed to consider whether it was more probable than not that a bonafide pre-arrangement had been entered into for the sharing of expenses.

[2] Boeing Company v Shipman, (5 Cir., 1969) 411 F 2d 365

[3] Weeks v Latter-Day Saints Hospital (10 Cir., 1969) 418 F 2d 1035

[4] M. C. Carlisle & Co. v Cross (1 Cir., 1967) 386 F 2d 672

who may *reasonably* disagree. For example if in a malpractice case against a dentist something went wrong to injure the patient and the expert witness testified that what went wrong could occur just as well by non-negligent treatment as by negligent treatment a jury will not be permitted to speculate.[5] Circumstantial evidence must be of sufficient substance to rise to the dignity of inferring the probability as distinguished from the possibility of negligence. Such dignity of probable negligence does not exist when in a case against a window manufacturer it is shown that the injured workman was using the window casement for its unintended use as a ladder to climb up the building.[6]

The "More Probable than Not" Rule

What if certain evidence produces a reasonable inference in both directions, one showing fault and one equally as persuasive showing no fault? In that case there would still be speculation if each of the opposing inferences to be drawn were of equal weight. No rule of evidence can justify a court putting a case to the jury if the jury must speculate to arrive at a verdict.[7]

Here is where the "more probable than not" rule comes into play. What we call a rule is really not a rule, but rather a tentative "stepping stone" finding of fact made by the trial judge in order to decide whether as a matter of law there is substantial evidence for jury consideration. If among the competing inferences to be drawn from certain circumstantial evidence one of them has a more rational quality than the others in the opinion of the trial judge based upon his personal understanding of the common experience of mankind, then he finds that such particular inference preponderates over other possible inferences. If the particular preponderating inference points in favor of the plaintiff and against the defendant, the trial judge finds that the evidence shows "more probably than not" the defendant was causatively negligent. Having so found, he concludes there is substantial evidence to put the plaintiff's case to the jury. If he cannot find that the needed inference has any preponderating quality, he grants the motion for directed verdict.

---

[5] Smith v Reitman, (DC., Cir., 1967) 389 F 2d 303

[6] McCready v United Iron & Steel Co., (10 Cir., 1959) 272 F 2d 700

[7] Carter v John Hennes Trucking Co. (7 Cir., 1954) 210 F 2d 443

While "more probable than not" is not unique in Oregon[8] it has flourished there as a rule to test circumstantial evidence. One of the most articulate expressions of "more probable than not" is found in *Kaufman v Fisher,* (Or., 1962) 371 P2d 948. In that wrongful death case plaintiff's decedent was occupant of a jeep driven by defendant's decedent. In the course of a hunting trip which took the jeep up a narrow muddy hillside road, the jeep went over the bank, killing both occupant and driver. Only evidence of possible negligence was tire tracks of the jeep first swinging to the up-side of the road before veering off to the down-side and over the bank where the jeep was found. In reversing the trial judge for not letting the case go to the jury, the Oregon Supreme Court explained the "more probable than not" rule (p. 953):

> 8. Whether the inference of negligence is drawn from specific conduct or simply from the fact that the accident happened, the test of preponderating probabilities is the same; in either case plaintiff can get to the jury if there is a rational basis for concluding that it was more probable than not that the defendant's failure to exercise reasonable care was the cause of the accident.
>
> . . . The determination of where the probabilities lie must, ordinarily, be made upon the basis of past experience as it is seen and appraised by the court. "These are the judgments of 'common sense' " 2 Harper & James, Torts #15.2, p. 879 (1956).
>
> The conclusion thus reached by the trial judge is tentative only because the jury may conclude otherwise. Therefore, although we frequently speak in terms of our own examination of the probabilities [e.g. *Secanti v Jones,* 223 Or. 598, 606, 349, P2d 274, 277 (1960); *Eitel v Times,* 221 Or. 585, 593, 352 P2d 485 (1960)] we are simply saying that because we are of the opinion that the probability of the defendant's negligence is greater than the probability of other causes, the jury is entitled to reach the same conclusion, although it is not required to do so.

---

[8] Prosser, Torts (2d ed 1955) #42 p. 200; 2 Harper & James, Law of Torts, #19.4, pp. 1068–1069 (1956); James, Jury Control Devices, 47 Va. L. Rev. 218 (1961); Peairs v Florida Publishing Co., (Fla., 1961) 132 So. 2d 561; it was more probable than not that negligence of ferry company caused injury, Sketo v Olympic Ferries, Inc., (9 Cir., 1971) 436 F2d 1107.

**Not Everything Put to Jury
Under "More Probable than Not"**

In Oregon "more probable than not" is a realistically applied rule and not one to let everything go to the jury. Shortly after *Kaufman v Fisher,* supra came *Southern Pacific Co. v Campbell McLean, Inc.* (Or., 1962) 376 P2d 77. In that action to recover property damage for a negligently burned-down saw mill, the Oregon Supreme Court affirmed the non-suit granted against the plaintiff. At most, it was proven that an electric circuit had been over-fused. The short circuit could have been caused by the fire just as well as having caused the fire. Nor, would the Oregon Supreme Court let stand a plaintiff's verdict in *Conger v Dant & Russell, Inc.* (Or., 1968) 443 P2d 201 on basis of "more probable than not." There the plaintiff's fishing boat was damaged when it struck a submerged sinker log in a small river opposite a saw mill whose workboat regularly towed rafts of logs of the same brand across the river in vicinity of the sinker log. It was more probable than not that the workboat permitted the sinker log to escape from one of its rafts it had towed except for one thing: a tugboat owned by a third person operated about a quarter of a mile up river. This tug had also handled the same log rafts with the same log brand. Proximity of the workboat to point of accident might have made its probability more preponderating over the activities of the tugboat except for the fact that the river had a six foot tide and water at different times flowed in opposite directions. Also, sinker logs can very well float for some time from some other place before becoming lodged at a certain point in the mud bottom of a river. Here was speculation at its worst.

Another case where the Oregon Supreme Court would not let the jury speculate under "more probable than not" was in *Coburn v Utah Home Fire Ins. Co.,* (Or., 1962) 375 P2d 1022. In that case the plaintiff had to prove that a small vessel which sunk at her mooring in New Orleans was due to a peril of the sea. The only proof was that after the vessel had been pumped out the leak in her hull appeared to be in a hose connection from engine to an underwater outlet, the hose appearing to have been cut or burst from the inside out. Plaintiff claimed that clam shells in the area had somehow worked up into the hose to cause the rupture. A judgment n.o.v. for defendant was affirmed on appeal. Here "more probable than not" was a very close question.

Perhaps the most widely encountered situation for testing the worth of "more probable than not" is found in those cases of head-on collisions between motor vehicles where the only evidence of who was on the wrong side of the road is position of vehicles after collision, location of impact debris and possibly gouge marks on the highway. Cases pro and con have been collected.[9]

Sufficient here to say that if there is some significant fact such as oil and broken glass all on one side of the road[10] or vegetables from a truck in collision all on one side of the road[11] or gouge or skid marks which can be identified as being made by one of the vehicles prior to impact[12] a preponderating probability may be developed sufficient for jury consideration.[13] In short, by finding a little personality in the debris of a head-on collision, you can get to the jury; otherwise, not.

In *Arrow Transportation Co. v Northwest Grocery Co.,* (Ore., 1971) 482 P2d, 519 a gasoline tanker collided with a grocery truck on a highway bridge. All went up in flames. While it was not thought that any semblance could be made of the debris, the grocery truck owner was permitted to let the jury find that it was "more probable than not" that at time of impact it was on its proper side of the road because: (1) its cargo of groceries at impact was thrown forward and not run over by the grocery truck; (2) rear wheels of the grocery truck were well on its side of the road; (3) unless the grocery truck had traveled 40 feet forward after impact, the collision could not have occurred on the wrong side of the road.

From the same facts, the owner of the gasoline tanker reasoned that the grocery truck upon entering the bridge had its right front wheel strike a curbing which caused the cab of the grocery truck (semi tractor-trailer) to swerve left into the left front of the tanker which, in turn, deflected the grocery truck's cab to the right and caused the trailer of the tanker to jackknife into the grocery truck's cab. The Supreme Court of Oregon held that the jury could have reasonably drawn an inference for or against either party or theory.

---

[9] ANNO: Automobiles—Place of Impact—Proof, 77 ALR 29 580
[10] Stark's Admrx. v Herndon's Adm. (Ky., 1942) 166 SW 2d 828
[11] Morris v Fortier (Calif., 1943) 138 P 2d 368
[12] Tracy v Guibbini (Calif., 1937) 66 P 2d 675
[13] Evjeh v Packer City Transit Line, Inc. (Wis., 1960) 100 NW 2d 580

Of interest here is whether the Oregon Supreme Court, in *Arrow Transportation Co. v Northwest Grocery Co.,* supra is liberalizing the "preponderating probability" concept announced in *Kaufman v Fisher,* supra, by holding that where two conflicting inferences may be drawn from the facts, one of them need not preponderate over the other if both may be reasonably drawn from the evidence. The Court stated:

> The rule of law quoted does not mean that the probabilities are equally divided if half the jurors would find one way and half the other. The probabilities also are not evenly balanced if the trial court or the judges of an appellate court have difficulty in determining what inferences should be drawn. Once the court determines that inferences can be drawn favorable to the defendant or plaintiff the fact finder decides which inference is most convincing. The probabilities are equally divided only if there is nothing in the evidence from which a reasonable juror can make a choice.

The "more probable than not" rule, however understood, has not been beyond criticism. Professor James contends that as a test for sufficiency of evidence it gives the court little guidance and great latitude.[14] Professor Jaffe sees either an unresolved tension or a contradiction in the rule that a judge is to direct a verdict for the defendant if the probabilities are evenly balanced, but is not to direct a verdict if reasonable men might differ as to whether they are equally balanced.[15] In the area of causation Professor Green believes that it is literal nonsense for a court to attempt to find whether the "probabilities" are that it was the defendant which caused the plaintiff's injuries.[16] In light of this and other criticism we hope for the sake of making a more definite measuring stick that the Supreme Court of Oregon will be sticking with the rule of "preponderating probabilities" as described in *Kaufman v Fisher,* supra and not slip into a rule that a case must go to the jury if two competing inferences are each reasonable but neither is more persuasive than the other. After all, a plaintiff has the burden of proof and should the case go to the jury it will be instructed that if the evidence in his favor does not preponderate over that favoring the defendant he does not carry his necessary burden of proof. It seems to us more consistent with the

---

[14] James—Jury Control Devices, 47 Va. L. Rev. 218 (1961)
[15] Jaffe, 1 Buffalo L. Rev. 1, 2 (1951)
[16] Green, 60 Mich. L. Rev. 543 (1962)

jury standard and far more specific for a court to tentatively determine whether it is more probable than not that the defendant was causatively negligent than for it to retreat to deciding whether two evenly balanced inferences are each reasonable.

The "Res Ipsa Loquitur" Doctrine

The Latin phrase *"res ipsa loquitur"* means in English that: "The thing speaks for itself." In law it is a well developed rule of evidence.[17] It is, however, nothing more than the application of the "more probable than not" rule restricted to the happening of unusual accidents. The doctrine of *res ipsa loquitur* is more restrictive in application than "more probable than not" and is inclusive within the later rule.

Whether called a doctrine or a rule or what, *res ipsa loquitur* remains to be the permissible drawing of an inference from an occurrence that the cause of an injury is probably, but not necessarily, the negligent act or omission of the defendant.[18] A most comprehensive definition of *res ipsa loquitur* couched in terms of probabilities has come out of the California Supreme Court in *Zentz v Coca Cola Bottling Co. of Fresno,* (Calif. S. Ct. en banc, 1952) 247 P2d 344 at page 349:

> . . . as a general rule, *res ipsa loquitur* applies where the accident is of such a nature that it can be said, in the light of past experience, that it probably was the result of negligence by someone and that the defendant is probably the person who is responsible. In determining whether such probabilities exist with regard to a particular occurrence, the courts have relied upon common knowledge and the testimony of expert witnesses, and they have considered the circumstances relating to the accident in each particular case, such as the extent of control exercised by the defendant, the plaintiff's own conduct, the likelihood of negligence by some third person, and, in some situations, evidence that the defendant is better able than the plaintiff to explain what happened. All of these matters have been treated as aids to help the court in determining whether the accident

[17] Revlon v Buchanan (5 Cir., 1959) 271 F 2d 795

[18] Sweeney v Erving, (1913) 228 U.S. 233, 240; Gailbreath v Homestead Fire Ins. Co. (9 Cir., 1950) 185 F2d 361, 364

was of such a nature that the injury was more probably than not the result of the defendant's negligence.

As we see it, there are three criteria to be employed in appraising sufficiency of evidence to make out a *res ipsa loquitur* case, together with three judicial policy considerations which courts sometimes employ to either put or not put a case to the jury.

The Unusual Which Suggests Negligence

An exploding bottle of carbonated soft drink is unusual and does call for an explanation by someone if it causes injury.[19] On the other hand, it is not so unusual for a train in approaching a station to stop unexpectedly, and when such a stop causes a conductor on the train to become injured, he cannot use *res ipsa loquitur* to get to the jury.[20] Nor is it unusual to expect a wall of an already gutted building to fall down while a contractor is in process of further demolishing the structure.[21]

Aside from the accident being an unusual occurrence, it must also have a suggestion of negligence on the part of someone. It is certainly unusual for a jet airplane to explode in mid-air and drop burning fuel to burn a building, but there is nothing in the event to suggest negligence.[22] However, have the same airplane come in for a landing and prove that just prior to touching down one of its jet engines stopped functioning and you have not only the unusual, but also a strong inference that had the engine been properly inspected or maintained, it would not have failed at the critical moment.[23] Likewise, if an automobile parked on a hill unattended gets free to roll down the hill and strike a pedestrian, the event is not only unusual, but infers that the automobile owner somehow did not properly park his automobile.[24]

Usually both the unusual accident, together with circumstances inferring negligence, are a combined necessity for *res ipsa loquitur*.

---

[19] Zentz v Coca Cola Bottling Co. of Fresno (Calif., 1952) 247 P 1d 344, 349

[20] Herdman v Penn. R. R. Co. (1957) 352 U.S. 518

[21] Carothers v Olshan (Tex., 1947) 198 S. W. 2d 941

[22] Williams v United States (5 Cir., 1955) 218 F 1d 473

[23] Lobel v American Airlines (2 Cir., 1951) 192 F 2d 217

[24] Lewis v Wolk (Ky., 1950) 228 SW 2d 432, 16 ALR 2d 974

However, in *Lux Art Van Service, Inc. v Pollard* (9 Cir., 1965) 344 F2d 883, circumstances inferring negligence without the unusual were alone sufficient to apply *res ipsa loquitur.* Ordinarily common carriers who transport livestock are not presumed to be negligent if the livestock get sick or die in course of transit as livestock can get sick, irrespective of the care employed in their transportation. In this case, however, *res ipsa loquitur* was applied when it was shown that the horses died of heat exhaustion after being hauled in a trailer for 10½ hours across a hot desert. An autopsy on the horses showed they were exhausted about 1½ hours before death.

Probability That Defendant Had Control of Event

It used to be that *res ipsa loquitur* failed to get the case to the jury unless it was shown that the instrumentality causing the harm was in the defendant's exclusive control.[25] Now, it seems that the proof for placing the blame upon the defendant is satisfied if it shows that the defendant is probably the person responsible.[26] In fact, in some limited situations, if there is question as to which of several defendants are responsible, the court will infer that each and all are responsible. In *Weeks v Latter Day Saints Hospital,* (10 Cir., 1969) 418 F2d 1035 the Court directed a verdict in favor of plaintiff against several doctors and the hospital under doctrine of *res ipsa loquitur* where it was shown that a small boy was burned by a table heater while being operated upon in surgery, and it could not be shown which of the several defendants may have "goofed." The verdict was directed in favor of plaintiff because collectively all of the defendants were in a better position to explain what happened than the small boy on the operating table.

Of course, in this business of "pointing the finger" at the defendant as the one probably negligent, the injured plaintiff is not overlooked. If the proof does not remove the injured plaintiff's conduct as a source of the cause of injury, he cannot rely upon *res ipsa loquitur.* For example, where the plaintiff has loaded a syphon bottle of carbonated water and he is injured when, in using the bottle, the head comes off to strike him in the face, he can forget about getting

---

[25] Yellow Cab Co. v Hodgson (Colo., 1932) 14 P 2d 1081
[26] Zentz v Coca Cola Bottling Co. of Fresno (Calif., 1952) 247 P 2d 344, 349

to the jury against the manufacturer under *res ipsa loquitur.*[27] On the other hand, if the injured patron is sitting on a stool at a restaurant counter and it collapses to cause injury, his participation does not prevent employment of *res ipsa loquitur.*[28]

In the product liability case the injured purchaser of the product usually sues both the retailer from whom the product was purchased as well as the manufacturer of the product. As a plaintiff, the purchaser can often fall between two chairs. Where the customer is injured when picking up a bottle of carbonated water in a serve-yourself store and it explodes to cause injury, the customer has a clear *res ipsa loquitur* case against the retailer but not against the bottler.[29] However, the customer could make a case against the bottler instead of the retailer if it was established that upon receipt of the bottle in the retail store until the explosion the bottle had been properly stored and not improperly handled.[30]

Even when given the unusual happening with an inference of negligence, the most difficulty in using *res ipsa loquitur* to get to a jury is encountered in proving that one particular defendant rather than someone else had control over the instrument causing the accident. It is for this reason that an injured passenger cannot rely upon *res ipsa loquitur* to sue both the driver of the automobile in which he was riding and the driver of the other vehicle involved in the collision.[31] The same holds true where a longshoreman is killed when he becomes wedged between the barge of one person and the scow of another while they are being maneuvered.[32]

By all means it must not be forgotten that even though *res ipsa loquitur* might be rejected by the court for getting a plaintiff's case to the jury, circumstantial evidence under "more probable than not" may still be justified to infer negligence on part of a particular defendant. Where a worker is crushed between a loading dock of a warehouse and a de-railed railroad car, the circumstances may infer negligence in the derailment and be sufficient even though *res ipsa loquitur* cannot be applied.[33] While *res ipsa loquitur* is a broad

---

[27] Levy v Ridde Mfg. Co. (N.J., 1951) 80 Atl. 2d 629

[28] Gow v Multnomah Hotel (Or., 1950) 224 P 2d 552; 228 P 2d 791

[29] Copher v Barbee (Mo., 1962) 361 SW 2d 137

[30] Sanders v Glenshaw Glass Co., (3 Cir., 1953) 204 F 2d 436; Gordon v Aztec Brewing Co., (Calif., 1949) 203 P 2d 522

[31] Estes v Estes (Mo., 1939) 127 SW 2d 78, 79

[32] Petition of Central R. Co. of New Jersey (SDNY, 1954) 121 F. Supp. 813

[33] Ramsouer v Midland Valley R. Co., (8 Cir., 1943) 134 F 2d 101

theory in the sense it infers negligence just from the happening of an accident, sometimes it is too narrow because necessary principles are required to be applied lest any unexplained accident be sufficient to infer negligence. In such event general circumstantial evidence may still be sufficient. In *Otis Elevator Co. v Robinson* (5 Cir., 1961) 287 F2d 62 *res ipsa loquitur* was not applicable but the circumstance that Otis had undertaken to repair the elevator three times before it dropped to cause injury was a circumstance to infer negligence on part of Otis. As the Court stated at page 65:

> Proof by circumstantial evidence is not confined to the narrower limits of *res ipsa loquitur* which, as we have pointed out . . . is simply a facet of the general law that verdicts may rest upon circumstantial evidence . . .

Policy Considerations for Applying Res Ipsa Loquitur

Overlaying the mentioned criteria for determining the sufficiency of the evidence to permit the application of *res ipsa loquitur* are several policy considerations—arbitraries, so to speak, which courts at varying times and in varying instances give as reason at law for either permitting or not permitting a case to go to the jury under the theory of *res ipsa loquitur*. These judicial policies apply only to *res ipsa loquitur* and not circumstantial evidence or its "more probable than not" rule.

First, where it appears that the defendant has under his control ultra-hazardous products such as explosives, wild animals or dangerous chemicals, he has imposed upon him under the law the highest degree of care. If such extra-hazardous products, while in his control, cause injury to others, he will be liable for damages under *res ipsa loquitur* absent a most persuasive explanation to rebut the strong inference of negligence.[34] Of course, as to the injured passenger or the shipper of damaged freight, the same high degree of care is owed by the common carrier and *res ipsa loquitur* is applicable for the same policy reason.[35] It is interesting when a passenger of a bus is injured in a collision between bus and another vehicle and sues both bus company and driver of the other car. At least in Missouri, the injured bus passenger

---

[34] American Glycerin Co. v Brown (5 Cir., 1929) 30 F2d 316 Selby v Osage Torpedo Co., (Okla., 1925) 241 P. 130

[35] Hall v Nashville * C. R. Co. (1871) 13 Wall (U.S.) 367

has *res ipsa loquitur* to get to the jury on his case against the bus company. He must prove specific negligence to recover against the driver of the other vehicle. However, if he goes so far as to prove the other vehicle solely responsible for the collision *res ipsa loquitur* is withdrawn as a crutch so as to prevent recovery against the bus company.[36]

A second judicial policy which will cause a court to apply *res ipsa loquitur* even when some of the factual elements to the doctrine appear weak or missing is in the clear case where it is evident that the defendant is in a far better position to know whether negligence caused the injury than the injured plaintiff. A good illustration is the case where a patient is injured while being operated upon by a staff of surgeons, nurses and hospital attendants.[37] This situation must, however, be distinguished from the malpractice case where a poor result is equally probable with non-negligent treatment as with negligent treatment[38] or where it is only speculation as to how much of the patient's neck injury arose from the negligent operation or the accident which required the operation.[39] Superior knowledge of defendant to that of plaintiff will justify application of *res ipsa loquitur*. However, where an automobile inexplicably leaves the road and the driver had superior knowledge of cause, his death in accident will not preclude application of *res ipsa loquitur*.[40]

There remains a third judicial policy infrequently invoked to deny *res ipsa loquitur* to an otherwise deserving plaintiff. Where it appears that the plaintiff himself should know more about the cause of the injury than the defendant[41] or where it appears there was available to the plaintiff direct evidence to establish negligence and he chooses instead to rely upon *res ipsa loquitur* the courts will not evoke *res ipsa loquitur*.[42]

---

[36] Roehswelter v St. Louis Public Service Co., (Mo., 1949) 224 SW 2d 569

[37] Weeks v Latter-Day Saints Hospital (10 Cir., 1969) 418 F 2d 1035; Ybarra v Spangard (Calif., 1945) 154 P 2d 687; Cavero v Franklin General Benevolent Society (Calif., 1950) 223 P2d 471

[38] Smith v Reitman (D.C. Cir., 1967) 389 F 2d 303

[39] Rudick v Prineville Memorial Hospital, (9 Cir., 1963) 319 F 2d 764

[40] Ehrlich v Merritt (3 Cir., 1938) 96 F2d 251; Weller v Worstall (Ohio, 1934) 197 NE 410, affirmed in 196 NE 637; Anno: Automobile—Leaving Road—Res Ipsa Loquitur, 79 ALR2d 6

[41] Monsanto Chemical Co. v Payne (5 Cir., 1966) 354 F 2d 965

[42] Winslow v Ohio Bus Line Co., (Ohio, 1947) 73 NE 2d 504, 507

Single Vehicle Inexplicably Leaving Highway

A particular area where *res ipsa loquitur* is often employed is in the case where a motor vehicle inexplicably leaves the road to injure another and the driver (or his administrator) is sued for damages. All of what we have mentioned is involved in these types of cases which are collected in Annotation: "Automobile—Leaving Road—*Res Ipsa Loquitur*," 79 ALR2d 6.

Res ipsa loquitur is also frequently employed in the FELA cases involving injured railroad workers and the Jones Act cases involving injured seamen. This class of case has been well annotated.[43] The Court of Appeals for the Ninth Circuit has held that as to FELA and Jones Act cases, the injured workman has his own special *res ipsa loquitur* doctrine to get him to the jury on the question of causation.[44]

Pyramiding of Inference upon Inference Not Necessarily Fatal

The most common attack upon the sufficiency of a circumstantial evidence case is the argument that the plaintiff's chain of proof involves an impermissible pyramiding of inference upon inference. If any hard and fast rule of evidence ever prevented the basing of an inference upon an inference it has been pretty well dissipated.[45]

Most all reasoning is based upon deducing one fact from another fact with the other fact often having first been deduced from still a further fact. The only fallacy that may occur in such a chain of reasoning is where a deduced fact is based upon circumstantial evidence that is either unreliable or too remote or too conjectural. If there must be a rule it should be the principle that an inference cannot be based upon an inference that is too remote or conjectural; not than an inference can never be based upon another inference. Thus, in a civil case, if the first inference is a reasonably probable one it may be used as a basis for a succeeding inference.[46] Conspiracy is

---

[43] Injury on Ship—Res Ipsa Loquitur, 1 ALR 3d 642

[44] Admiral Towing Co. v Woolen (9 Cir., 1961) 290 F 2d 641

[45] ANNO: "Inference on Inference," 5 ALR 3d 100

[46] Fegles Constr. Co. v Mc Laughlin Constr. Co., (9 Cir., 1953) 205 F 2d 637; Vaccarezza v Sabquinetti, (Calif., 1945) 163 P 2d 470

practically always established by circumstantial evidence.[47] Any hard and fast rule preventing inference upon inference would frustrate proof of a conspiracy case.

The soundest approach to weighing the sufficiency of a circumstantial evidence case where one inference must be based upon another is to be sure that the basic inference is not too remote or conjectural. In a wrongful death case you will not get very far if you depend upon inferring defendant's negligence from the presumption of care accorded the plaintiff's decedent as the presumption of care runs to both defendant and decedent.[48]

Pertinent Law Review Articles on Circumstantial Evidence

"How to Win a Pedestrian Case without the Plaintiff and without Eyewitnesses," Herbert Murphy, *The Practical Lawyer,* Vol. 11 No. 7 (1965)

"The Anatomy of Proof in Civil Actions," Joe W. Sanders, Associate Justice, Supreme Court of Louisiana, *Louisiana Law Review,* Vol. 28, p. 297 (1968)

"The Validity of an Inference on an Inference in Iowa," Max A. Gors, *Drake Law Review,* Vol. 19, p. 452 (1970)

"Evidence—Testimony as to Position of Vehicles After Collision Insufficient," R. E. B. Jr., *Tennessee Law Review,* Vol. 29, p. 304 (1962)

"Relevancy and the Theory of Probability," William B. Stoebuck, *Iowa Law Review,* Vol. 51, p. 849 (1966)

---

[47] Cooper v United States (8 Cir., 1925) 9 F 2d 216
[48] Looney v Metropolitan R. Co., (1906) 200 U.S. 480

Circumstantial Evidence— 6
Implied Consent—
Implied-in-Fact Contracts

This venture into the wonderland of inference drawing would not be complete without considering implied consent in general and implied in fact contracts in particular. Whether the circumstantial evidence has as its target the fact of consent or the making of an offer or acceptance in order to create a contract the ultimate objective is that of finding a person's intent. Almost a century ago Lord Bowen, J. made the classic statement that: "The state of a man's mind is as much a fact as the state of his digestion."[1]

Implied Consent

Before reaching implied-in-fact contracts it is useful to recognize how courts, upon circumstantial evidence, have impliedly found that persons have consented to one thing or another.

Whether the driver of an automobile involved in collision was driving with permission of the owner will be implied from the circumstance of the owner having seen him drive the car before and making no objection.[2]

Where notice or knowledge on part of a defendant is essential to recovery, the jury may imply such notice or knowledge from facts showing that the defendant had a duty of inquiry as well as means of

---

[1] Commissioner of IRS v Culbertson (1949) 337 U.S. 733, 743n

[2] Lumberman's Mutual Casualty Co. v Pother, (Ill., 1968) 243 NE2d 40, 45

acquiring the knowledge,[3] or a reasonable person under the circumstances in position of the defendant had means of knowledge available and would have used it.[4]

A person will be impliedly found to have waived a substantial legal right through his conduct upon clear and unequivocal evidence showing his intent to give up the right of which he was aware.[5]

Where necessary, it will be found that an implied invitation was extended to the driver of a delivery truck to drive upon the unloading area of an industrial plant but not as to other areas where he need not be.[6]

A way of necessity will be implied from a transaction where the owner of a single parcel of land conveys a portion of it to another and the only reasonable ingress or egress to the portion conveyed is over the portion remaining of the parcel.[7]

A "resulting trust" will be implied from what persons do with property of others.[8]

Under the most compelling of circumstances, a testator may make a devise by implications drawn from his will.[9]

Where a principal appoints an agent the authority for the agent to employ others on a commission may be implied from evidence showing that agents of such type ordinarily have such power.[10]

Ordering goods for a particular use may imply warranty of seller that the goods delivered are fit for their intended use.[11] Likewise, in sale of ordinary goods, a warranty by the seller that the goods are of merchantable quality will be implied.[12]

Where a new law or constitutional amendment is enacted by a legislature which is inconsistent with and repugnant to an older one the intent of the legislature to repeal the older one will be implied.[13]

---

[3] McCausland v Davis, (Fla., 1967) 204 S2d 334, 335

[4] Blackburn v Norman Estates, Inc. (Ohio, 1967) 232 NE2d 442, 445; Black v Public Service Elect. & Gas Co., (NJ, 1968) 237 A2d 495, 499

[5] United States v Chichester, (9 Cir., 1963) 312 F2d 275, 283

[6] Moss v Nooter Corp., (Mo., 1961) 344 SW2d 647, 652

[7] Wagner v Fairlamb (Colo., 1963) 379 P2d 165, 168

[8] Hereford Land Co. v Globe Industries, Inc. (Tex., 1965) 387 SW2d 771, 775

[9] In re Selner's Estate (NY., 1941) 26 NYS2d 783, 787

[10] Masuda v Kawasaki Dockyard Co., (2 Cir., 1964) 328 F2d 662, 664

[11] Carney v Sears, Roebuck & Co., (4 Cir., 1962) 309 F2d 300, 303

[12] Sylvia Coal Co. v Mercury Coal & Coke Co., (W. Va., 1967) 156 SE2d 1, 7

[13] Johnston v Hicks, (Ga., 1969) 170 SE2d 410

Implied-in-Fact Contracts

Contracts between parties often take several forms or combination of forms. An express contract is one where the parties express intent to contract by either written or oral words. An implied-in-fact contract is one where the intent to contract is expressed by conduct—sometimes active and sometimes passive.[14] In this chapter we are not concerned with an "implied-in-law" contract which is also described as a "quasi" contract. This latter type of contract is really no contract at all. An "implied-in-law," or so called "quasi," contract is nothing more than a duty imposed upon a person by a court as a matter of law to pay another money under the fiction of implied contract in order to prevent unjust enrichment.[15]

Since nothing could be more remote from an actual contract than the wrongful extortion of money by threat of litigation,[16] it becomes critically important that a person's conduct points unequivocally to an intent to contract before finding him so obligated. Usually the implication of contract comes into issue through conduct evidencing intent to accept an express offer or through a request for service which another performs. Frequently parties enter into a written contract leaving unsaid things which later must be construed as implied covenants if the written contract is to be given effect.

An Agreement to Later Agree—Not a Contract

In considering circumstantial evidence to determine whether an implied-in-fact contract was made there very often is the threshold question of whether the conduct of the parties under consideration evidenced an actual meeting of the minds or was at best negotiations with only an implied promise to make a contract at some future date.

Since this situation can often arise in the construction business where prime contractors in bidding for public work use offers from sub-contractors and suppliers, we illustrate the point by discussing

---

[14] Western Contracting Corp. v Sooner Cons. Co., (Okla., 1966) 256 F. Supp. 163, 167

[15] Fidelity & Deposit Co. of Md. v Harris, (9 Cir., 1966) 360 F2d 402, 410

[16] Wallace v Hines, (1920) 253 U.S. 66, 68

Merritt-Chapman & Scott Corp. v Gunderson Bros. Eng. Corp., (9 Cir., 1962) 305 F2d 659, certiorari denied (with two dissents) in 371 U.S. 935. In that case Gunderson Bros. as supplier offered to MCS to furnish a million dollars' worth of spillway gates for a large hydro-electric dam to be built on the Columbia River should MCS become the successful bidder. MCS was the successful bidder, and in entering into the prime contract, it named Gunderson Bros, as the supplier of the spillway gates. For several months thereafter MCS had telephone conversations with Gunderson Bros. in which MCS asked that quotations on other related machinery be given and that Gunderson Bros. do certain things which it would not otherwise have done had it not understood that its spillway gate offer had been accepted. Finally, when it became advantageous to MCS to do so it gave the spillway gate job to another supplier. Gunderson Bros. sued MCS for breach of contract. A federal jury returned a verdict in favor of Gunderson Bros. for its lost profits after finding that MCS by its words and conduct had accepted the Gunderson Bros. offer. The Court of Appeals for the Ninth Circuit reversed the judgment, holding that the evidence was insufficient to show that MCS had accepted the Gunderson Bros. offer. In doing so it stated:

> This case bristles with indicia of negotiations. In the very first instance of contact between the parties after the offer was made, MCS proposed an arrangement considerably different than that which was submitted by Gunderson. From that point on, all further contact between litigants came to nothing more than offers and counter-offers. MCS certainly manifested an intention to enter into a contract with Gunderson at some time in the future, and MCS may very well have taken advantage of Gunderson, but contract with Gunderson it did not.

For the other side of the coin read: *Hill v Waxberg,* (9 Cir., 1956) 237 F2d 936 and the two Washington cases of *Western Asphalt Co. v Valle,* (Wn., 1946) 171 P2d 159 and *Milone & Tucci, Inc. v Bonafide Builders, Inc.,* (Wn., 1956) 301 P2d 756.

Furnishing Things or Services

A most common situation which gives rise to an implied-in-fact contract is where one person with or without request furnishes things or services to another without expressing an intent to be paid. Let us take a set of facts which could make an excellent question in some bar examination.

Suppose a nice but unsophisticated lady from somewhere in the mid-west (beyond Chicago) makes her first visit to New York City. While there she has lunch in an exquisite dining room of a famous hotel. She becomes enamoured with the pastry. Upon learning that the pastry was an exclusive creation of the hotel's pastry chef, she asks to meet the chef. Upon his arrival at her table, she compliments him about his pastry and then, after telling him that she sometimes at home tries her hand at making pastry, she asks the chef if he would give her the recipe in order that she might make the pastry to serve to the women of her bridge club. The chef does. Upon return home this nice lady finds a bill from the chef for $250.00. When a demand from a collection agency arrives a month later, she rushes to your law office and with tears in her eyes asks you if she is required to pay the chef $250.00. What do you tell her?

Your search of the cases shows that generally when one requests a thing or service from another, there usually arises an implied-in-fact agreement to pay a reasonable price for that which was furnished.[17] Even if no request is made, if expectation of payment is manifested at the time the thing or service is furnished, a like implication will arise.[18] However, the matter of whether compensation is expected or intended usually rests upon the facts indicating whether the recipient as a reasonable person might have believed the thing or service was not a gratuity.[19]

It is clear that the unsophisticated client of yours and the pastry chef are miles apart on the matter of payment. You probably tell your client to return the recipe (whether used or not) and deny liability. This she does. However, the chef means business, as a month later he sues your client and you have your chance to defend her cause and your advice.

At this point you look further into the law and find that sometimes when a stranger furnishes things or services, the matter of payment is presumed while the contrary presumption comes into play when a relative furnishes the thing or service.[20] However, the chef

[17] Callan v Andrews, (7 Cir., 1931) 48 F2d 118; Grepke v General Electric Co., (8 Cir., 1960) 280 F2d 508

[18] Vaught v Charleston Nat. Bank, (10 Cir., 1933) 62 F2d 817; Chem-Tronix Laboratories, Inc. v Solocast Co. (Conn. 1968) 258 A2d 110, 113

[19] Ross Eng. Co. v Pace, (4 Cir., 1946) 153 F2d 35, 45

[20] Re Roger's Estate (Kan., 1959) 334 P2d 830

should not be too smug about the presumption in his favor as some courts believe that a presumption in this type of case should not be entertained as often the matter of the relationship of the parties is of little importance.[21] You know your case will turn on a question of fact.

We conclude by saying that if the pastry chef is foolish enough to come to your client's home town to have his day in court, you should be smart enough to demand a trial by jury. With your client's peers or their husbands sitting on the jury, you can't lose.

Furnishing Ideas for the Boss

Implied in fact contract litigation often springs from an employer asking employees for suggestions on how to better run the business, or even in the case without request where an employee gives his boss an idea which is later adopted by the company. The fact that the written invitation for ideas from employees contains a provision that the matter of compensation for the idea is to be exclusively for employer determination does not necessarily prevent an implied in fact agreement to pay compensation from becoming a jury question.[22]

However, where an employee gives an idea to his company to use he cannot claim compensation unless the expectation for compensation is indicated at time of delivery of the idea to the boss. Where an employee invents an improvement to an ice cream freezer which is adopted by the employer, the employee will be "frozen out" of compensation if the idea for compensation only appears to have been an afterthought.[23]

An idea which can be the subject of an implied-in-fact agreement for compensation need not be novel in order to recover as the disclosure of the idea to the boss may be of substantial benefit to the company.[24] If one is employed for purpose of creating inventions it is implied that he will assign his patent rights to his employer, but if he is not so specifically employed, the implication is otherwise.[25]

As a general rule the voluntary furnishing of things or services to another cannot in itself create evidence sufficient to infer an agree-

---

[21] Blenard v Blenard, (Md., 1946) 45 A2d 335, 339; Simmons v Simmons, (Okla., 1960) 357 P2d 949

[22] Osborn v Boeing Airplane Company (9 Cir., 1962) 309 F2d 99

[23] Woodruff v New State Ice Co., (10 Cir., 1952) 197 F2d 36

[24] Donahue v Ziv Television Programs, (Calif., 1966) 245 CA2d 593

[25] Salterini v Schneider, (NY, 1943) 45 NYS2d 645

ment to pay.[26] There are, however, some business transactions where obligations are implied. For example, where upon request one goes surety for another there is an implied promise to indemnify if the surety is called upon to pay.[27] Likewise, if money is paid by one person to another at his request or request of a third person, there is an implied promise that it will be repaid with interest.[28]

Whatever evidence you may present to prove an implied-in-fact contract, it must show contract terms with sufficient certainty to enable the contract to be enforced.[29] Indefiniteness may arise from lack of showing time, price or property involved in the contract.[30] However, once the intent to contract is established, the court as a rule will stretch as far as possible to find the contract terms to be sufficiently definite.[31]

Implied Covenants to Express Contracts

Parties to a contract are bound by its implied covenants as well as its express covenants.[32] Circumstances surrounding the entering into the contract, customs of the particular trade and conduct of the parties during performance of an express contract all come into play in determining if an implied covenant is necessary to give effect to an express contract, and if so, what the implied covenant might be.

The general principle is that only when it is necessary to give effect to an express contract will a non-expressed covenant be implied and then only when the implied covenant is not inconsistent with any covenant expressed in the contract.[33]

In *Wood v Lucy, Lady Duff-Gordon,* (NY, 1917) 118 NE 214 the plaintiff had become Lady Duff-Gordon's exclusive agent for one year to sell her endorsements to fashion people and split profits with Lady Duff-Gordon. However, Lady Duff-Gordon did not give the plaintiff an opportunity to purvey her endorsements as she did this

---

[26] Stevens v Continental Can Co., (6 Cir., 1962) 308 F2d 100

[27] Felton v Finley, (Idaho, 1949) 209 P2d 899

[28] Island Petroleum Co. v Commissioner, IRS, (4 Cir., 1932) 57 F2d 992

[29] Castor v Coppock, (8 Cir., 1954) 211 F2d 136; W. C. Shepherd Co., Inc. v Royal Indemnity, (5 Cir., 1951) 192 F2d 710

[30] Schwartz v Inspiration Gold Mining Co., (Mont., 1936) 15 F. Supp. 1030

[31] Armstrong v Southern Production Co., Inc., (5 Cir., 1950) 182 F2d 238

[32] Baltimore & Ohio R. Co. v United States, (1923) 261 U.S. 592

[33] Republic Pictures Corp. v Rogers, (9 Cir., 1954) 213 F2d 662, 665

herself. When plaintiff sued for breach of contract, Lady Duff-Gordon claimed lack of mutuality of obligation because plaintiff in the writing had not promised to do anything. Judge Cardozo found an implied promise on part of plaintiff to use reasonable efforts to act as her exclusive agent. The Court stated:

> The law has outgrown its primitive stage of formalism when the precise word was the sovereign talisman, and every slip was fatal. It takes a broader view today. A promise may be lacking, and yet the whole writing may be 'instinct with an obligation' imperfectly expressed. (citing cases) If that is so, there is a contract.

So it is with implied covenants to express contracts. Covenants are usually implied to express contracts in two situations: One, where the implication is so clearly within the contemplation of the parties that it was unnecessary to put it in writing; and another, where the implied covenant was probably beyond the thoughts of both parties but is necessary to be implied if the contract is to be given effect.

Thus, where a party acknowledges a debt it is implied that he is also promising to pay the debt.[34] Where a dealer agrees to stock a manufacturer's spark plugs and sell them to the trade it is implicit that the manufacturer is obligated to accept and fill the dealer's orders.[35] In almost every contract there is an implied covenant that each party will cooperate and not hinder the other in his performance of the contract.[36]

While the custom and usages of a particular trade can be used as an aid to interpret an ambiguous covenant of a contract, such custom and usage cannot in itself form basis of a contract or add to its terms, except to the restricted extent of supplying a needed implied term in order to effectuate the intent of the contracting parties. Thus, as to a contract involving the purchase and sale of hops where the contract is silent as to how the hops are to be inspected, a known custom can furnish evidence to support an implied-in-fact term to the contract.[37]

---

[34] New York Casualty Co. v Sinclair Refining Co., (10 Cir. 1939) 108 F2d 65

[35] Mills-Morris Co. v Champion Spark Plug Co., (6 Cir., 1925) 7 F2d 38

[36] The Murmanill Corp. v Simkins, (5 Cir., 1958) 251 F2d 33; Vanadium Corp. of America v Fidelity & Deposit Co. of Maryland, (2 Cir., 1947) 159 F2d 105

[37] John I. Haas, Inc. v Wellman (9 Cir., 1951) 186 F2d 862

The Maritime Implied-in-Fact Indemnity Contract

Perhaps the most important and complex implied-in-fact contract of present time is that fashioned by the Supreme Court of the United States in *Ryan Stevedoring Co. v Pan-Atlantic SS. Corp.*, (1956) 350 U.S. 124. In that case the Supreme Court held that when a stevedore company places its longshoremen aboard a ship to handle cargo with use of the ship's cargo gear the stevedore by implication of fact not only warrants that it will perform a workmanlike stevedore service but as well promises to indemnify and hold harmless the shipowner if by its failure to perform a workmanlike service a longshoreman is injured and as a consequence the shipowner finds himself cast in damages because the stevedore's breach rendered the ship unseaworthy.

It is interesting to understand why the Supreme Court fashioned an implied-in-fact indemnity arrangement when already the common law gave indemnification through *quasi* contract.[38] This was once the author's pet subject.[39]

In the beginning the true seaman who sailed the seas as a member of the crew of a ship had unseaworthiness as basis for recovery for personal injuries. The Jones Act[40] gave him, in addition, a right of action for shipowner's negligence. The Longshoremen's and Harbor Workers Act[41] gave the longshoreman a workman compensation system comparable to those offered by states to shore-side workers. Usually, the longshoreman was employed by an independent stevedore and when injured the longshoreman could not sue his employer but could sue the shipowner as a third person either for causative unseaworthiness of the vessel or his causative negligence.

In 1946 the Supreme Court in *Seas Shipping Co. v Sieracki,* (1946) 328 U.S. 85 waved its magic wand and ordained that longshoremen, while not crew members, were nevertheless seamen as they were doing work traditionally done by seamen. The shipowner owes a duty to seamen to maintain its ship and her gear in a reasonably fit condition and failing that, the shipowner becomes absolutely liable

---

[38] Portel v United States, (SDNY, 1949) 85 F. Supp. 458; The S. S Samovar (Calif., 1947) 72 F. Supp. 574

[39] William F. White, "A New Look at the Shipowner's Right-Over for Shipboard Injuries," Stanford Law Review, Vol. 12, No. 4, July, 1960

[40] 46 U.S.C. Section 688

[41] 33 U.S.C. Section 901 et seq

for resulting injury.[42] What constitutes unseaworthiness has been extended beyond maintenance of ship and gear to some very ridiculous extremes.[43] As always, the seaman's contributory negligence does not bar his recovery but only goes to mitigate his damages. With *Sieracki,* supra the shipowner found himself owing a duty to maintain a seaworthy ship to both his crew members and the longshoremen employed by the stevedore to handle cargo.

Here is what has become the eternal triangle: The longshoreman as a seaman sues the shipowner as a third person and the shipowner impleads the stevedore to seek indemnity because the stevedore brought about the liability. Often it is the stevedore and its longshoremen who either renders the ship unseaworthy or brings into play an unseaworthy condition to cause injury.[44] The shipowner in such situation without a right over against the stevedore takes it on the chin for the faults of the stevedore. Where both stevedore and shipowner were at fault some lower courts had allowed contribution between these two co-tortfeasors.[45] However, the idea of balancing the equities between longshoreman, shipowner and stevedore was short-lived. In *Halcyon Lines v Haenn Ship Ceiling & Refitting Corp.,* (1952) 342 U.S. 282 the Supreme Court refused to permit the rule of comparative negligence to come into play as between stevedore and shipowner although it sanctioned the long-standing comparative negligence concept as between longshoreman and shipowner.

We believe that because of its unwillingness to overrule *Halcyon,* supra the Supreme Court in correcting the inequitable position in which it had placed the shipowner by its *Sieracki* decision fashioned an implied-in-fact warranty in *Ryan.* Those who follow the sea can readily see an implied-in-fact understanding so far as the stevedore rendering a workmanlike service. It is obvious that if the chief mate met the stevedore's walking boss on the quarter deck and asked him if he would promise to render a workmanlike service, that the reply would be an emphatic "Yes." It is more difficult, however, to imagine that the Chief Mate could extract from the walking boss a promise to indemnify. While the warranty in *Ryan,* flies the flag of "implied-in-fact," it is to our thinking more of a hybrid of both an implied-in-fact and an implied-in-law understanding.

---

[42] Mitchell v Trawler Racer, Inc., (1960) 362 U.S. 539

[43] Ferguson v Moore–McCormack Lines, Inc. (1957) 352 US 521

[44] Crumady v The Joachim Hendrick Fisser, (1959) 358 U.S. 423

[45] Portel v United States, (SDNY, 1949) 85 F. Supp. 458; The S.S. Samovar (Calif., 1947) 72 F. Supp. 574

What has happened since is that trying to juggle at one time both *Sieracki, Halcyon* and *Ryan*, the Supreme Court has created more problems than it has solved. When both are at fault, shifting the full package of the loss from shipowner to stevedore is as inequitable to the stevedore as it was to the shipowner when he could not do so. If shipowner under implied contract could pass matters to the stevedore, why shouldn't the stevedore pass matters to the injured longshoreman, particularly when he has been found contributorily negligent? No reason in logic exists except that the courts put a quick stop to so extending such right over actions.[46]

If the stevedore made an implied-in-fact warranty to the shipowner to perform a workmanlike service at peril of paying indemnity if he failed, why did not the shipowner at the same time make an implied-in-fact warranty to the stevedore that his ship was a safe place for the longshoremen to work and if it wasn't, that he would respond in indemnity? These questions and others are still churning in the admiralty law and here is not the place to delve deeper into them. Apparently, the lower courts seem reluctant to solve these doctrinal problems short of Supreme Court or Congressional guidance.

In *McLaughlin v Trelleborgs Angfartygs* A/B, (2 Cir., 1969) 408 F2d 1334 the stevedore pleaded that the Court should be sufficiently resourceful to find some way to avoid the apparently irrational result whereby a shipowner who supplied a defective hoist emerges scot-free and a stevedore who did nothing more than innocently recruit a careless workman from a hiring hall pays the full bill for the workman's injury and the ship's defense against the claim. This plea met sympathetic ears, but nothing more as the Court stated:

> So long as *Halcyon vs Haenn*, Supra 342 U.S. 282 remains on the books, inferior federal courts will do better to abstain from further adventures in this wonderland and leave doctrinal development to the Supreme Court, unless current congressional interest in the complex problems arising from the creation of a new class of land-based seamen by the *Sieracki* decision, 328 U.S. (1946), should result in the knot being cut in a more drastic fashion.

---

[46] Nicroli v Den Norske Afrika—OG Australielinie (2 Cir., 1964) 332 F2d 651

Pertinent Law Review Articles on Implied Contracts

"An Appraisal of Judicial Reluctance to Imply an Indemnity Contract in Time-Barred Breach of Warranty Suits," *St. John's Law Review,* Vol. 39, p. 361 (1965)

"Implied-Contract Substitutes for Fair Trade Act Non-signer Provisions," *Georgetown Law Journal,* Vol. 55, p. 923 (1967)

"Implied Warranty Extending to Persons Not in Privity of Contract with Seller," Daniel F. Thomas, *Maryland Law Review,* Vol. 21, p. 247 (1961)

"Conditional Offer Implied from a Request to Submit Proposals," Mona Salyer Lambird, *Maryland Law Review,* Vol. 22, p. 225 (1962)

Filling in the Chinks—   7
Presumptions—
Judicial Notice

In the case thin on its facts there are apt to be several holes, cracks or crevices in the evidentiary wall. These chinks must be patched. Your case based upon direct evidence can have as many chinks as the one based upon circumstantial evidence. For example, you prove that a condition exists at one time, but it is not at the critical time of the accident. What about that? This is where an understanding and awareness of presumptions and judicial notice can come to your aid.

"Inferences" and "Presumptions" Distinguished

In the last three chapters we have explored the fine art of inference drawing. Here, we deal in presumptions. What's the difference? Unfortunately, there is nothing more confusing and involved than understanding the differences between an inference and a presumption unless it is a plate of spaghetti. Both bench and bar often term an "inference" as a "permissible presumption" or a "presumption of fact" while true presumptions are often called "presumptions at law" or "necessary inferences." As trial lawyers we are only interested in functional differences and their procedural effects.

In Oregon as elsewhere there are two kinds of indirect evidence: (1) Inferences and (2) Presumptions.[1] An inference is a deduction

---

[1] Oregon Rev. Statute 41.310

which the jury makes from the facts proved, without an express direction of law to that effect.[2] On the other hand, a presumption is a deduction which the law expressly directs to be made from particular facts.[3]

Procedural effects of these terms are clearly explained in *Rehm v United States,* (EDNY, 1960) 183 F. Supp. 157. In that case an Air Force airplane inexplicably struck an automobile which was minding its own business on a highway. Plaintiff moved for summary judgment on liability on basis there was no genuine dispute over the facts and that a *res ipsa loquitur* case was established. Summary judgment was denied. After explaining that a prima facie case consisted of that quantum of evidence tending to prove each material fact that a plaintiff must introduce to sustain his burden of going forward with the evidence and thus render himself immune from a non-suit, the Court defined a true presumption:

> The term "presumption" has been used loosely to mean a "permissible inference" in some instances and a "necessary inference" in other instances. A true presumption arises when the plaintiff establishes to the satisfaction of the fact-trier the basic facts which *require* a finding of the presumed fact. When a true presumption arises, the defendant must come forward and rebut the presumption or suffer a directed verdict. It is because of the failure to define such terms that considerable confusion is reflected in many cases concerned with the procedural effects of the doctrine of *res ipsa loquitur,* when it is held to apply. Rosenthal, The Procedural Effects of *Res Ipsa Loquitur* in New York, 22 Corn. L.Q. 39 (1936)

Otherwise stated: a presumption is an inference which the law directs a jury to draw from a given set of facts while an "inference" is a conclusion of fact which the jury may but need not draw from a given set of facts.[4] The procedural consequence is that an inference gets a plaintiff to the jury while a presumption gets the plaintiff a directed verdict *IF* the only fact issue turns on the presumption and the defendant fails to go forward with evidence to rebut the presumption. A procedural plus for the true presumption is that if it be an inference *required* by law to be drawn by the jury and is not rebutted,

---

[2] Oregon Rev. Statutes 41.320

[3] Oregon Rev. Statutes, 41.340

[4] Pendergrast v United States, (DC Cir. 1969) 416 F2d 776

the party in whose favor the presumption runs should be entitled to have the court instruct the jury that it must find the ultimate fact.

Some confusion can be cleared up by understanding that a given set of facts can and often gives rise simultaneously to both an inference and a presumption. For example, when a moving vessel hits a stationary object such as a bridge, there is a presumption that the vessel was negligent.[5] This presumption shifts the burden of going forward to the moving vessel. If the defending vessel offers evidence to the contrary, the presumption which is nothing more than a rule of law disappears.[6] However, what is forgotten is that while the presumption as a rule of law disappears, the inference of negligence drawn from the fact that the moving object struck the stationary object remains as evidence to be weighed by the fact finder along with the direct evidence tending to show freedom from negligence.[7]

Thus, a presumption is not evidence but a rule of law requiring the inference unless rebutted and in that sense has a greater quality than an inference. However, in the sense that the inference is evidence, it has a greater quality than the presumption. In *California Western State Life Ins. Co. v Vaughan*, (9 Cir., 1948) 165 F2d 945 which involved the question of whether decedent had falsified his application for life insurance, it was argued that under Washington law a presumption is not evidence but only a rule to shift the burden of going forward and since it disappeared upon the defendant's proof of a false application that the insurance company should have a directed verdict. However, the Court of Appeals, while agreeing that the presumption disappeared upon being controverted, held, nevertheless, that there was an inference from the circumstances which made the ultimate fact one for jury determination. It is suggested that in considering the presumptions under discussion that they be critically examined for rationality to support an inference should the presumption go out the window and evidence in form of an inference from circumstantial evidence become sorely needed to erect a solid wall of evidence.

---

[5] The Oregon, (1895) 158 U.S. 186; Pacific Tow Boat Co. v States Marine Corp., (9 Cir., 1960) 276 F2d 745, 750

[6] Pennsylvania R. R. Co. v S. S. Marie Leonhardt, (3 Cir., 1963) 320 F2d 262

[7] Wigmore, Evidence (3rd ed., 1940) Section 2491; State of Oregon v Tug GO-GETTER, (Ore., 1969) 299 F. Supp. 269

How State-Created Presumptions Work
in the Federal Courts

Since true presumptions arise from law and inferences only from common sense reasoning, the question is what law gives rise to presumptions. No doubt in earlier days presumptions sprang from the common law. Now it appears to us that most presumptions are statutory, either springing from state statutes which codify earlier common law principles or create new ones or federal statutes which are enacted to shift where thought best the burden of going forward with evidence. Without attempting to run the gamut of all statutory presumptions, we consider how these presumptions, particularly state statutory presumptions, work in the federal courts.

A step toward uniform use by federal courts of statutory presumptions came in the enactment of Rule 43(a) of the Federal Rules of Civil Procedure which reads in part:

> . . . In any case, the statute or rule which favors the reception of the evidence governs and the evidence shall be presented according to the most convenient method prescribed in any of the statutes or rules to which reference is made. . . .

Rule 43(a) makes reference to statutes and rules of the United States, courts of the United States on hearing of suits in equity, as well as rules applied in courts of general jurisdiction of the State in which the United States District Court is located.

The language "rule which favors the reception of the evidence" in Rule 43(a) has been used by District Courts to adopt and apply state evidentiary and procedural rules in all District Court cases irrespective of whether jurisdiction is based upon diversity of citizenship or rests in equity or admiralty. The District Court need not apply state rules when not as liberal or are incompatible with federal rules. The District Court cannot, however, reach beyond its own state for state rules.

In *Weber v Continental Casualty Co.*, (10 Cir., 1967) 379 F2d 729 the action was upon a California life insurance policy with the fact issue being whether the decedent died by drowning or by reason of a contemporaneous heart attack. The trial was held in Oklahoma. Under California law the pertinent presumption in California then constituted evidence which would have made a case for the plaintiff. Under Oklahoma law the pertinent presumption was merely a procedural tool which disappeared upon introduction of evidence rebutting the presumption. It was held that although California controlled the substantive law of the case, Oklahoma as the forum of the District Court controlled the procedural law of the case. Hence, the District Court had to accept Oklahoma law on the effect of the presumption and could not reach to California for presumption law more favorable to the plaintiff.

It must also be kept in mind that a state statutory presumption must be relevant to the case before a District Court will apply it. In *Mayfield Casualty Co. v Williams,* (5 Cir., 1967) 377 F2d 389 a directed verdict for plaintiff was reversed on appeal. Plaintiff sued an insurance company directly upon a liability insurance policy and relied upon a Tennessee statutory presumption that made the registered owner presumably the operator of an automobile or its driver, if not the owner, presumably in the employ and acting within his scope of employment by the registered owner. The Court of Appeals reversed because it considered that the Tennessee law was never intended to be applied to an action based upon the omnibus clause of a liability insurance policy.

Go into the District Court familiar with all presumptions afforded in the State where the District Court is located. But do not expect the District Court to accept a state created presumption that is in conflict with federal law.[8]

Rebuttable Presumptions Useful
in Completing Facts for a Case

Most rebuttable presumptions go to filling the chinks in the wall of necessary evidence. Unfortunately many court decisions fail to indicate the source of the presumption, i.e. a state or federal statute or the common law. Many rebuttable presumptions are nothing more than codified inferences. A caveat: If the presumption stems from a state statute or code it can only be used in the state wherein the District Court has Jurisdiction.[9] Also, many of the presumptions set

---

[8] Weyerhaeuser Timber Co. v Marshall, (9 Cir. 1939) 102 F2d 78, 81
[9] Broderick v McGuire, (Conn. 1934) 174 A. 314, 94 ALR 890

forth below are indicated as being created by a state statute. However, these state codified presumptions are likewise codified in other states although the language might vary. Get your ideas here but check out the presumptions in the law of the forum.

A Thing once Proved to Exist Continues as Long as is Usual with Things of that Nature: This rebuttable presumption is one of the most prevalently used in civil litigation. For example, prove the vessel's navigation lights were burning prior to the collision and it will be presumed that they were burning at time of collision.[10]

Can this presumption work backwards? It is usually thought not because by its very terms it only flows in a forward direction. However, while codified as a rebuttable presumption it is really nothing more than a common sense inference. As an inference in the right situation the presumption of continuity can work backwards. A worn and decayed floor shown to exist 1½ months after the accident has been presumed to exist at time of the accident because floors do not become worn or decayed in 1½ months.[11] Where a vessel is damaged by reason of a broken pile upon her arrival at a wharf it will be presumed that the broken pile existed long enough to have imparted constructive knowledge on the wharf owner in absence of the wharf owner coming forth with evidence of a recent inspection where the piling was not found broken.[12]

The continuity presumption and inference of backward relation gained currency in business relationships in *McFarland v Gregory* (2 Cir., 1970) 425 F2d 443. In that case the issue was whether a person's proven intent to obstruct another person from exercising his stock option existed at an earlier date. While not applying the backward inference, the Court recognized the principle by holding:

> The continuity presumption and the presumption of backward relation appear to be reasonable grounds on which to draw inferences where (1) a situation or the circumstances surrounding it do not go through an apparent material change and (2) the lapse of time is not great enough to suggest that unknown circumstances or courses, in the normal course of events, will have changed the situation. Each case must rest on its own bottom.

---

[10] Hess Tankship Co. v S.S. M. L. Gosney (ED,Va 1963) 230 F. Supp. 1 Oregon Rev. Statutes 41.360 (32)

[11] F. W. Woolworth Co. v Seckinger, (5 Cir., 1942) 125 F2d 97

[12] Berwind-White Coal Mining Co. v City of New York (2 Cir., 1931) 48 F2d 105

So, when you need a backward flow, don't give up the ship merely because the presumption is cast in terms of a forward flow.[13]

Things Have Happened According to the Ordinary Course of Nature and the Ordinary Habits of Life: Under this usual general presumption,[14] there arise a number of other similar presumptions. There is a presumption against suicide.[15] It is presumed that one exercises due care for his own concern and safety.[16] But do not expect this last mentioned presumption to carry you to a jury if the decedent is shown to have piloted an airplane into a mountain while flying at a low elevation contrary to regulations of a federal aviation agency.[17]

It is presumed that an adult is mentally competent even though a year after signing a contract the person may have been adjudicated an incompetent.[18]

It is presumed that a person intends the natural and probable consequences of his acts.[19]

It has even been presumed that a person is just before he is generous.[20]

A person not heard from in seven years is presumed dead.[21]

A writing is presumed to be truly dated.[22]

A person is presumed identified by identity of his name.[23]

An uninterrupted adverse possession of real property for 20 years or more has been held pursuant to a written conveyance.[24]

Presumptions Founded Upon Public Policy as well as Reason: Many of the usual presumptions found codified by most states have been created for reasons of public policy although they also have logic for their justification. Among these are the following:

All adult males are presumed capable of producing offspring.[25]

---

[13] Girardi v Gates Rubber Co., (9 Cir. 1963) 325 F2d 196, 203; Allen v Matson Navigation Co., (9 Cir. 1958) 255 F2d 273, 281

[14] Oregon Rev. Statutes, 41.360(28)

[15] National Life & Acc. Ins. Co. v Graham, (8 Cir., 1962) 301 F2d 439

[16] Schultz & Lindsay Const. Co. v Erickson, (8 Cir., 1965) 352 F2d 425

[17] Gatenby v Altoona Aviation Corp., (W.D. Pa., 1967) 268 F. Supp. 599, affirmed in (3 Cir., 1969) 407 F2d 443

[18] Smith v Atlas Contracting Co., (D.C., 1964) 235 F. Supp. 225; Katopodis v Liberian S/T Olympic Sun, (E.D. Va., 1968) 282 F. Supp. 369

[19] Rankin v Farmers Elevator Mut. Ins. Co., (10 Cir., 1968) 393 F2d 718

[20] Ottenberg v Ottenberg, (D.C. 1961) 194 F. Supp. 98

[21] Oregon Rev. Statutes, 41.360(26)

[22] Oregon Rev. Statutes, 41.360 (23)

[23] Oregon Rev. Statutes, 41.360 (25)

[24] Oregon Rev. Statutes, 41.360 (37)

[25] Hamilton Nat. Bank of Chattanooga v United States, (E.D. Tenn. 1965) 236 F. Supp. 1005, affirmed in 367 F2d 554

All persons have knowledge of pertinent law.[26] However, a taxpayer at time of receiving securities will not be chargeable with knowing of subsequently created regulations.[27]

United States mails are regularly handled.[28] Letter which is properly sealed, stamped, addressed and deposited in the United States mail will reach addressee and be received by him in due course.[29]

A telegram properly dispatched has been received.[30]

State courts will enforce rights secured by the United States Constitution.[31]

Official duty has been regularly performed.[32]

Everyone (including attorneys) discharge their duties, both legal and moral.[33]

When one endeavors to exercise his right under law he does so in a legal manner.[34]

That an injunction issued by a court will be obeyed.[35]

A person acting in a public office was regularly appointed to it.[36]

A court, or judge acting as such, whether in this state or any other state or country, was acting in the lawful exercise of his jurisdiction.[37]

A judicial record, while not conclusive, does still correctly determine or set forth the rights of the parties.[38]

All matters within an issue were submitted to the jury, and passed upon by them.[39]

A man and woman deporting themselves as husband and wife have entered into a lawful contract of marriage.[40]

A child born in lawful wedlock, there being no decree of separation from bed and board, is legitimate.[41]

---

26 United States v Yazell, (1966) 382 U.S. 341

27 Eger v C. I. R. (2 Cir., 1968) 393 F2d 243

28 Federal Ins. Co. v Summers, (1 Cir., 1968) 403 F2d 971

29 Charlson Realty Co. v United States, (Ct. Cl., 1967) 384 F2d 434

30 Wagner Tractor Inc. v Shields (9 Cir., 1967) 381 F2d 441

31 Eubanks v State of Florida, (Fla., 1965) 242 F. Supp. 472

32 United States v Jones, (9 Cir., 1949) 176 F2d 278; Oregon Rev. Statutes, 41.360 (15)

33 Dorf v Relles, (7 Cir., 1966) 355 F2d 488

34 TRW, Inc. v N.L.R.B., (6 Cir., 1968) 393 F2d 771

35 United States v Raines, (Ga., 1961) 203 F. Supp. 147

36 Oregon Rev. Statutes, 41.360 (14)

37 Oregon Rev. Statutes, 41.360 (16)

38 Oregon Rev. Statutes, 41.360 (17)

39 Oregon Rev. Statutes, 41.360 (18)

40 Oregon Rev. Statutes, 41.360 (30)

41 Oregon Rev. Statutes, 41.360 (31)

The law has been obeyed.[42]

A document or writing more than twenty years old is genuine, when it has been generally acted upon as genuine by persons having an interest in the question, and its custody has been satisfactorily explained.[43]

A printed and published book purporting to be printed and published by public authority was so printed and published.[44]

A printed and published book purporting to contain reports of cases determined in the tribunals of the state or country where the book is published contains correct reports of such cases.[45]

A trustee or other whose duty it was to convey real property to a particular person has actually conveyed it to him, when such presumption is necessary to perfect the title of the person or his successor in interest.[46]

Presumptions in Aid of Business Transactions: A number of rebuttable presumptions are useful in filling out a case involving business and corporate transactions. Among these include:

It is presumed that everyone acts in good faith.[47]

Private transactions are fair and regular.[48] The ordinary course of business has been followed.[49]

A subcontractor has knowledge of the terms of the general building contract (where state law requires him to be familiar with the building contract).[50]

Director of a corporation knew of the corporation's deficit position.[51]

Director of a corporation knows of those things which corporate books or minutes of directors' meeting disclose.[52]

An importer engaged in marketing imports knew how imported products were to be used.[53]

---

[42] Oregon Rev. Statutes, 41.360 (33)

[43] Oregon Rev. Statutes, 41.360 (34)

[44] Oregon Rev. Statutes, 41.360 (35)

[45] Oregon Rev. Statutes, 41.360 (36)

[46] Oregon Rev. Statutes, 41.360 (38)

[47] In Re Las Colinas, (P.R., 1968) 294 F. Supp. 582

[48] Johnson v Barton, (WD Va., 1966) 251 F. Supp. 474; United States v Kansas Gas & Elec. Co., (Kan., 1963) 215 F. Supp. 532

[49] Oregon Rev. Statutes, 41.360 (20)

[50] National Brick & Supply Co. v Baylor (DC, 1962) 299 F2d 454

[51] De Pinto v Provident Sec. Life Ins. Co., (9 Cir., 1967) 374 F2d 37

[52] Myzel v Fields, (8 Cir., 1967) 386 F2d 718

[53] Viking Importrade, Inc. v United States (Customs Ct., 1967) 273 F. Supp. 394

An insurance company knows the contents of its insurance policy.[54]

Salaries fixed by a corporation's board of directors are reasonable and proper.[55]

That a bank or other corporation is in possession and control of its own books and records.[56]

That a stockholder invests with knowledge of corporate liabilities.[57]

Money paid by one to another was due to the latter.[58]

A thing delivered by one to another belonged to the latter.[59]

An obligation delivered to the debtor has been paid.[60]

Former rent or installments of a debt have been paid when a receipt for latter is produced.[61]

Things in the possession of a person are owned by him.[62]

A person is the owner of property from exercising acts of ownership over it or from common reputation of his ownership.[63]

A person in possession of an order on himself, for the payment of money or the delivery of a thing, has paid the money or delivered the thing accordingly.[64]

A promissory note or bill of exchange was given or endorsed for a sufficient consideration.[65]

An indorsement of a negotiable promissory note, or bill of exchange, was made at the time and place of making the note or bill.[66]

Persons acting as copartners have entered into a contract of copartnership.[67]

Except in regular course of trade, every sale of personal property, capable of immediate delivery to the purchaser, and every assignment of such property, by way of mortgage or security, or upon any condi-

---

[54] Walker v American Ice Co., (DC, 1966) 254 F. Supp. 736

[55] Capitol Market Limited v United States (Hawaii, 1962) 207 F. Supp. 376

[56] In Re Equitable Plan Co., (SDNY, 1960) 185 F. Supp. 57, modified in Ings v Ferguson, (2 Cir., 1960) 282 F2d 149

[57] Myzel v Fields, (8 Cir., 1967) 386 F2d 718

[58] Oregon Revised Statutes, 41.360 (7)

[59] Oregon Revised Statutes, 41.360 (8)

[60] Oregon Revised Statutes, 41.360 (9)

[61] Oregon Revised Statutes, 41.360 (10)

[62] Oregon Revised Statutes, 41.360 (11)

[63] Oregon Revised Statutes, 41.360 (12)

[64] Oregon Revised Statutes, 41.360 (13)

[65] Oregon Revised Statutes, 41.360 (21)

[66] Oregon Revised Statutes, 41.360 (22)

[67] Oregon Revised Statutes, 41.360 (29)

tion whatever, unless accompanied by an immediate delivery, and followed by an actual and continued change of possession, creates a presumption of fraud as against the creditors of the seller or assignor, during his possession, or as against subsequent purchasers in good faith and for a valuable consideration. This is disputable only by making it appear on the part of the person claiming under such sale or assignment that the same was made in good faith, for a sufficient consideration, and without intent to defraud such creditors or purchasers; but this presumption does not exist in the case of a mortgage filed or recorded as provided by law.[68]

Presumptions Useful in Carrying Burden of Persuasion: There are a group of usual presumptions that cannot by themselves patch up chinks in the wall but which, nevertheless, can be effectively used to persuade either court or jury that your case rather than your opponent's is sounder on the facts. Where by statute these presumptions are required to be made in absence of evidence to the contrary, you can perhaps have the court specifically instruct in respect to such presumptions. If so, you have the aid of the court in persuading the jury and a better ally cannot be had.

Failure of party to introduce evidence within his possession creates the presumption that if produced it would be unfavorable to his position. In *Hoffman v C.I.R.,* (3 Cir., 1961) 298 F2d 784 the taxpayer had meager books in court which neither proved nor disproved the factual contention. However, he did not place them in evidence so the court drew the inference that had the books been produced, they would be against the taxpayer's position. Think about that result before resting your case.[69]

This same presumption goes to failing to produce a witness as well as records, but as to a witness, the presumption should be applied, if at all, with great caution.[70] The reason for caution is that there can often be reasons unrelated to the case why it is awkward to produce a witness seemingly under a party's control. Another caveat: Failure of a party to testify and thus give rise to an adverse presumption cannot be used by the adverse party to create a prima facie case which he otherwise does not have.[71]

---

[68] Oregon Revised Statutes, 41.360 (39)

[69] Oregon Revised Statutes, 41.360 (5)

[70] Mammoth Oil Co. v United States, (1927) 275 U.S. 13, 32; Schoenberg v C.I.R., (8 Cir., 1962) 302 F2d 416

[71] Transcontinental Gas & Pipe Line Corp. v Mobile Drilling Barge Mr. Charlie, (5 Cir., 1970) 424 F2d 684

Of course, wilfully suppressed evidence or a showing that records have been tampered with can well presume you right out of the ball game.[72]

It has also been held that where one party has the burden of proving a negative fact and the evidence is shown to be available to the other party and the other party fails to produce such evidence it will be presumed that the negative fact has been established.[73]

Where a party claims an issue is controlled by foreign law and does not prove the foreign law the court is justified in presuming the foreign law, if proved, would be the same as the law of the forum.[74]

Finally, what is not a presumption but rather rhetoric of Judge John R. Brown, known for his colorful written opinions, is the presumption that judges are "sophisticated uninitiates."[75]

Conclusive Presumptions Are Really Rules of Substantive Law

Conclusive presumptions are those which the law does not permit to be contradicted by evidence. An example is the record of a court of competent jurisdiction.[76] There are very few conclusive presumptions and most of them are the creatures of a state legislature. The reason all evidence is excluded from rebutting a conclusive presumption is because its admission would injure some other cause more than it would help the cause of truth, and because the avoidance of that injury is considered of more consequence than the possible harm to the cause of truth.[77] A conclusive presumption for this reason is really a rule of substantive law.[78]

Oregon has codified its conclusive presumptions which appear to be little different from those in other states. They are:[79]

---

[72] United States for use of C. H. Benton, Inc. v Roelof Construction Co., (9 Cir., 1969) 418 F2d 1328

[73] Campbell v United States, (1961) 365 U.S. 85, 96; Allstate Finance Corp. v Zimmerman, (5 Cir., 1964) 330 F2d 740

[74] 1700 Ocean Avenue Corp. v GBR Associates, (9 Cir., 1966) 354 F2d 993

[75] Dallas Typographical Union No. 173 v A. H. Belo Corp., (5 Cir., 1967) 372 F2d 577

[76] Oregon Revised Statutes, 41.130

[77] United States v Provident Trust Co., (1934) 291 U.S. 272

[78] Ellis v Henderson (5 Cir., 1953) 204 F2d 173; C.I.R. v Clark, (7 Cir., 1953) 202 F2d 94

[79] Oregon Revised Statutes, 41.350

(1) An intent to murder, from the deliberate use of a deadly weapon, causing death within a year.

(2) A malicious and guilty intent, from the deliberate commission of an unlawful act, for the purpose of injuring another.

(3) The truth of the facts recited from the recital in a written instrument, between the parties thereto, their representatives or successors in interest by a subsequnt title; but this rule does not apply to the recital of a consideration.

(4) Whenever a party has, by his own declaration, act or omission, intentionally and deliberately led another to believe a particular thing true, and to act upon such belief, he shall not, in any litigation arising out of such declaration, act or omission, be permitted to falsify it.

(5) A tenant is not permitted to deny the title of his landlord at the time of the commencement of the relation.

(6) The issue of a wife cohabiting with her husband, who is not impotent, is legitimate.

(7) The judgment, decree or order of a court, when declared by statute to be conclusive; but the judgment, decree or order shall be pleaded, if there be an opportunity to do so; and if there be no opportunity, it may be used as evidence with like effect.

(8) Any other presumption which by statute is expressly made conclusive.

Constitutionality of Presumptions: Conclusive Presumptions in Particular

Since conclusive presumptions reflect policy of the state and are arbitrary for the most part, they are greatly suspect of being unconstitutional where logic is lacking in their nature.[80] It seems, however, courts will not strike down as unconstitutional conclusive presumptions unless they affect personal rights guaranteed by the Constitution.[81]

In *United States v Bowen*, (3 Cir., 1969) 414 F2d 1268 the

---

[80] Ellis v Henderson, (La., 1953) 204 F2d 173
[81] United States v Jones, (9 Cir., 1949) 176 F2d 278, 288–289

defendant was convicted for failure to report for induction into the Armed Forces. He was mailed a notice. Regulation 32 CFR No. 1641.3 made proof of mailing notice to defendant as being conclusive proof that the notice was received. The Court of Appeals reversed, holding that such conclusive presumption violated the due process clause of the Fifth Amendment.

Where a statute without logic or reason seeks to make proof of one fact to shift the burden of going forward to defendant to prove an ultimate fact, it has been stricken as being in violation of the Fourteenth Amendment. In *Morrison v California,* (1934) 291 U.S. 82, 90 the California Alien Land Law, (Calif. Stat. 1927, p. 880, c 528) sought to make proof that defendant owned or occupied agricultural land sufficient to require defendant to prove he was not a citizen ineligible to own or occupy the land. As to this statute, the Supreme Court stated:

> Possession of agricultural land by one not shown to be ineligible for citizenship is an act that carries with it not even a hint of criminality. To prove such possession without more is to take hardly a step forward in support of an indictment. No such probability of wrongdoing grows out of the naked fact of use or occupation as to awaken a belief that the user or occupier is guilty if he fails to come forward with excuse or explanation. . . .

Judicial Notice Can Be Taken of
Facts of Common Knowledge

To patch up chinks in your solid wall of evidence you should request the trier of fact, if need be, to take judicial notice of those facts pertinent to your case which are of such general notoriety that they are assumed to be already known to the court. Judicial notice is merely a substitute for the conventional method of taking evidence to establish facts.[82]

Basically, judicial notice will be taken of facts of common knowledge relating to common articles, devices, utilities, and operations.[83] However, on fact questions a court should not use the doctrine of judicial notice to go outside the record unless facts are truly those of

---

[82] Grand Opera Company v Twentieth Century Fox-Film Corp., (7 Cir., 1956) 235 F2d 303

[83] Application of Polson, (Cust. & Pat. Ct. 1966) 368 F2d 267

common knowledge and capable of certain verification.[84] Jurors, like the court, are supposed to possess commonly known facts and may bring them into their consideration of the case.[85] The court is not justified in taking judicial notice of other particular cases and the facts adjudicated therein.[86] However, a court judicially knows the facts of current history and can consider such without evidence.[87] Furthermore, a judge may resort to any means he deems safe to refresh his memory respecting matters of which he should have judicial knowledge.[88]

The most important thing to remember is to request the court to either take judicial notice or to instruct the jury that it may take judicial notice of those critical facts in the case on which evidence has not been introduced, but upon which you wish judicial notice to be taken. You have no complaint if you do not direct the court to take judicial notice.[89]

Facts of Which Federal Courts Have Taken Judicial Notice

Business Matters: Commercial and industrial expansion in relevant areas. *Dixie Highway Express, Inc. v United States,* (Miss. 1968) 287 F. Supp. 473.

Common knowledge matters: Navigation buoys are liable to be extinguished, *Humble Oil & Refining Co. v Tug Crochet,* (La., 1968) 288 F. Supp. 147. Facts relating to commonly used articles and devices, *Application of Poison, Cust. & Pat. App.,* (D.C. Cir., 1966) 368 F2d 267. Facts of common knowledge and capable of being verified, *Alvary v United States,* (2 Cir., 1962) 302 F2d 790.

Demographic Facts: Federal decennial census, *Grills v Branigin* (Ind., 1968) 284 F. Supp. 176. Gross population inequality among legislative districts, *Magraw v Donovan,* (Minn., 1958) 163 F. Supp. 184.

---

[84] Alvary v United States, (2 Cir., 1962) 302 F2d 790

[85] Gault v Poor Sisters of St. Francis Seraph of Perpetual Adoration, Inc., (5 Cir., 1967) 375 F2d 539

[86] Woodward v United States, (Iowa, 1952) 106 F. Supp. 14, affirmed in 208 F2d 893

[87] National Maritime Union of America v Herzog (1948) 334 U.S. 854, below in 78 F. Supp. 146

[88] Rank v Krug, (Calif., 1950) 90 F. Supp. 773

[89] Kenosha Auto Transport Corp. v Lowe Seed Co., (7 Cir., 1966) 362 F2d 765; Gediman v Anheuser Busch, Inc., (2 Cir., 1962) 299 F2d 537

Economic Facts: Trading range and the mean trading price of stocks listed on a national stock exchange, *Baumel v Rosen,* (Md., 1968) 283 F. Supp. 128.

Geographic Facts: That new and old Parkway in Washington, D.C. is now a single highway, *United States v Washington, Va. and Maryland Coach Co.,* (D.C. 1967) 268 F. Supp. 34, reversed on other grounds in 398 F2d 765.

Government Records and Documents: Tariffs, regulations and orders of administrative agencies. *Carter v American Tel. & Tel. Co.,* (5 Cir., 1966) 365 F2d 486.

Hazardous Conditions: Some persons have been admitted to United States under Mutual Education and Cultural Exchange Act of 1961 whose standards are very high, *Glorioso v Immigration and Naturalization Service,* (7 Cir., 1967) 386 F2d 664.

Historical Facts: Hong Kong is a British Crown Colony, whose Government has not undertaken to persecute anyone, *Fong Sen v U.S. Immigration and Naturalization Service,* (La., 1956) 137 F. Supp. 236, affirmed in 234 F2d 656.

Judgments: State judgment ordering forfeiture of fund to county, *United States v Bleasby,* (2 Cir., 1958) 257 F2d 278.

Judicial Practices: Inherent power and authority of state trial and appellate courts to advance matters on their calendars, *Southern Pacific Co. v Devitt,* (Ariz., 1968) 288 F. Supp. 570.

Judicial Records and Papers: The complaint filed by a federal agency in action to condemn land, *Travis v Pennyrite Rural Elec. Coop.* (5 Cir., 1968) 399 F2d 726. Prior proceedings in own District Court, *Prepakt Concrete Co. v Augusto Menendez Const. Co.,* (P. R., 1968) 293 F. Supp. 638.

Jurisdictional Matters: That a Presidential Commission had terminated prior to action against Commission, *Skolnick v Parsons,* (7 Cir., 1968) 397 F2d 523. That plaintiff, who claimed jurisdiction by reason of diversity of citizenship had his residence called into question in prior actions, *Euge v Trantina,* (Mo., 1969) 298 F. Supp. 873.

Medical Matters: That cancer is a latent disease and requires early treatment, *Franklin Life Ins. Co. v W. J. Champion & Co.,* (6 Cir., 1965) 350 F2d 115. That a spinal fusion is painful and often dangerous, *Henninger v Celebrezze,* (6 Cir., 1965) 349 F2d

808. That general practitioners still purport to treat the whole man, *Massachusetts Mut. Life Ins. Co. v Brei*, (2 Cir., 1962) 311 F2d 463.

Military Matters: That Americans in military service have been stationed in Japan since 1945, *Gates v P. F. Collier, Inc.*, (Hawaii, 1966) 256 F. Supp. 204, affirmed in 378 F2d 888.

Patents: Letters patent, *Feathercombs, Inc. v Solo Products Corp.* (2 Cir., 1962) 306 F2d 251. That a patent does not always confer a monopoly over a particular commodity, *Northern Pac. Ry. Co. v United States*, (1958) 356 U.S. 1.

Postal Matters: Second class mail does not travel as fast as first class mail, *Protein Foundation, Inc. v Brenner*, (D.C. 1966) 260 F. Supp. 519. Mail between two cities 10 miles apart should arrive within 24 hours, *Hetman v Fruit Growers Exp. Co.*, (N.J., 1961) 200 F. Supp. 234.

Products, Manufacture and Production: That coffee and tea used at a refreshment counter originated outside of Louisiana, *Adams v Fazzio Real Estate Co.*, (La., 1967) 268 F. Supp. 630, affirmed in 396 F2d 146. Manufacture of intoxicating liquors was not lawful in a particular county, *United States v Fine*, (Tenn., 1968) 293 F. Supp. 189.

Public Laws and Statutes: Statutory laws and judicial decisions of all States, *Board of Education of Independent School District 20, Muskogee County, Okla. v State of Oklahoma*, (Okla., 1968) 286 F. Supp. 8⁴5; affirmed in 409 F2d 665.

Public Officials and Their Conduct: Official signatures of State and Federal officials, *Hagen v Porter*, (9 Cir., 1946) 156 F2d 362. That a State Supreme Court justice resigned, *Romiti v Kerner*, (Ill., 1966) 256 F. Supp. 35.

Reputation: That a former Major General was well known and subject to nationwide news reports while on active duty, *Walker v Courier-Journal & Louisville Times Co.*, (Ky., 1965) F. Supp. 231, reversed on other grounds in 368 F2d 189. That persons who are defamed tend to lose opportunities which they cannot prove at law. *Afro-American Pub. Co. v Jaffe*, (D.C. Cir., 1966) 366 F2d 649.

Scientific Facts: Rocks in most places on certain plains are of no substantial size, *Coyle v Gardner* (Hawaii, 1969) 298 F. Supp. 609. Where cypress trees grow pine trees do not, *Fox v City of West Palm*

Beach (5 Cir., 1967) 383 F2d 189. That a modern automobile can be started and moved in a very few seconds, *Serratoni v Chesapeake & O. Ry. Co.,* (6 Cir., 1964) 333 F2d 621. Weather during summer, *Buchanan v Rhodes,* (Ohio, 1966) 249 F. Supp. 860.

Sociological Data: Official and accredited social studies of the Black Muslim Movement, *Cooper v Pate,* (7 Cir., 1963) 324 F2d 165, reversed on other grounds in 378 U.S. 546. That there exists a severe housing shortage, *Chadwick v Stokes* (3 Cir., 1947) 162 F2d 122.

Tax Consciousness of the American Public: Reason to instruct jury that damage award is not subject to income taxes, *Domeracki v Humble Oil & Refining Co.,* (3 Cir., 1971) 443 F2d 1245.

Voting and Election Matters: That in Delaware as in other states there is a direct and reliable relationship between the number of inhabitants in an area and the number of electors and that the ratio is relatively stable, *Sincock v Duffy,* (Del. 1963) 215 F. Supp. 169, affirmed in 377 U.S. 695.

Miscellaneous Matters: Few if any merchant vessels are commonly controlled with railroads, *Long Beach Banana Distributors, Inc. v Atchison, Topeka & Santa Fe Ry. Co.,* (9 Cir., 1969) 407 F2d 1173. Ladies high heels are not meant to be flexible, *Ronci v Eastern Plastics Corp.,* (1 Cir., 1968) 396 F2d 890. Tug with 12 foot draft could not travel closer to shore than the three-fathom line, *Mobile Towing & Wrecking Co. v A Dredge* (Fla., 1969) 299 F. Supp. 358. Cornflower is not used in Hawaii for making leis. *Coyle v Gardner* (Hawaii, 1969) 298 F. Supp. 609. Petroleum is a mixture of hydrocarbons and other substances, *Northern Natural Gas Co. v Grounds,* (Kan., 1968) 292 F. Supp. 619. Technological processes are constantly being modified and improved, *Struthers Scientific & Intern Corp. v General Foods Corp.,* (Texas, 1968) 290 F. Supp. 122.

**Pertinent Law Review Articles on
Presumptions and Judicial Notice**

"Judicial Notice in the Proposed Federal Rules of Evidence," *Washington University Law Quarterly,* Vol. 1969, p. 453 (1969)

"Judicial Notice and the California Evidence Code," Thomas Kongsgaard, *Hastings Law Journal,* Vol. 18, p. 117 (1966)

"The Law of Presumptions: A Look at Confusion, Kentucky Style," Robert G. Lawson, *Kentucky Law Journal,* Vol. 57, p. 7 (1969)

"Presumptions—A View at Chaos," by John E. Stumbo, *Washburn Law Journal,* Vol. 3, p. 182 (1964)

"The Law of Rebuttable Presumptions in Maine," *Maine Law Review,* Vol. 23, p. 175 (1971)

"Presumptions in the Washington Supreme Court," Paul L. Stritmatter, *Gonzaga Law Review,* Vol. 5, p. 198 (1970)

"The Effect of a Rebuttable Presumption in Montana," Gregory L. Hanson, *Montana Law Review,* Vol. 31, p. 97 (1969)

"Presumptions and their Treatment under the Law of Ohio," H. S. Subrin, *Ohio State Law Journal,* Vol. 26, p. 175 (1965)

"Conflicting Presumptions: An Evaluation of the Solution Proposed by Uniform Rule 15," Edward C. Mengel, Jr., *Villanova Law Review,* Vol. 10, p. 324 (1965)

"Burden of Production of Evidence: A Function of a Burden of Persuasion," John T. McNaughton, *Harvard Law Review,* Vol. 68, p. 1382. (1955)

Where Evidence Has Been Found Insufficient   8

There is no end to the number of cases where courts have held the evidence to be sufficient for jury consideration. On the other hand, cases where courts have granted directed verdicts or entered judgments n.o.v. because of insufficient evidence are not so great in number as to preclude their consideration. For this practical reason we present in this chapter federal cases holding evidence to be insufficient. Finding one in point with your case can give you ammunition for arguing for or against a directed verdict. While the trial judge must rationalize upon the evidence before him, the presenting of a comparable case for his consideration permits him to compare and distinguish and this very challenge gives body and action to the trial judge's rationalization process. However, before reaching the cases, a very practical *caveat* is in order, one that runs through many of the cases next to be considered.

Double Talk—Is the Testimony Really Like It Sounds?

In considering sufficiency of evidence, beware of illusory evidence. The witness may have impressed you, but did he really say something sufficiently specific to complete the essential elements in your case? How many times have you read the transcript of a deposition or of the trial itself and discovered that while you thought you had gotten a responsive answer to a question asked, it really wasn't so? It is rather late to find the record on appeal lacking in substantial evidence after you have won a large verdict and it is under attack on appeal. We here offer one illustration of illusory evidence that really was not as formidable as it must have sounded at the trial. In *Ashworth Transfer Inc. v United States,* (Utah, 1970) 315 F. Supp. 199 a three-judge District Court was reviewing an order of the Interstate Commerce Commission which had granted a certificate of public convenience and necessity for the transportation of dangerous explosives. Did the evidence support the Commission's finding of fact that several shippers had shown a need for the proposed motor carrier service? In holding that the Commission's finding of "need" lacked rational support by substantial evidence the Court described the insufficient evidence thusly:

> . . . Alleging that its demand for mining supplies "included explosives", a gold mining operator indicated its need for motor carrier service in general was small but frequent and continuing. What part of this need related to explosives is not specified. The other shipper who mentioned explosives stated that explosives were received "together with all types of ranching materials", and also that development of tungsten ore reserves of approximately three million tons is "contemplated in the near future" and would require shipment of those explosives "necessary to properly conduct a mining operation". Neither user indicated volume frequency or type of explosives used, and there was no showing that they had sought to avail themselves of the services of carriers who had pre-existing authority to serve them. . . .

So, with the above warning to cut with surgical precision into the evidence to decide whether it is sufficiently substantial for jury consideration, we pass to the cases where the federal courts for one reason or another have found the evidence insufficient.

Not Enough to Prove Negligence

Truck struck plaintiff pedestrian crossing highway. No proof of negligence. Verdict directed for defendant.[1]

In automobile collision defendant admitted brakes of his car were defective. Plaintiff's motion for directed verdict was denied. After verdict for defendant, Court of Appeals reversed denial of plaintiff's motion for directed verdict.[2]

Train, while switching, had cars across road crossing on dark

---

[1] Robinson v City Express, Inc., (D.C., Cir., 1962) 298 F2d 677
[2] Hanley v Heckler, (3 Cir., 1967) 380 F2d 986

foggy night. Plaintiff driver ran into railroad car on crossing. It was error for not granting railroad's motion for directed verdict because there was no showing the train had been long enough on the crossing to permit a brakeman to put out a warning signal.[3]

Proof showed that oil station manager in returning repaired car to customer was acting for himself as an independent contractor and not employee so verdict was directed in favor of defendant oil company.[4]

Plaintiff showed nothing more than a collision between decedent's truck and defendant's motor bus so verdict direct for defendant.[5]

Law required proof of willfully injuring the plaintiff. Plaintiff only showed that oil station attendant carelessly jerked gas hose causing customer to trip. Directed verdict for defendant.[6]

Boy lingering on railroad track struck by train. "Subsequent" negligence of railroad not proved for failure to show locomotive engineer had actual knowledge of boy's peril in time to stop train. Verdict directed for railroad.[7] Verdict directed for railroad where locomotive with brakeman at head of locomotive as lookout struck track walker. No negligence.[7a] In railroad crossing case the only evidence of cause of death was decedent's own negligence so verdict directed for railroad.[8]

In railroad crossing case no evidence showed locomotive engineer negligent in failure to blow whistle or apply brakes. Negative evidence of witness not hearing whistle insufficient because it was not shown he was in a position to have heard whistle had it been blown.[9]

Defendant truck driver was traveling in daylight 24–30 m.p.h. under speed limit on highway. After verdict for plaintiff, defendant's motion for a directed verdict was denied. On appeal denial was reversed for lack of proof of negligence.[10]

Twelve-year-old boy passenger on train apparently wandered to vestibule of passenger car through a non-defective closed door. He

---

[3] Norfolk, Southern Ry. Co. v Swindell, (4 Cir., 1943) 139 F2d 71

[4] Stanolind Oil & Gas Co. v Trosclair, (5 Cir., 1948) 166 F2d 229

[5] Medina v All Am. Bus Lines, (5 Cir., 1945) 152 F2d 61

[6] Drake v Iowa Mut. Ins. Co. (5 Cir., 1960) 274 F2d 818

[7] Hentley v Atlantic Coast R. Co., (5 Cir., 1955) 224 F2d 929

[7A] Brown v Seaboard Airline Railroad, (5 Cir., 1970) 434 F2d 1101

[8] Melancoh v Southern Pac. Co. (5 Cir., 1965) 344 F2d

[9] Brinks v Chesapeake & O. Ry. Co., (6 Cir., 1968) 398 F2d 889

[10] Hall v Marshall, (6 Cir., 1968) 394 F2d 790

was found dead on railroad road bed. Judgment for plaintiff reversed on appeal for lack of proving railroad negligent.[11]

Locomotive engineer, while bringing train into a switch yard, was struck on head by a thrown object. Case dismissed after plaintiff's opening statement. On appeal, dismissal was reversed as there was some evidence that objects had been thrown in yard before, which could infer that railroad did not give the engineer a safe place to work.[12]

Car owner cut his eyeball as he leaned over in driver's seat and somehow struck his eye on edge of glass on vent in window. Judgment n.o.v. after plaintiff's verdict was affirmed on appeal as there was no evidence of automobile manufacturer having foreseeability of a driver so acting to injure himself.[13]

In product liability case, appellate court found trial court clearly erroneous in finding that the manufacturer of belt on a combine negligent as there was no evidence that the belt was defective.[14]

In Arkansas it was presumed that an employee driving employer's truck was acting in scope of his employment. However, when driver admitted accident occurred while on the way to see his relative, the presumption was rebutted and verdict directed in favor of employer.[15]

Failure to keep lookout not proved as fireman on locomotive had no duty to warn engineer of automobile slowly approaching railroad crossing until last minute when it appeared automobile was not going to stop and at such time it would have been too late to stop train.[16]

When automobile passenger was suing the driver for injuries received in collision and admitted she was not a compensating passenger, the verdict was properly directed for defendant.[17]

When airline passenger falls on ramp upon entering an airplane fails to show any defect in ramp, a verdict will be directed for the defendant.[18]

Only when it is very clear that testimony is contrary to physical facts is a directed verdict justified.[19]

---

[11] Norfolk & W. Ry. Co. v Estepp, (6 Cir., 1953) 204 F2d 880

[12] Reynolds v Penn. R. R. Co., (7 Cir., 1959) 267 F2d 231

[13] Schneider v Chrysler Motors Corp., (8 Cir., 1968) 401 F2d 549

[14] United States Rubber Co. v Bauer, (8 Cir., 1963) 319 F2d 463

[15] Capital Transp. Co. v Armour & Co., (8 Cir., 1952) 200 F2d 722

[16] Roth v Swanson, (Minn., 1944) 145 F2d 262

[17] Vogrin v Hedstrom, (8 Cir., 1955) 220 F2d 863

[18] Ozark Air Lines v Larimer, (8 Cir., 1965) 352 F2d 9

[19] Kansas City Public Service Co. v Shephard, (10 Cir., 1950) 184 F2d 945; Vale v Indiana County Theaters, (3 Cir., 1941) 120 F2d 495

In a railroad crossing case where the evidence shows the motorist took no precaution to determine if train was coming, a verdict will be directed for defendant railroad.[20]

Where a passenger in chartered airplane sues employer of dead pilot, a verdict in favor of plaintiff will be directed where evidence shows airplane crashed into mountain while flying at a low elevation contrary to regulations.[21]

Where defendant truck driver runs into a stationary scaffold to injure a workman-plaintiff on the scaffold, a verdict will be directed for plaintiff-workman.[22]

In railroad crossing case, the railroad crossing signal was in plain view of the plaintiff motorist for all but a fraction of a second. Verdict directed for railroad.[23]

Verdict directed for defendant bus company in case where passenger was thrown to floor as bus started up because Michigan law, ever since 1892, was that the starting up of a bus could not be basis for negligence.[24]

In a malicious prosecution case against a police officer who arrested plaintiff for attempting to molest a girl, case was dismissed as evidence of policeman having a love motive during arrest was too remote to establish ulterior motive for arrest.[25]

A malicious prosecution case against lady who erroneously identified plaintiff as a rapist was dismissed because the evidence was not sufficient to show the lady knowingly made wrong identification.[26]

A summary judgment for defendant was granted when defendant manufactured the blasting caps for U.S. Navy thirteen years before they exploded aboard a non-Navy ship. No evidence to show defendant had duty to warn.[27]

---

[20] Mast v Illinois Cent. R. Co., (N.D. Iowa, 1948) 79 F. Supp. 149 affirmed in 176 F2d 157 (8 Cir., 1949)

[21] Gatenby v Altoona Aviation Corp., (WD., Pa., 1967) 268 F. Supp. 599

[22] Baumann v Maloney Concrete Co., (D.C., 1967) 278 F. Supp. 463

[23] Palisi v Louisville & Nashville R. Co., (Miss., 1964) 226 F. Supp. 651

[24] Barnett v City of Detroit, (Mich., 1956) 139 F. Supp. 134, affirmed in 245 F2d 445

[25] Richards v Swanson, (SDNY, 1968) 283 F. Supp. 476

[26] Wehrle v Brooks, (N. Carolina, 1966) 269 F. Supp. 785 affirmed in 379 F2d 288

[27] Littlehale v E. I. duPont de Nemours & Co., (SDNY, 1966) 268 F. Supp. 791

Not Enough to Prove Causation

A verdict was directed for defendant hospital in a malpractice case as there was no relevance between patient's post-operation infection and negligence of hospital in permitting a street-clothed person to wheel plaintiff to operating room.[28]

In intersection collision between automobile defendant and truck plaintiff it was claimed that had defendant looked to the left, she would have seen truck in time to avoid collision, but the evidence showed that had she looked, the speed of truck gave defendant only two seconds in which to avoid collision, and this was insufficient. Denial of directed verdict was reversed on appeal.[29]

Where plaintiff was required to prove that a front-end loader came in contact with a brick wall which fell in order to recover under an insurance policy, it was insufficient to prove loader pushed dirt against wall which did not fall down until 30 minutes later.[30]

Inference of negligence can only go one way against plaintiff motorist when shown he drove to railroad crossing, stopped and then proceeded across tracks to be hit by train. Verdict directed.[31]

In a malpractice case, plaintiff's action was dismissed as the evidence was not sufficient to show how much of the plaintiff's neck injury was caused by a previous accident and how much by the alleged malpractice.[32]

Where an automobile struck a pole and an autopsy showed the driver died of a heart attack, *res ipsa loquitur* was not sufficient to put the case to the jury on causation.[33]

Passenger riding in station wagon sued the driver claiming he was negligent because he had cardboard in side window of station wagon in violation of a statute. Station wagon was struck from behind. Verdict directed for defendant because violation of statute did not cause accident.[34]

Defendant parked his car in violation of statute by leaving rear of car extending out from curb. Plaintiff child stepped from curb past

---

[28] Denneny v Siegel, (3 Cir., 1969) 407 F2d 433

[29] Haldeman v Bell Tel. Co. of Pa. (3 Cir., 1967) 387 F2d 557

[30] Miller v Boston Ins. Co., (5 Cir., 1959) 271 F2d 9

[31] Pratt v New York Cent. R. Co., (7 Cir., 1964) 339 F2d 964

[32] Rudick v Prineville Memorial Hospital, (9 Cir., 1963) 319 F2d 764

[33] Van Dyke v Merchants Indemnity Corp., (ED Wis., 1963) 215 F. Supp. 428

[34] Idzojtoc v Penn. RR Co., (WD Pa., 1969) 47 F.R.D. 25

rear of defendant's car and into street where she was struck by another car. Verdict was directed for defendant as unlawful parking did not contribute to accident.[35]

In action on life insurance policy the opinion of expert witness that a blow on the decedent's head caused his death was valueless because it was based on hypothesis that decedent was in bed 45 days before death. Proof was he had gone to bed the day before he died.[36]

Not Enough to Prove Damages

In fraud case where plaintiff was awarded exemplary damages, the appellate court reversed plaintiff's judgment and granted new trial unless plaintiff remitted exemplary damages. This was because there was no evidence sufficient to justify exemplary damages.[37]

In a wrongful death case the appellate court reversed as being clearly erroneous the trial court's finding of fact that had decedent lived for the next five years following death he would not have earned any net income in face of evidence that in five years prior to death the decedent earned $418,000 and expert opinion evidence predicted that the new business venture in which decedent was engaged at time of death he would have earned $80,000 per year.[38]

Plaintiff's case for conversion of tractor parts by defendant was dismissed because court could not reasonably determine from the evidence the amount or value of the parts converted.[39]

Not Enough to Prove Insurance Policy or Contract Cases

In a most imponderable case to recover on a life insurance policy which excluded suicide, the insured was found alone with a discharged shotgun which had been fired and which had killed him. On question of whether the fatality was accidental or suicidal, jury found against the insurance company. The District Court denied defendant's

---

[35] Almond v Pollon, (ED Pa., 1961) 198 F. Supp. 301 affirmed in 300 F2d 763
[36] Troutman v Mutual Life Ins. Co. of N.Y., (6 Cir., 1942) 125 F2d 769
[37] Bankers Life & Casualty Co. v Kirtley, (8 Cir., 1962) 307 F2d 418
[38] Noel v United Aircraft Corp., (3 Cir., 1965) 342 F2d 232, 239
[39] Gebrueder Kulenkempft & Co. v Bousman, (ED, Wis., 1969) 301 F. Supp.

motion for judgment n.o.v. The Court of Appeals reversed for lack of evidence as to who pulled the trigger. The Supreme Court of the United States again reversed in favor of the beneficiary, holding the evidence was sufficient for the jury.[40]

In action by employee against group insurer on policy carried by the employer for the benefit of his employees, a verdict directed in favor of plaintiff was reversed on appeal because evidence was not sufficient to prove required notice by employer to the insurer. Employee had been laid off during month of October. Employer maintained with insurer two different policies, one employee-contributory and the other a non-contributory policy. The employer only gave notice on the non-contributory policy, and neither the employee nor the employer contributed as required to the other policy for the month of October.[41]

In action on liability insurance policy defense was non-cooperation of insured in stating injured person was in his employ. At the accident trial, the insured testified the injured person was employed by the insured, though other testimony was to the contrary. In action on policy, defendant failed to prove insured lied and verdict was directed for plaintiff.[42]

When injured workman sued supplier of cement-head to oil rig, the supplier brought third party complaint for indemnity against the driller. Third party complaint was dismissed because there was no agreement for driller to indemnify supplier and the allegations of injured workman's complaint against supplier alleged active negligence of supplier, which if proven could not in any event entitle supplier to indemnity.[43]

Verdict directed for defendant life insurance company was affirmed as the undisputed evidence showed that the insured had deliberately lied on his application for insurance.[44]

Eighteen-year-old boy just home from college was so clearly a member of the household and excluded from insurance policy benefits that the verdict against the insurance company was set aside on appeal.[45]

---

[40] Dick v New York Life Ins. Co. (1959) 359 U.S. 437

[41] Equitable Life Assur. Soc. v Larocco, (3 Cir., 1933) 68 F2d 451

[42] Church v American Casualty Co., (3 Cir., 1933) 64 F2d 266

[43] Lumbermen's Mutual Ins. Co. v Bowman, (10 Cir., 1963) 313 F2d 381

[44] Rhodes v Metropolitan Life Ins. Co., (5 Cir., 1949) 172 F2d 183

[45] State Farm Mutual Automobile Ins. Co. v Borg, (8 Cir., 1968) 396 F2d 740

Finding of the Secretary of Health that child was not living in the home of the wage earner was not supported by substantial evidence and was set aside.[46]

In action on fidelity bond of employee, evidence of a shortage in the employer's inventory was not sufficient to find that the employee stole it.[47]

Where written demand is necessary in action on insurance policy an equivocal letter from insurer referring to a previous demand was not sufficient to prove written demand by insured. Directed verdict for insurance company was affirmed on appeal.[48]

Where policy required written notice of claim, an investigation of accident by insurance adjuster was not sufficient to waive notice requirement. Verdict directed for defendant was affirmed.[49]

Not Enough to Prove Tax Cases

In tax refund case whether or not a family partnership is valid is ordinarily a question of fact, but when inferences are all pointed to creation of only an anticipated assignment of property to children, it becomes a question of law.[50]

Whether repairs to taxpayer's real property constituted an expense or a capital investment because being part of a general rehabilitation plan is fact for jury. Denial of directed verdict for Government was affirmed.[51]

In income tax case the law of Spain in reference to a nonresident alien is a question of fact, but for the court and not the jury to decide.[52]

Not Enough to Prove Cases Concerning Business Transactions

In a libel and slander suit plaintiff's attorney in opening statement made no mention of relationship between personal defendant

---

[46] Gaston v Gardner, (S. Carolina, 1965) 247 F. Supp. 441

[47] Fort Smith Tobacco & Candy Co. v American Guarantee & Liability Ins. Co., (SD Iowa, 1962) 208 F. Supp. 244

[48] Ketona Chemical Corp. v Globe Indemnity Co., (5 Cir., 1969) 404 F2d 181

[49] Alexander v Standard Acceptance Ins. Co., (10 Cir., 1941) 122 F2d 995

[50] United States v Ramos, (9 Cir., 1968) 393 F2d 618

[51] United States v Wehrli, (10 Cir., 1968) 400 F2d 686

[52] Crespo v United States, (Ct. Cl., 1968) 399 F2d 191

and his corporations and proved none so verdict was directed for defendant corporations.[53]

Purchaser of automatic pin setting machines sued seller for loss of benefit of his contractual bargain as a result of newer models being put on the market. The evidence was insufficient to show that value of machines which plaintiff purchased had fallen.[54]

In land owner's action against general contractor's surety for damages resulting in sub-contractor failing to properly replace iron pipe with clay pipe, the action against surety was dismissed because land owner had made contract direct with sub-contractor and not through general contracts.[55]

In action against railroad for damage to shipment in railroad car due to flood, the defense of the railroad was an Act of God. Verdict was directed for railroad because it had placed car on highest ground possible and never before had floods reached the high ground.[56]

Where owner of oyster bed sued a pulp company for pollution which damaged oysters, verdict was directed for defendant because plaintiff, while having the opportunity to do so, did not present sufficient scientific evidence to tie pulp pollution to oyster deaths.[57]

Not Enough to Prove NLRB Unfair Labor Charges

It is unrealistic to attribute to employer a discriminatory motive for discharging an employee when a lawful reason existed. Fact that employer was without knowledge of employee's attempt to slow down production must be rejected.[58]

In 3,000 pages of testimony there was not sufficient evidence to prove employer had knowledge that a forelady was urging other employees to join an employee association.[59]

Proof that the employer dominated procedures for adjusting grievances of employees did not infer that the employer also dominated a subsequently organized employees' organization.[60]

---

[53] Brown v Collins, (D.C., 1968) 402 F2d 209

[54] Classic Bowl, Inc. v A. M. F. Pinspotters, Inc., (7 Cir., 1968) 403 F2d 463

[55] Twin City Plaza, Inc. v Central Surety Ins. Corp., (8 Cir., 1969) 409 F2d 1195

[56] Farr Co. v Union Pac. R., (10 Cir., 1939) 106 F2d 437

[57] Olympia Oyster Co. v Rayonier, Inc., (WD, Wash., 1964) 229 F. Supp. 855

[58] NLRB v Kaye, (7 Cir., 1959) 272 F2d 112

[59] Cupples Co. Mfgs. Co. v NLRB, (8 Cir., 1939) 106 F2d 100

[60] NLRB v Standard Oil Co., (10 Cir., 1942) 124 F2d 895

Not Enough to Prove Anti-Trust Cases

In a treble damage action under Sherman and Clayton Acts plaintiff cannot establish conspiracy that distributor "cleared" pictures for release in other theatres in city and not plaintiff's theatre to injure plaintiff without showing the "clearance" unreasonable and was used to further scheme against plaintiff.[61] In anti-trust price fixing case, fact finder cannot speculate as to conspiracy. It is insufficient to only prove: (1) parallel price activity; (2) nothing from which belonging to a conspiracy can be inferred; or (3) unilateral dealing without proof of intent to monopolize.[62]

Not Enough to Prove in Miscellaneous Cases

In action on promissory notes evidence was insufficient to prove that bank president breached a fiduciary duty to mother of son who signed note of son as an accomodation endorser on basis of a telephone conversation had with bank president. As to another note, the evidence was insufficient to prove whether it was the bank president or the son who deceived the mother.[63]

---

[61] Ayers v Pastime Amusement Co., (S. Carolina, 1968) 283 F. Supp. 773

[62] Fiumara v Texaco, Inc., (E.D. Pa., 1962) 204 F. Supp. 544

[63] Giblin v Beeler, (10 Cir., 1968) 396 F2d 584

Making Meaningful
Findings of Fact
9

Webster's dictionary tells us that a "fact" is a thing done, an actuality or information having objective reality. We all know that a trial court, sitting without a jury, receives evidence concerning things done and based thereon makes findings of fact. From these findings the trial court concludes that one of the parties as a matter of law is entitled to a judgment and so enters it.

Findings of Fact—the Most Vital Step to Judgment

What is often not appreciated is the reality that the judicial determination of what the essential facts are in a controversy is the prime function of the trial court when sitting without a jury. Sometimes this determination can become excruciatingly difficult. While only an intermediate step in the judicial process, fact finding is the most important step of all. As Chief Justice Burger put it: ". . . the facts are more often 'the whole ball game'." In any given case findings of fact serve several significant purposes.

Only by knowing what facts the court found can it be determined whether the court's conclusion of law is right or wrong.[1]

Only by considering the basic facts as found by the court can it be determined whether or not the court's discussion of law in its opinion constitutes its holding or is nothing more than dictum.[2]

Only by making specific findings of fact can the trial court satisfy

---

[1] American Cyanamin Co. v Union Reliance (5 Cir., 1962) 306 F2d 135

[2] Capella v Zurich Gen. Acc.—Liability Ins. Co. (5 Cir., 1952) 194 F2d 558, 559; Podgorski v United States (Pa., 1949) 87 F. Supp. 731, 733

itself that it has dealt fully and properly with all issues before it for determination.[3]

Only by proper findings of fact can the evidentiary grist of the mill be sifted and ground into a concise product much like a loaf of bread so that it can be served to the appellate court in such a package that it can be readily weighed for its sufficiency as a matter of law.[4]

Findings of fact also take on a collateral importance. Without specific findings of fact it would be impossible to determine whether a judgment entered against a plaintiff bars his re-litigation of the same issue in another case under the principles of either *res judicata* or collateral estopple.[5]

Perhaps more important of all, the trial judge with the duty to make specific findings of fact will more likely than otherwise listen attentively to the witnesses as the evidence goes in, read exhibits, make notes and resolve the critical issues of fact upon which a case must turn. When the case is tried before a jury, the court can sometimes become little more than an umpire calling the strikes as the evidence goes in and keeping order in the court room. Not so when the case is tried before the court. In the later situation the trial court undertakes the full responsibility for delivering a just judgment.

The purpose and function of findings of fact has been explained very well by the Court in *Hartford-Empire Co. v Shawkee Mfg. Co.,* (3 Cir., 1944) 147 F2d 532 at 535.

> A finding of fact is not the goal of the judicial process nor is it the relief which a court of justice accords a litigant. On the contrary, it is merely an intermediate step in the judicial process of deciding a controversy. Its office is to distill from the evidence which has been adduced at the trial of a disputed issue the pertinent facts which must be known by the court in order to enable it to determine and apply the relevant rules of law and thereupon to grant appropriate relief to the litigants.

Practice: Rule 52 of Federal Rules of Civil Procedure

An excellent point of departure for considering the practice of fact finding is Rule 52 of the Federal Rules of Civil Procedure en-

---

[3] In Re Las Colinas, Inc., (1 Cir., 1970) 426 F2d 1005
[4] Hurwitz v Hurwitz (D.C., Cir., 1943) 136 F2d 796
[5] United States v Forness (2 Cir., 1942) 125 F2d 928, cert. denied 316 U.S. 694

titled "Findings by the Court."[6] The present Rule 52 has finally consolidated under one roof the fact finding rule for law, equity and
admiralty cases in the federal judicial system. As will be seen, the
present Rule has a simplified post-judgment mode for objecting to or
seeking amendments or additions to findings of fact upon which the
entered judgment has been based. It also eliminates much need for
objecting or the taking of exceptions during the trial in order for
counsel to protect his client's record. More significantly, the present
Rule 52 for once makes it clear that the trial court may include its
own findings of fact in its written opinion or memorandum of decision.

A meaningful discussion of the principles of fact-finding can be
had by considering the facets of Rule 52. It should be kept in mind,
however, that the principles of fact-finding under Rule 52 are equally
as applicable to the judicial process in the courts of the fifty States;
subject, of course, to possible peculiar state practice. If admiralty cases
appear more frequently than others, it is because this type of case
turns most frequently upon the determination of critical fact issues,
and the courts sitting in admiralty have had much to say about adequate and inadequate findings of fact. Attorneys in other fields of civil
litigation can well borrow a page from the admiralty courts on fact
finding without having to know about admiralty practice which otherwise has been considered a special breed of cat. Since the former Admiralty Rule 46-½[7] is essentially the same as present Rule 52, decisions under the former admiralty rule are as valid as those under
the present Rule 52.[8]

Rule 52 reads:[9]

(a) *Effect.* In all actions tried upon the facts without a jury
or with an advisory jury, the court shall find the facts specially
and state separately its conclusions of law thereon and direct the
entry of the appropriate judgment; and in granting or refusing
interlocutory injunctions the court shall similarly set forth the
findings of fact and conclusions of law which constitute the

---

[6] 28 USCA Rule 52(a) As amended December 27, 1946, effective March 19,
1948

[7] Rule 46-1/2 Findings of Fact and Conclusions of Law.
    In deciding cases of admiralty and maritime jurisdiction the court of first in-
stance shall find the facts specially and state separately its conclusions of law
thereon; and its findings and conclusions shall be entered of record and, if an appeal
is taken from the decree, shall be included by the clerk in the record which is certi-
fied to the Appellate Court under Rule 49. (Rule adopted June 2, 1930, effective
October 1, 1930. A similar Equity rule was adopted at the same time.)

[8] Ramos v Matson Navigation Co. (9 Cir., 1963) 316 F2d 128

[9] 28 USCA Rule 52

grounds of its action. Requests for findings are not necessary for purposes of review. Findings of fact shall not be set aside unless clearly erroneous, and due regard shall be given to the opportunity of the trial court to judge of the credibility of the witnesses. The findings of a master, to the extent that the court adopts them, shall be considered as the findings of the court. If an opinion or memorandum of decision is filed, it will be sufficient if the findings of fact and conclusions of law appear therein. Findings of fact and conclusions of law are unnecessary on decisions of motions under Rules 12 or 56 or any other motion except as provided in Rule 41 (b). As amended Dec. 27, 1946, effective March 19, 1948.

(b) *Amendment.* Upon motion of a party made not later than 10 days after entry of judgment the court may amend its findings or make additional findings and may amend the judgment accordingly. The motion may be made with a motion for a new trial pursuant to Rule 59. When findings of facts are made in actions tried by the court without a jury, the question of the sufficiency of the evidence to support the findings may thereafter be raised whether or not the party raising the question has made in the district court an objection to such findings or has made a motion to amend them or a motion for judgment.

Notes of the Advisory Committee on Amendments to Rules[10] point out that Rule 52 applies to both courts sitting without a jury as well as those sitting with an *advisory* jury. It, of course, supercedes the former Equity rule 70 and former Admiralty Rule 46-½, but adopts the essence of both of these former rules. It also puts to rest the question of the propriety of a court incorporating its findings of fact into its written opinion or memorandum of decision. By so doing, Rule 52 is encouraging trial judges to fashion their own findings of fact in their own decisions and not, except in exceptional cases, have the attorney for the prevailing party prepare the findings of fact.[11]

Leave Some Meat on the Conclusionary Bone

While it was once the rule that only ultimate facts need be found,[12] Rule 52 adds a new dimension. More is now required than brief con-

---

[10] Notes of Adv. Com.—28 USCA—52(a) p. 15

[11] United States v Forness, (2 Cir., 1942) 125 F2d 928, cert. denied in 316 U.S. 694. United States v Crescent Amusement Co. (1944) 323 U.S. 173

[12] Union Consol. Silver Min. Co. v Taylor (1879) 100 U.S. 37 25 L. Ed 541

clusionary ultimate findings of fact. There must be sufficient special findings to comply with Rule 52 so that the findings of fact become meaningful to the appellate court.

While conciseness should be strived for in the making of findings of fact they should, nevertheless, have enough meat on the conclusionary bone to permit an appellate court to tell whether the ultimate judgment is based on the facts found rather than upon an undisclosed improper standard of law.[13]

Trial judges and attorneys can well keep in mind the statement of the Supreme Court in *Dalehite v United States,* 346 U.S. 15 at 24, about concise but meaningful findings of fact:

> ... Fed. Rule Civ. Proc., Rule 52(a), in terms, contemplates a system of findings which are "or fact" and which are "concise." The well-recognized difficulty of distinguishing between law and fact clearly does not absolve district courts of their duty in hard and complex cases to make a studied effort toward definiteness. Statements conclusory in nature are to be eschewed in favor of statements of the preliminary and basic facts on which the District Court relied. *Kelly vs Everglades Drainage District,* 319 U.S. 415, and cases cited. Otherwise, their findings are useless for appellate purposes. In this particular case, no proper review could be exercised by taking the "fact" findings of "negligence" at face value. And, to the extent that they are of law, of course they are not binding on appeal. *E.G., Great Atlantic & Pacific Tea Co. vs Supermarket Equipment Corp.,* 340 U.S. 147, 153–154, and concurring opinion at 155–156.

In *Ramos v Matson Navigation Co.,* (9 Cir., 1963) 316 F2d 128 the Court held that conclusions that a ship was seaworthy and her owner not negligent were findings of fact not to be upset unless clearly erroneous. At the same time it stated it is good practice for the trial court to make enough findings as to what happened so that the appellate court can appraise the ultimate findings.

General, Special, Ultimate and "Stepping Stone" Findings

It can generally be said that there are two kinds of findings— general and special. Within the "special" kind there are three grades, namely: Ultimate, Subsidiary ("stepping stone") and Evidentiary.

---

[13] Commissioner Internal Revenue v Duberstein (1960) 363 U.S. 278, 80 S. Ct. 1190, 4 L. Ed 2d 1218; Berger v Berger, (3 Cir., 1971) 439 F2d 1008

A general finding is in reality no finding at all but merely a recital that one party is entitled to judgment against the other.[14] Some state jurisdictions require that a request be made of the court at the commencement of the trial for special findings or entitlement thereto is waived.[15] Rule 52(a) of the Federal Rules of Civil Procedure requires the trial court to make special findings whether requested or not. Most states now require special findings.[16]

As you have perhaps already surmised, special findings comprise a number of separate but related findings of specific facts essential to support the judgment to be rendered. However, in this regard it is well to keep in mind that there are several grades of special findings. Generally speaking, there is the specific finding of an "ultimate fact," i.e. that the defendant was denied right of counsel.[17] Then, there is what is sometimes called a "subsidiary" finding,[18] or a "mediate" finding,[19] or as we like best, a "stepping stone" finding.[18] The cases sometimes refer to "evidentiary" findings. These "evidentiary" findings, where they consist only of a narration of the evidence, are improper and inadequate as findings of fact. While appellate review will later be discussed in Chapter 11, it should be mentioned here that it is important to distinguish between "ultimate" and "subsidiary" findings as each partakes of a different quality that affects scope of appellate re-

---

[14] "A general finding is like a general verdict of a jury, by which the court finds generally in favor of one of the parties and against the other"—*Larsen v Martin* (1943) 172 Or. 605 143 P. 2d 239; Norris v Jackson, 9 Wall., 125, 19 L. Ed. 608

[15] For example, Oregon Revised Statutes, 17.431 provides:
"(1) Whenever any party appearing in a civil proceeding tried by the court, whether at law, in equity or otherwise, so demands prior to the commencement of the trial, the court shall make special findings of fact, and shall state separately its conclusions of law therefrom.
(2) In the absence of such demand for special findings the court may make either general or special findings."

[16] Arkansas, Civ. Code (Crawford, 1934) § 364; California, Code Civ. Proc. (Deering, 1937) §§ 632, 634; Colorado, 1 Stat. Ann. (1935) Code Civ. Proc. §§ 232, 291 (in actions before referees or for possession of and damages to land); Connecticut, Gen. Stats. §§ 5660, 5664; Idaho 1 Code Ann. 2 Gen. Laws (Ter. Ed., 1932) ch. 214, § 23; Minnesota, 2 Stat. (Mason, 1927) § 9311; Nevada, 4 Comp. Laws (Hillyer, 1929) §§ 8783–8784; New Jersey, Sup. Ct. Rule 113, 2 N.J. Misc. 1197, 1239 (1924); New Mexico, Stat. Ann. (Courtright, 1929) §§ 105–813; North Carolina, Code (1935) § 569; North Dakota, 2 Comp. Laws Ann. (1913) § 7641; Oregon, 1 Code Ann. (1930) §§ 2–502; South Carolina, Code (Michie, 1932) § 649; South Dakota, 1 Comp. Laws (1929) §§ 2525–2526; Utah, Rev. Stat. Ann. (1933) § 104–26–2, 104–26–3; Vermont (where jury trial waived), Pub. Laws (1933) § 2069; Washington, 2 Rev. Stat. Ann. (Remington, 1932) § 367; Wisconsin, Stat. (1935) § 270.33.

[17] That "defendant was denied right of counsel" is an ultimate fact, O'Keith v Johnston (9 Cir., 1942) 129 F2d 889, 890

[18] A "subsidiary finding sometimes called a 'stepping stone finding.' " Sandall v Haskins (Utah, 1943) 137 P2d 819, 822

[19] The Evergreens v Nunan, (2 Cir., 1944) 141 F2d 927

view. The difference between subsidiary and ultimate findings may also become significant if collateral estopple or *res adjudica* becomes important. For example, in *The Evergreens v Nunan,* (2 Cir., 1941) 141 F2d 927 it was held that findings in one case whether "subsidiary" or "ultimate" can collaterally estop a party from litigating an identical "ultimate" fact in a subsequent action, but not so in respect to re-litigating a "subsidiary" fact in the later action.

Quality of Findings Vary with Different Proofs and Cases

Findings of fact vary in quality. By quality we do not mean the wisdom of the trial court finding on the evidence one thing instead of another but, rather, the degree of conclusiveness which the appellate court attaches to the finding. Otherwise put: The staying power of the finding on review.

Generally, trial courts control the facts and appellate courts the law. In the federal judicial system the appellate court will not upset a trial court's finding of fact unless it concludes from the evidence or lack of evidence that it is clearly erroneous. While the "unless clearly erroneous" rule will be more fully treated in Chapter 11 which considers appellate review of facts, it seems appropriate here to mention several situations where an appellate court will sometimes let down the bars of "unless clearly erroneous" to upset a finding in order to reach a just result.

You can be reasonably sure that if your case on review involves broad social principles of our Governmental system or personal liberties guaranteed by the United States Constitution the federal appellate courts and particularly the United States Supreme Court will not let the "unless clearly erroneous" rule stand in the way of reversing, if need be, a finding of fact. Of what we speak is seen in *Baumgartner v United States* (1944) 322 U.S. 665. In that case the Supreme Court had before it the revocation of a citizen's naturalization certificate. Two courts below had found as a fact that the citizen had intentionally lied when years before he had applied for citizenship. In upsetting the finding of fact in order to reverse the judgment of revocation, the Supreme Court candidly stated that because of the social and Constitutional importance of the particular case, it was not giving the deference to the findings of the lower courts as it would otherwise have done in an ordinary case.

The rigor of "unless clearly erroneous" is also weakened by appellate courts in reviewing facts in cases where at the trial level the burden of proof has been increased from a "preponderance" of the evidence to "clear and convincing" evidence. *Schneiderman vs United States,* (1943) 320 U.S. 118. If the trial court in certain cases must be more demanding in respect to burden of proof, it is reasonable that the appellate court take a keener look at the proof with less deference to the lower court's finding in order to make sure the trial court in fact applied the heavier burden of proof.

Some appellate courts have given less deference to a trial court's finding when it is based primarily on writings such as depositions, contracts and letters rather than oral testimony.[20] This is likewise true where an ultimate finding of fact such as "negligence" is under attack. Reason for this approach to an ultimate finding of negligence is that "negligence" has entwined in it the standard upon which the finding is measured, i.e. that which the mythical reasonable person would do nor not do.[21]

Court-Fashioned versus Attorney-Fashioned Findings of Fact

With present Rule 52 clearly encouraging trial courts whenever possible to fashion their own findings of fact in their own written opinions or memorandum of decision, it is relevant to look at the wisdom of trial courts making their own findings as against adopting findings proposed by the attorney for the prevailing party.

The ideal, of course, is for every trial judge upon the close of evidence to retire to his chambers, consider his recollections, consult his notes, read pertinent exhibits and dictate his findings of fact and conclusions of law. But in the workaday judicial world the ideal is often hard to accomplish with congested trial calendars such as they are. Then again every case is different. One may involve estimating the veracity of a plaintiff who claims injuries which have at best a subjective base. Another may involve a collision at sea with a judge needing to keep in mind the courses, speeds, signals and sea conditions as two vessels steam into the jaws of collision. Still another may be a complicated fraud case with alleged conspiracies, or an intricate patent

---

[20] Midwood Associates v C. I. R. (2 Cir., 1940) 115 F2d 871, 872; Walters Trust v C. I. R. (3 Cir., 1942) 127 F2d 101

[21] Mamiye Bros. v Barber S. S. Co. (2 Cir., 1966) 360 F2d 774

case with numerous exhibits, or an anti-trust case that can go on and on for months on end.

In *Polarusoil—Sandefjord,* (2 Cir., 1956) 236 F2d 270, the Court of Appeals for the Second Circuit commended the trial court which heard a ship collision case and promptly dictated his findings of fact after close of evidence and before the feel of the evidence left his recollection of events. It also recognized that many more complicated cases could not admit to such prompt judicial determinations.

A number of appellate courts have expressed their desire to be confronted with court fashioned findings rather than attorney proposed findings. Several appellate courts have expressed the idea that they will give greater weight to findings fashioned by the trial judge than to attorney-fashioned findings. However, no court as yet has held that attorney-fashioned findings are any different or any less a set of findings than the court-fashioned kind.

For a busy trial judge it would seem that common sense applied on a case to case basis as to method of manufacturing findings of fact would be the most practical rule. After all, the judge must, to one degree or another, weigh the evidence and reach conclusions of fact before deciding who is to win and which counsel becomes that of the prevailing party. If the case is not too complex evidentiary-wise, it should be practical for the court to take the additional step of dictating his own findings of fact. The trial judge should realize that judge-fashioned findings often carry a certain badge of personal analysis and determination that may dissuade an appellate court from reversing in a doubtful case. Of course, in a complex technical case the better part of valor might be to have the attorney for the prevailing party submit proposed findings of fact. Once this is done the trial court can then edit and carefully consider the proposed findings before lodging. In *Farley v United States,* (9 Cir., 1958) 252 F2d 85 the trial judge had plaintiff's attorney prepare the findings which described the plaintiff's personal injuries, leaving the trial judge to fill in the amount of money awarded. Either plaintiff's attorney overdid it or the judge underdid it, as the Court of Appeals found the findings clearly erroneous and remanded the case to the trial court to either change the description of injury or increase the amount originally awarded. It is an undesirable practice for a court to accept findings from one party *haec verba.*[22]

---

[22] United States v Howard, (3 Cir., 1966) 360 F2d 373

One danger built into court-fashioned findings is that of commingling fact and law and in so doing arrive at findings which are neither precise nor clear.[23] In any event, no matter how the findings are manufactured, they should not be a mere recital or discourse of evidence.[24] Nor should they be "boiler plate" affirming the allegations of a pleading. Court versus attorney-fashioned findings are thoroughly discussed in *The Charles L. D.*, (5 Cir., 1962) 298 F2d 733.

Settling Findings—
First Too Little—Then Too Much

When the trial court decides a case and orders the attorney for the prevailing party to prepare proposed findings of fact and conclusions of law, the attorney for that party is immediately confronted with deciding what facts to propose and how extensive the findings shall become. A narration of the evidence sometimes found in reports of administrative agencies is not proper findings in a court of law. However, determining to what extent bare ultimate facts should be supported by subsidiary findings can often become difficult. The type of case and the complexity of the evidence best dictates the extensiveness of proper and meaningful findings of fact. For instance, no one can quarrel with a court in a personal injury case finding the ultimate fact that the plaintiff was generally damaged in amount of $10,000. On the other hand, when the Court is confronted with amount of damages sustained for the repair of a vessel where there is a mixture of both collision and non-collision repair, it is another story. In the later case the Court should specify the items which comprise the total amount of damages found due.[25]

Let us consider the findings in the complicated securities fraud case of *Errion v Connell*, (9 Cir., 1956) 236 F2d 447, particularly the work and frustration that went into the settlement of the findings which the Court of Appeals ultimately held not to be clearly erroneous. That was a case brought by a defrauded eighty-year-old widow against a number of defendants to recover damages for her losses. It was tried before Judge Lindberg in the United States District Court at Seattle, Washington. Jurisdiction was founded under the civil

---

[23] Koehler v United States (7 Cir., 1953) 200 F2d 588

[24] In Re Hill Store Co., (W. Va., 1939) 28 F. Supp. 785, 787

[25] Araxos v Frota National de Petroleiros, (3 Cir., 1965) 348 F2d 33

remedy implied from Section 10(b) of the Securities Exchange Act of 1934 and Rule 10B-5 of the Securities and Exchange Commission. Several theories were pleaded, including one seeking pecuniary restitution. To reach all of the defendants through a judgment a civil conspiracy to defraud was alleged and proved. After seven days of trial, the Court orally announced its decision in favor of the widow-plaintiff and ordered her attorney to prepare findings of fact and conclusions of law. It took three contested hearings and more time than it took to try the case in order to settle the controversial findings of fact. First proposed findings were pure ultimate findings of fact and objected to as being insufficient in spelling out the alleged conspiracy and the connection of certain defendants therewith. The second proposed findings were objected to as too detailed and evidentiary in nature instead of being ultimate facts. The third set of proposed findings which were less than evidentiary and more than ultimate findings of fact were accepted by the Court still over objections of defendants. It was this series of continued objection to findings which did more than anything else to prevent the defendants from securing a reversal on appeal. Had the defendants not objected to the first proposed findings and had they for lack of objection been adopted by the Court, plaintiff would have been vulnerable on appeal. This was true not only because plaintiff had left out a jurisdictional finding that violations of the Securities Exchange Act occurred in the State of Washington, but because the findings led to support a theory of pecuniary restitution. It was not until the second proposed findings were being drafted that plaintiff's attorney came to the horrible realization that some of the conspiring defendants could not be required to make restitution when they were not a party to any transaction and had nothing to restore.

Thanks to objecting defendants, plaintiff had a competent set of findings of fact when the case reached the Court of Appeals. Certain defendants claimed they were not liable because of not receiving any of the "loot." However, by this time the findings spelled out precisely how, when and in what amount each defendant participated in the "loot." Evidentiary wise it took thirty-eight exhibits and a diagram to explain to the trial court the cash flow. Moral of all this is that if findings are poorly proposed, the better strategy sometimes is not to keep objecting until they become improved.

What Happens When Findings of Fact Are Inadequate?

What happens when neither the trial judge nor the attorney for the unsuccessful party cares little about findings proposed by counsel for the successful party? One thing that can happen is having the Court of Appeals remand the case to the trial court for better findings as was done in *Brown Paper Co. v Irvin,* (8 Cir., 1943) 134 F2d 337, 338. That case had as its ingredients much equivocal and confused evidence pertaining to whether or not the plaintiff had an agreement with defendants to pay plaintiff a "finder fee" for defendants acquiring plant property. Apparently a nebulous contract was made, cancelled and later re-instated. The trial court had plaintiff's counsel prepare the findings of fact and conclusions of law which were adopted without challenge by anyone. When the Court of Appeals got the case it found that the findings of fact of the trial court were nothing more than a confusing recital of the evidence and that under conclusions of law an attempt was made to state ultimate facts. Holding that findings of fact should be a clear and concise statement of the ultimate facts and not a statement, report, or recapitulation of evidence from which the ultimate facts might flow, the Court of Appeals remanded the case with instructions to the trial court to make new and better findings. It told the trial court (p. 338):

> The findings of fact in this case should constitute unequivocal answers to the following questions: (1) Did Irvin have an agreement? (2) If so, when was it made, what were its terms, and was it ever revoked or cancelled? (3) If so, when if at all, was it re-instated and by whom? (4) Was Irvin the procuring cause of the contract?

The Court of Appeals even went further. It *requested* the trial court to submit in addition to new findings a memorandum pointing to the specific evidence in the record upon which he relied to support each of the findings as so made. One can well imagine that plaintiff's counsel's "stock" dropped to a new low with the particular trial judge who relied upon him to present competent findings only to have the Court of Appeals of the Eighth Circuit give him a decisional lecture on how to make findings of fact and conclusions of law.

Still another result can happen where findings of fact are inadequate on appeal. In *Zack Metal Co. v S. S. Birmingham City,* (2 Cir., 1962) 311 F2d 334, a defendant shipowner successfully defended the plaintiff's first appeal, he thought. The case was remanded to the trial court because of inadequate findings. With better findings, plaintiff appealed again. Defendant won again. However, when defendant moved to have its costs for the first appeal assessed against plaintiff, the Court of Appeals denied such costs, because the shipowner defendant could have prevented the remand on the first appeal by requesting the trial court to make appropriate and adequate findings for purpose of review.

Where the trial court makes no findings of fact whatsoever, the appellate court will generally remand to trial court with direction to make findings.[26] Sometimes, however, the appellate court will not remand for findings if from the evidence it is shown that lack of findings of fact was not prejudicial to the appellant.[27] On rare occasions, where findings of fact are made by the trial court, but they lack an essential finding or are otherwise inadequate, a Court of Appeals will amplify or remedy the trial court's finding on its own. This is particularly true where most of the evidence was presented to the trial court through depositions.[28] Of course, if the judgment turned purely on a question of law, the trial court does not need to make any findings.[29] Generally, however, it is not an appellate court's business to make findings of fact and inadequate findings usually require remand to the trial court with order to make adequate findings.[30]

Even the most conscientious trial court can overlook an essential finding of fact when such essential finding is not in dispute. After all, the primary duty of the trial court is to resolve disputed questions of fact. In such a case the appellate court may itself furnish the essential finding based upon the undisputed facts of record rather than remanding the case for further findings. However, the rule is that adequate formal findings are necessary and if ever excused it is only in the case where the trial court determines a question of law based upon agreed or undisputed facts.[31]

---

26 Domeracki v Gulf Oil Corp., (3 Cir., 1965) 342 F2d 219; Victory Towing Co. v Bordelon, (5 Cir., 1955) 219 F2d 540; Jones v Beto, (5 Cir., 1971) 448 F2d 1259

27 Lucky Lindy (5 Cir., 1935) 1935 AMC 553; Leighton v One Williams Street Fund, Inc. (★★ Cir., 1965) 343 F2d 565

28 Petition of the United States—The F.S. 231 (2 Cir., 1949) 178 F2d 243 Parker Bros. & Co. v De Forest, (5 Cir., 1955) 221 F2d 377

29 Rogers et al v Alaska S. S. Co. (9 Cir., 1961) 290 F2d 116

30 Deering-Milliken & Co. v Modern-Aire of Hollywood, (9 Cir., 1956) 231 F2d 623; Employers Liability Assur. Corp. v Weeden (★★ Cir., 1960) 274 F2d 809; Peper v Cedarbrook Farms, Inc., (3 Cir., 1971) 437 F2d 1209

31 Yanich v Barber (9 Cir., 1956) 232 F2d 939; Philadelphia Marine Trade Ass'n. v International Longshoremen Local 1291, (3 Cir., 1966) 365 F2d 295

Findings of fact are inadequate when they fail to include a finding on an essential fact. Finding a defendant negligent without also finding that the negligence was a proximate cause of plaintiff's injuries renders the finding of negligence irrelevant and the set of findings inadequate for lack of a finding on proximate cause. For example, finding that an employer failed to furnish a safe place to work because of poor lighting is irrelevant in absence of a further finding that the poor lighting caused the employee to become injured.[32] Likewise, finding that a small boat owner was negligent in failing to tie his beached boat to the shore accomplishes nothing in absence of a finding that such failure contributed to an ensuing collision.[33]

A less apparent inadequacy of findings of fact can come about by finding an ultimate fact but failing to find an essentially related "stepping stone" finding. Suppose a court finds that a defendant corporation had notice of a poor condition of things and was negligent. Since a corporate entity cannot acquire any knowledge or commit any act or omission unless it is by or through a human being—officer or employee—it becomes important for the court to further find as a fact which officer or employee of the corporate defendant knew or should have known of the poor condition or was otherwise negligent. This is particularly true where the injured plaintiff happens to be an officer or employee of the corporate defendant and is charged with a duty of knowing or finding out about a condition or to otherwise behave in a negligent-free manner. Obviously it would be error to find the corporate defendant liable only through the negligent acts or omissions of the injured plaintiff-employee. On appeal the appellate court should not be left in wonderment as to whether the trial court found the corporate defendant liable because of the neglect of the plaintiff or because of the neglect of some other employee.

A finding of fact can also be inadequate when it is a crucial fact upon which negligence or non-negligence turns and it appears to the appellate court to be contrary to the evidence. In such a situation the appellate court will remand the case to the trial court for a new trial so that the trial court can, upon the evidence, make its own determination of the crucial fact. This was exactly what was done in *Tug Port of Bandon,* (9 Cir., 1966) 367 F2d 857. There a tug owner moved from his anchored position off the coral atoll of Kure Island at 1:00 P.M. The trial court found no negligence because he found the change of

---

[32] Shaver Transportation Co. v Alaska Freight Lines (9 Cir., 1963) 315 F2d 97
[33] Claybon v Evansville Veneer & Lumber Co. (Indiana, 1947), 73 NE2d 698

wind did not occur until noon of the particular day and the tug owner was not negligent in changing his anchorage within an hour of the shift in wind. However, because the evidence showed that the shift in wind occurred about the break of day, a finding of fact consistent with the evidence would make a finding of non-negligence clearly erroneous unless based on some other subsidiary finding. Only the trial judge on remand could fairly determine consistent findings as he had something in mind. Of what we have just spoken is a different situation from one where the critical ultimate finding of negligence is unsupported by the evidence and for that reason clearly erroneous. In the later situation reversal is in order.[34]

A finding that the plaintiff "has sustained the burden of proof" to a particular issue is not an adequate finding of fact on that issue, but is in nature of a conclusion,[35] nor is a finding that no co-tenancy existed between plaintiff and defendant a sufficient finding of fact.[36]

What Are Not Findings of Fact?

A stated conclusion that the evidence is not sufficient to prove a fact is not a finding of fact even though the trial court might call it that.[37] Likewise, some courts distinguish a "conclusion of fact" from a "finding of fact."[38] A statement by the trial court in an oral opinion is not a finding of fact where a formal opinion is thereafter entered. The oral statement cannot be used to impeach the formal opinion.[39] Otherwise expressed: the trial court cannot be lashed to the mast by oral comments it might make at the conclusion of the trial which later appear inconsistent with its subsequent findings of fact.[40]

Notes of a trial judge who dies before decision cannot serve as findings of fact or even be considered by a second judge who undertakes to re-try and decide the case upon the transcript of the evidence in the first trial.[41] Nor, can a trial judge receive into evidence findings

---

[34] Vastola v Conn. Protective System, (Conn., 1946) 47 ATL. 2d 844, 73 NE 2d 698

[35] United States v Jefferson Elec. Mfg. Co. (1934) 291 U.S. 386

[36] Kahn v Central Smelting Co. (1880) 102 U.S. 641

[37] Alfs v Compagnie Gen. Transatlantique (Wash., 1963) 385 P 2d 53

[38] Monetaire Min. Co. v Columbus Rexall Consol. Mines, (Utah, 1918) 174 Pac. 172

[39] Rawson Admx. v Calmar S. S. Corp. (9 Cir., 1962) 304 F2d 202

[40] Deep Sea Tankers, Ltd. v The Long Branch (2 Cir., 1957) 242 F2d 433

[41] Brown & Root v Amer. Home Assur., (5 Cir., 1965) 353 F2d 113

of fact made in another related case and use such findings as a predicate for his own finding that the defendant was negligent.[42] While it is best to have all findings of fact in a single document, it is not reversible error if the findings appear in several documents. At least prior to present Rule 52 it has been held that an opinion of the trial court is no substitute for formal findings of fact.[43]

Nothing Can Be Done After Notice of Appeal Is Filed

Once notice of appeal from a judgment has been filed, jurisdiction leaves the trial court and rests in the appellate court so that no party to the action in the trial court can move to have the trial court amend or correct any of its findings of fact.[44] Much the same is true where the appellate court dismisses an appeal and the trial court thereafter attempts to make supplemental findings to its original findings. Such supplemental findings will be vacated on a writ of mandamus.[45]

Pertinent Law Review Articles on
Making Meaningful Findings of Fact

"Findings of Fact," United States District Judge James M. Carter and Bruce V. Wagner, L.L.B., University of San Diego, School of Law, *San Diego Law Review,* Vol. 1, p. 13 (1964)

"Federal Civil Rule 52 as it Relates to Bond Litigation," Francis L. Kenney, Jr., *Insurance Counsel Journal,* Vol. 35, p. 242 (1968)

---

[42] West Coast Term. Co. v Luckenbach S. S. Co., (9 Cir., 1965) 349 F2d 568

[43] Interstate Circuit, Inc. v United States, (1938) 304 U.S. 55

[44] Pan Cargo Shipping Corp. v United States, (SDNY, 1960) 180 F. Supp. 8

[45] Madden, Req. Director, NLRB v Judge J. Sam Perry (7 Cir., 1959) 264 F2d 169

Judicial Review of   10
Findings of
Administrative Agencies

The federal bureaucracy feeds on facts. The agencies spew regulations and orders. Each agency is usually created by an Act of Congress which defines the power and purpose of the creature. Agency action beyond Congressional power or purpose is invalid. The agency process for promulgating and enforcing regulations and issuing orders has at its heart the finding of facts, usually, but not always, made as result of an adversary proceeding in which evidence is produced to establish a base for the facts to be found.

Because our Constitution requires separation of governmental powers on the one hand and, on the other, due process of law, the matter of judicial review has become an exceedingly complex kettle of fish. Agencies should be able to act freely within their respective spheres and at the same time the courts should be permitted to oversee agency action to the limited extent of seeing to it that action taken is legal and due process afforded to affected persons. The easiest way agency action can become arbitrary or capricious is to permit it to occur without substantial evidence to support findings of fact and without good reason being affirmatively and patently shown to justify the action. This is why the law of facts is important in the system of judicial review.

To better understand the scope of judicial review of agency findings we first mention several requirements necessary to obtain judicial review. To make this chapter particularly practical we will conclude it by showing how and where to go to get judicially reviewed the action of many of the federal offices and agencies.

The Federal Administration Procedure Act (hereafter "APA")[1] is the backbone to agency procedure designed to assure due process within agency proceedings and on judicial review of agency action. Agencies subject to judicial review include with but few exceptions[2] every authority of the Government of the United States be it an official, a commission, a corporation or a board.

Right of Review—"Standing to Sue"

Any person suffering a legal wrong because of agency action, or adversely affected or aggrieved by agency action within the meaning of a relevant statute, is entitled to judicial review thereof. APA Sec. 10(a)(#702).

For a plaintiff to complain in court of agency action he must show two things: (1) Truly being aggrieved which is usually evidenced by showing that he has a "stake" in the outcome of the litigation; and (2) that his aggrievement i relevant to the jurisdictional Act which defines the power and purpose of the agency whose action is under attack.

The first mentioned test is usually easy. Any client coming into your office who is willing to commit himself to a fee to which you are entitled for you to spend the skill and time to prosecute an action for judicial review can well be expected to have a "stake" in the matter.

It is the second test of "relevancy" that plaintiffs usually flunk. For example, in *Rasmussen v United States*, (8 Cir., 1970) 421 F2d 776 two cities and a state agency were not held to have standing to sue the Postmaster General for review of his order discontinuing use of railroads for delivery of first class mail. The reason was that the statute under which the Postmaster General acted had as its purpose the efficient operation of the Post Office and not the subsidization of railroads.

---

[1] Presently codified in 5 U.S.C. Sec. 551–575 and Sec. 701–706. Originally enacted June 11, 1946, Chap. 324, 60 Stat. 237 and 243. Prior to 1964 codified in 5 U.S.C. Sec. 1,001 (a) et seq and Sec. 1009 et seq. Cases will refer to both codifications.

[2] Authorities excepted from application of APA include: (1) the Congress; (2) the courts of the United States; (3) the governments of the territories or possessions of the United States and the District of Columbia; (4) courts martial and military commissions and military authority exercised in the field in time of war or in occupied territory; (5) agencies composed of representatives of parties to disputes determined by them; (6) functions conferred by sections 1738, 1739, 1743 and 1744 of title 12; chapter 2 of title 41; or sections 1622, 1884, 1891–1902, and former section 1641(b)(2), of title 50, appendix of United States Code.

Even the requirement of "relevancy" is being relaxed by the courts. As long as the plaintiff can show he is *arguably* within the zone of interest to be protected by the agency he can meet the relevancy test.[3] In fact, one court would throw "relevancy" out the window if it could.[4]

Certain Agency Actions Are Not Subject to Review

There are certain agency actions insulated from judicial review. They are those actions where the jurisdictional Act of the Agency precludes judicial review and those actions which the jurisdictional Act has committed to agency discretion by law.

This point of law is too complex for brief treatment. Suffice to say that you should be sure to read and understand both the legislative history of and the jurisdictional Act which created the agency whose action your client is about to attack.

The lack of express authority for judicial review in the Act is no evidence of intent that Congress intended to preclude judicial review.[5] Judicial review is presumed.[6] Courts will decline judicial review only where Congressional intent is established by the clearest and most cogent of evidence.[7]

Just because the jurisdictional Act states that agency action shall be final does not necessarily mean that judicial review is barred.[8] However, when the Act expressly states that certain action shall not be judicially reviewed that is another matter.[9] But given an opening, the courts will even circumvent such language. For example, in *Di Silvestre v United States,* (2 Cir., 1968) 405 F2d 150 a veteran sued the Veterans Administration for benefits to which he claimed to be entitled. At that point he had no standing to sue. However, when the Veterans Administration conceded he was entitled to the benefits except for its off-set counterclaim to recoup money either mistakenly paid to the

---

[3] Data Processing Service v Camp, (1969) 397 U.S. 150; Barlow v Collins, (1970) 397 U.S. 159

[4] Scanwell Laboratories, Inc. v Shaffer, (D.C. Cir., 1970) 424 F2d 859

[5] Stark v Wickard, (1944) 321 U.S. 288

[6] Abbott Laboratories v Gardner (1967) 387 U.S. 136

[7] Western Pac. R. Co. v Habermeyer (9 Cir., 1967) 382 F2d 1003, certiorari denied in 390 U.S. 980

[8] United States v William, (1929) 278 U.S. 255

[9] Fountain v United States, (Ct. Cl., 1970) 427 F2d 759; Merge v Troussi, (3 Cir., 1968) 394 F2d 79

veteran or obtained through fraudulent medical records, a judiciable controversy appeared in the counterclaim sufficient to give the veteran a standing to sue.

It is only discretion left to the agency *by law* which precludes judicial review. Here, again Congress must be shown to have intended to place unfettered discretion exclusively in the agency. These cases are the exception rather than the rule. Exclusive agency discretion is usually found in "permissive" and not "mandatory" legislation. Where the Secretary of the Interior "may" sell land or otherwise act his action is not subject to judicial review.[10]

Actions Reviewable—Ripeness for Review

Agency action made reviewable by statute and final agency action for which there is no other adequate remedy in a court are subject to judicial review. A preliminary, procedural, or intermediate agency action or ruling not directly reviewable is subject to review on the review of the final agency action.

Except as otherwise expressly required by statute, agency action otherwise final is final for the purpose of judicial review whether or not there has been presented or determined an application for a declaratory order, for any form of reconsideration, or, unless the agency otherwise requires by rule and provides that the action meanwhile is inoperative, for an appeal to superior agency authority. APA Sec. 10(c)(#704).

Again, read the jurisdictional Act and rules of the agency. Make sure the agency action is final but do not feel you must ask for reconsideration in order to exhaust your administrative remedy unless rules require.

Sometimes action involving agency rule-making can only be judicially reviewed when the agency commences enforcement proceedings. For a most compelling reason or a showing of great irreparable loss if your client must wait until enforcement proceedings are commenced before challenging a rule a court may permit pre-enforcement judicial review.[11] However, the reason had better be extraordinarily convincing.[12]

---

[10] United States v Walker, (9 Cir., 1969) 409, 477; Ferry v Udall (9 Cir., 1964) 336 F2d 706; Hamel v Nelson (Calif., 1963) 226 F. Supp. 96

[11] Abbott Laboratories v Gardner, (1967) 387 U.S. 136

[12] Toilet Goods Ass'n. v Gardner, (1967) 387 U.S. 158

Scope of Judicial Review Is Very Limited

Scope of judicial review of agency actions is set forth in APA Sec. 10(3)(#706). It provides that to the extent necessary to decision and when presented, the reviewing court shall decide all relevant questions of law, interpret constitutional and statutory provisions, and determine the meaning or applicability of the terms of an agency action. The review of findings of fact where most litigation centers comes in the "(2)" provision of the section which provides that the court shall:

(2) hold unlawful and set aside agency action, findings and conclusions found to be—

(A) arbitrary, capricious, an abuse of discretion, or otherwise not in accordance with law;

(B) contrary to constitutional right, power, privilege or immunity;

(C) in excess of statutory jurisdiction, authority, or limitations, or short of statutory right;

(D) without observance of procedure required by law;

(E) unsupported by substantial evidence in a case subject to sections 556 and 557 of this title or otherwise reviewed on the record of an agency hearing provided by statute; or

(F) unwarranted by the facts to the extent that the facts are subject to trial de novo by the reviewing court.

In making the foregoing determinations, the court shall review the whole record or those parts of it cited by a party, and due account shall be taken of the rule of prejudicial error.

The above standard for judicial review in most cases free reviewing courts of time-consuming and difficult tasks of weighing evidence and at the same time gives proper respect to the expertise of the administrative agency.[13] Of course, Section 10(e)(#706) of APA must be read in *pari materia* with the agency's jurisdictional Act.[14]

---

[13] Consolo v Federal Maritime Commission, (1966) 383 U.S. 607

[14] Willapoint Oysters Inc. v Ewing, (9 Cir., 1949) 174 F2d 676 certiorari denied in 338 U.S. 860

Setting Aside Agency Action As Being Arbitrary or Capricious

It is rare that a case of judicial review turns on pure law. More often than not there is inextricably involved in the agency action not only law but arbitrary and capricious action, abuse of discretion, inadequate findings of fact, as well as the not to be forgotten requirement that all findings must be supported by substantial evidence.

As used in Section 10(e) (#706) of APA the words "arbitrary" and "capricious" are not used in their approbrious or popular sense but rather in a technical sense of meaning that the agency action has no rational basis.[15]

Thus "arbitrary" covers "capricious" in this technical sense. While all findings not supported by evidence are arbitrary, both findings and agency orders can be arbitrary for other reasons.

The most authentic way of demonstrating arbitrary agency action is to cite cases where reviewing courts have struck down agency action for this reason.

The Labor Commissioner acted arbitrarily in finding that a longshoreman did not collapse and die within his employment when he suffered heart attack while urinating outside of his employer's office. *Wheatley v Adler,* (D.C., 1969) 407 F2d 307.

The Interstate Commerce Commission acted arbitrarily in finding that public convenience and necessity required entrance of a new truck service into a field of existing motor carriers when based only upon showing that proposed new service intended to supply pumps to pump up tires of mobile homes being transported. *National Trailer Convoy, Inc. v United States,* (Okl., 1968) 293 F. Supp. 634.

The Interstate Commerce Commission acted arbitrarily in a railroad rate hearing when it ordered sharing of a joint rate between several carriers based upon misleading system average cost studies where standard for dividing the revenue was "cost of handling" the traffic. *Aberdeen & Rockfish Co. v United States,* (La., 1967) 270 F. Supp. 695.

The Interstate Commerce Commission acted arbitrarily when it failed to state a reasonable basis to support its conclusion that the "full distributive costs of rail and barge services must be compared" to determine what mode of transportation has an inherent cost ad-

---

[15] Dell Publishing Co. v Summerfield, (D.C. 1961) 198 F. Supp. 843

vantage over the other; also when the rail cost study included passenger service revenue. *Louisville & N. R. Co. v United States,* (Ky., 1967) 268 F. Supp. 71.

The Interstate Commerce Commission acted arbitrarily when it canceled a proposed rate to transport single dwelling mobile homes because it held such transportation was beyond the commodity description of "Buildings complete, knocked down or in sections." *Pre Fab Transit Co. v United States,* (Ill., 1967) 262 F. Supp. 1009.

Federal Maritime Board (Commission) acted arbitrarily when it ordered a common carrier by water to cease transporting bananas under a contract arrangement for the reason that bananas are "susceptible of being transported in common carriage." Such order eliminated contract carriage of bananas in violation of Congressional intent. *Grace Lines v Federal Maritime Board,* (2 Cir., 1959) 263 F2d 709.

Secretary of Interior's order invalidating a mining claim after hearing was arbitrary as its basis was lack of good faith of claimant and that question was not clearly made an issue at the hearing. *Coleman v United States,* (9 Cir., 1966) 363 F2d 190.

Secretary of Interior acted arbitrarily in issuing oil and gas leases to applicants in an Alaska public land area prior to the area being opened for leasing by executive order of the President. Agency cannot frustrate judicial review by issuing confusing and conflicting orders. *Tallman v Udall,* (D.C., 1963) 324 F2d 411.

The Secretary of the Interior acted arbitrarily when person who attended hearing to oppose cancelation of his homestead filed timely notice of appeal from the examiner's report but was one day late in filing his supporting statement of reasons and dismissed the appeal. *Price v Udall,* (Alaska, 1968) 280 F. Supp. 293.

Federal Power Commission acted arbitrarily when it issued a rate order that did not provide for proper allowable expenses, taxes, depreciation and return. *Mississippi River Fuel Corp. v Federal Power Comm.* (DC, 1947) 163 F2d 433.

National Labor Relations Board acted arbitrarily when it refused to consider evidence. Evidence in form of exhibits had been introduced at a union representation hearing but somehow got waylaid in the Board's files. Later, in an unfair labor practice hearing on same controversy, the mislaid evidence was found but not used. *S. D. Warren Co. v N.L.R.B.,* (1 Cir., 1965) 342 F2d 814.

Setting Aside Agency Action for Abuse of Discretion

It appears rare that agency action is set aside for abuse of discretion aside and apart from being set aside for being arbitrary. Abuse of discretion is nevertheless reason for setting aside agency action.

An example of abuse of discretion is found in *Atewooftakewd v Udall,* (Okl., 1967) 277 F. Supp. 464. In that case the Secretary was found to have abused his discretion when he refused to approve a deceased Indian's last will and testament which devised his worldly goods to a niece and her children with whom the decedent had been living his past years. The Secretary refused approval because omitted from the will was an illegitimate daughter of decedent who had little contact with the Indian over the years.

Setting Aside Agency Action for Inadequate Findings of Fact

Under authority of findings "otherwise not in accordance with law" of Subsection (2)(A) of APA Sec 10 (e) (#706), reviewing courts frequently remand the case to the agency with instruction to make better findings. The Court never attempts to substitute its judgment for that of the agency but merely tells the agency to do a better job on its fact finding chore. In a judicial review case such outcome is at least a *quasi* victory as the aggrieved party may have a further hearing before the agency, or the agency may drop the matter, or, after making proper findings, it may take action contrary to that originally taken.

To begin with, an ultimate finding which merely recites statutory language or only refers to a "related" case is inadequate.[16]

Where the Commission, after making an order suspending proposed railroad rates, later makes an order vacating the suspension order because of "good cause" such finding is inadequate to state reason for taking reverse action.[17] However, a later case held the Commission need not give any reason for vacating a rate suspension

---

[16] Seatrain Lines v United States, (SDNY, 1958) 168 F. Supp. 819
[17] Amarillo-Borger Express v United States (Texas, 1956) 138 F. Supp. 411

order because no hearing was required for such action under Section 8(b) of APA, 5 U.S.C. #557(b).[18]

Where as with the Interstate Commerce Commission, Congress lays down its National Transportation Policy for the Commission to follow in regulating the various modes of surface transportation it behooves the Commission to make findings which show that it is heeding the Congressional policy.[19]

Adequate findings of fact are often necessary to protect a person's Constitutional rights. Rights are often whittled away by agency interpretation of language and sloughing over of facts. A good example is in *Mitchell Bros. Truck Lines v United States,* (Ore., 1967) 273 F. Supp. 430. In that case a motor carrier through grandfather rights had acquired a certificate from the Commission authorizing the transportation of "machinery." The Commission ordered the motor carrier to cease and desist from transporting "a truck with wrecker" within the generic commodity description of "machinery," claiming that the item had assumed a new identity even though it may have at one time been considered "machinery." The three judge Court remanded the case to the Commission for better findings, and in doing so stated:

> A careful, thoughtful and meticulous examination of the record discloses a deplorable lack of meaningful findings. The Commission, as a basis for its order, merely adopted the alleged findings of the examiners. This procedure, of course, was permissible if the findings of the latter have significance. We hold they have not. For example, the examiners under the heading *Discussion and Conclusions* find "The truck with wrecker (Ex. 3) has achieved an identity of its own, and is not mere machinery." They then go on to cite certain authorities in support of their statement. No factual basis can be found for the conclusion. Another example: "The steel dump bodies and crane and truck parts . . . were not destined to a contractor, and while they may have moving parts, they are not 'machinery' in the sense that they perform any function. . . .
>
> Throughout the alleged findings of the examiners and the order of the Commission, the references would seem to be to the present, or more recent views, definitions and philosophy of the Commission, rather than the generally accepted meaning of "machinery", and the views, definitions and philosophy of the

---

[18] Freeport Sulphur Co. v United States (SDNY, 1961) 199 F. Supp. 913, 916

[19] Schaffer Transp. Co. v United States (1957) 355 U.S. 83; Chicago, M. St. P. & P. R. Co. v State of Illinois, (1958) 355 U.S. 300; Stott v United States, (SDNY, 1958) 166 F. Supp. 851

Commission at the time of granting *The Lundstrom* Application
in 1939. Without clear, objective and precise findings in these
areas, we are powerless to intelligently exercise our decisional
function.

Findings of fact have been found to be inadequate in *Denver &
R. G. W. R. Co. v Union Pacific R. Co.,* (1955) 351 U.S. 321
(through route railroad order); *State of North Carolina v United
States,* (1944) 325 U.S. 507 (Order for intra state railroad rates to
be raised); *United States v Baltimore & O. R. Co.,* (1935) 293 U.S.
454, 465 (order requiring railroad to substitute power operated
reversing gear on locomotive for hand operated gear); *Florida v
United States,* (1930) 282 U.S. 194, 208 (findings too indefinite to
support order for intrastate freight rates to be reduced; *Cantlay &
Tanzola, Inc. v United States* (Calif., 1953) 115 F. Supp. 72 (proposed reduced petroleum rates); *Sindicato Puertorriqueno de Trabajadores v Hodgson,* (D.C., 1971) 448 F2d 1161 (Secretary of Agriculture wage order).

Setting Aside Agency Action for Lack of Substantial Evidence

Where a critical finding of fact is not supported by substantial
evidence it will be set aside on review under Subsection (2) (E) of
APA Sec. 10(E) (#706). However, agency action can only be
attacked for lack of evidentiary support where the action reviewed
stems from a hearing where evidence is required to be presented or
the making of a regulation where the agency's jurisdictional Act
requires the regulation to be made on the "record." APA, Sec 4
(#553).

That which constitutes substantial evidence sufficient to support
an agency finding is that quantity and quality of evidence deemed
sufficient to put the issue of fact to a jury if the issue was tried in a
court sitting with a jury.[20] Measuring a finding and supporting evidence in light of the equitable "unless clearly erroneous" rule is
improper in the judicial review of agency action.[21]

A most interesting case is that of *Bonica v Olesen,* (Calif.,
1954) 126 F. Supp. 398. In that case the Postmaster General cut off
mail delivery to an address in Los Angeles because it found that the

---

[20] Consolo v Federal Maritime Commission, (1966) 383 U.S. 607
[21] N.L.R.B. v Southland Mfg. Co. (4 Cir., 1952) 201 F2d 244

person at the address was using the mails to sell lewd and lascivious movie films of nude dancing girls. The evidence consisted of the movie films which the Postmaster had intercepted. On review the Court looked at all of the antics of the dancing girls and concluded that the evidence was insufficient to support a finding of lewdness and lasciviousness. Here is a clear case where the Court substituted its judgment for that of the Postmaster General. Only justification for such heresy is the decision that as a matter of law the finding lacked support of substantial evidence.

A mere scintilla of evidence plus an inference therefrom will not arise to the dignity of substantial evidence.[22]

Findings of the Interstate Commerce Commission in proceedings to modify certificate of public convenience and necessity obtained through "grandfather" rights are insufficient when they have no relevant subsidiary findings of bonafide service.[23] Or, when Commission ignores evidence of actual operation during "grandfather" period.[24]

Where the Interstate Commerce Commission grants a broad certificate of public convenience and necessity for a proposed motor carrier service the court on review will examine the evidence and whereas between some points of proposed service no evidence supports the need the proposed service will be deleted from the certificate.[25]

Findings by the Interstate Commerce Commission as to the justness and reasonableness of carrier rates will be set aside when not supported by evidence. "System average" cost studies of a carrier are usually regarded as being insufficient evidence.[26]

Further Reasons for Setting Aside Agency Action

Reasons for setting aside agency action less frequently arising than those already discussed are found in subsections "(B)," "(C)," "(D)," and "(F)" of APA Sec 10(e) (#706).

---

[22] Consolidated Edison Co. of N.Y. v N.L.R.B., (1938) 305 U.S. 197–229; N.L.R.B. v Columbia Enameling & Stamping Co. (1939) 306 U.S. 292; Universal Camera Corp., v N.L.R.B. (1951) 340 U.S. 474

[23] Nashua Motor Express, Inc. v United States, (NH., 1964) 230 F. Supp. 646

[24] Mayfield Sons Trucking Co. v United States, (Ga., 1964) 234 F. Supp. 655

[25] T.S.C. Motor Freight Lines, Inc. v United States, (Texas, 1960) 186 F. Supp. 777, 793

[26] Pacific Inland Tariff Bureau v United States, (Ore., 1955) 129 F. Supp. 472

Contrary to Constitutional Right, Power, Privilege or Immunity:
The Constitution usually comes into the judicial review of agency
action when the aggrieved party alleges he has been denied due process
of law under the Fifth Amendment as to either a procedural matter
such as notice and opportunity to be heard or because the agency
action has the effect of confiscating his property.[27] Short of impinging
on these rights Congress can provide that administrative agencies do
just about anything.[28]

In Excess of Statutory Jurisdiction: Prove that the agency action
is beyond the Congressional Act which defines the agency's power
and purpose and you can surely win your case on judicial review.

Without Observance of Procedure Required by Law: This reason
for setting aside agency action arises from the agency failing to give
procedural due process or conducting a proceeding in violation of
APA, Sec. 7 (#556) or Sec. 8 (#557). Due process was denied a
corporation where a Senate Sub-Committee questioned Fair Trade
Commissioners as to reasons for action taken by the Commission even
before a hearing examiner had made his initial decision on merits in
a divestiture proceeding.[29] Where a Social Security claimant was not
represented by counsel, and obviously unprepared and ignorant of
what facts might be significant, a hearing Examiner acted arbitrarily
and denied claimant due process when he discouraged claimant's wife
from representing claimant and excluded her from hearing room
during questioning of claimant.[30] Full and fair disclosure is an element
of a fair hearing and due process.[31]

*"Unwarranted by the Facts" Where Review Subject to Trial De
Novo:* Believe it or not there are a few rare instances where Congress
has provided that a court on judicial review of agency action may
consider agency findings as only prima facie evidence, receive further
evidence and otherwise review the action as on a trial de novo. One
case is under 7 U.S.C. #499g pertaining to the Secretary of Agriculture awarding reparations where perishable commodities are involved.[32] Another case is in review of deportation proceedings, where

---

[27] American Trucking Ass'n. v United States (1953) 344 U.S. 298, 320
[28] Cobb v Murrell, (5 Cir., 1967) 386 F2d 947
[29] Guenther v Morehead, (Iowa, 1967) 272 F. Supp. 721; J. B. Montgomery,
Inc. v United States, (Colo., 1962) 206 F. Supp. 455, affirmed in 376 U.S. 389
[30] Pillsbury Co. v F.T.C., (5 Cir., 1966) 354 F2d 952
[31] Coyle v Gardner, (Hawaii, 1969) 298 F. Supp. 609
[32] Grimm v Brown, (Calif., 1968) 291 F. Supp. 1011

U.S. citizenship is alleged.[33] Still another case is where the National Railroad Adjustment Board makes money awards.[34]

Aside from Congress authorizing judicial review by trial *de novo* it has been held that in any agency action under review the court may try *de novo* findings of fact which go only to a person's statutory right.[35]

How and Where to Go to Get Judicial Review

Generally, the form of action to file in a federal court to obtain judical review of an agency action is: First, to be that specified if any by the agency's jurisdictional Act; and Second, in absence thereof or should the specified remedy be inadequate then any applicable form of legal action that is deemed the most appropriate including an action for declaratory relief, a writ of prohibition, action for a mandatory injunction, or, in case of incarceration, a writ of habeas corpus.[36]

Except to the extent that prior, adequate, and exclusive opportunity for judicial review is provided by law, agency action is subject to judicial review in civil or criminal proceedings undertaken to judicially enforce the agency action. APA, Sec. 10(b) (#703). While the APA is not intended to modify existing remedies or create new ones for judicial review,[37] it did intend to simplify and make more flexible the avenues for judicial review.[38]

Following is general method of securing judicial review of actions of a number of federal officers and agencies:

Civil Service Commission—Removal or Discipline of Federal Employee: 5 U.S.C. Sec. 652; 5 U.S.C. Sec. 863. File action in District Court. *Jenkins v Macy,* (8 Cir., 1966) 357 F2d 62.

Commissioner of Internal Revenue (also National Enforcement Commission under Defense Production Act of 1950): 50 U.S. C.A.

---

[33] John J. Trombetta Co. v Goldstein and Procacci, (Pa., 1961) 198 F. Supp. 288

[34] Frank v Rogers (D.C. Cir., 1958) 253 F2d 889

[35] Russ v Southern Ry. Co. (6 Cir., 1964) 334 F2d 224

[36] United States ex rel, de Lucia v O'Donovan, (Ill., 1948) 82 F. Supp. 435, affirmed in 178 F2d 876

[37] St. Joseph Stock Yards Co. v United States (1936) 298 U.S. 38; Cox v United States, (9 Cir., 1946) 157 F2d 787; Big Table, Inc. v Schroeder, (Ill., 1960) 186 F. Supp. 254

[38] Kristensen v McGrath, (D.C. Cir., 1949) 179 F2d 796

Appendix 2159) District Court has jurisdiction to review determination of National Enforcement Commission in proceeding instituted by taxpayer against Commissioner of Internal Revenue for refund of taxes when the Commissioner disallowed salary payments as non-taxable solely because National Enforcement Commission (not subject to review) issued a "Certificate of Disallowance." *Oak Mfg. Co. v United States* (Ill. 1961) 193 F. Supp. 514.

Civil Aeronautics Board or Administrator: 49 U.S.C. Sec. 1371 et seq. File petition for review of order with U.S. Court of Appeals of Circuit wherein petitioner resides or in District of Columbia Circuit. Judgment of Court of Appeals reviewed by Supreme Court on petition for writ of certiorari. Note: Order respecting a foreign air carrier requiring approval of President is not subject to review. 49 U.S.C. Sec. 1486.

Federal Aviation Agency: File complaint for declaratory relief in District Court. *Dutchess County Aviation Adm. v Federal Aviation Agency,* (SDNY, 1966) 251 F. Supp. 426.

Comptroller of the Currency—Banking Act: 12 U.S.C. Sec. 36(e) Where controller acts without hearing (non-required) file complaint in District Court to set aside or enjoin action. District Court will hear *de novo* facts necessary to determine validity of Comptroller's action. 5 U.S.C. Sec. 706; *First National Bank of Smithfield, North Carolina v Saxon,* (4 Cir., 1965) 352 F2d 267.

Federal Communication Commission: 47 U.S.C. Sec. 201–222. File notice of appeal with U.S. Court of Appeals for the District of Columbia Circuit, concisely stating the nature of the proceeding from which appeal is taken, reasons upon which appellant intends to rely and proof of service on the Commission. Reviewed by Supreme Court on petition for writ of certiorari.

Federal Home Loan Bank Board or Federal Savings & Loan Ins. Corp.: 12 U.S.C. Sec. 1464(d) (1); 12 U.S.C. Sec. 1725(c) (4). File complaint for declaratory and injunctive relief in District Court. APA, Sec. 10 (#701); *Elliott v Federal Home Loan Bank Board,* (Calif. 1964) 233 F. Supp. 578, 588.

Federal Maritime Commission—Shipping Act, 1916: 46 U.S.C. 815. File petition to set aside order with U.S. Court of Appeals for the District of Columbia. Sec. 2 of Administrative Orders Review Act (64 Stat. 1129, as amended, 5 U.S.C. 1032(c); *Consolo v Federal Maritime Commission,* (1966) 383 U.S. 607.

Federal Power Commission—Natural Gas Act: 15 U.S.C. 717 et seq. Aggrieved person must first file petition for rehearing before Commission which is deemed denied in 30 days if not acted upon. Thereafter, within 60 days file petition in U.S. Court of Appeals for Circuit wherein natural gas company is located or in District of Columbia. Supreme Court will review either on petition for writ of certiorari or on Certification as provided in 28 U.S.C. Sec. 346–347.

Federal Trade Commission: 15 U.S.C. Sec. 41–77. File petition in Court of Appeals of any Circuit where matter in question occurred or defendant resides. Reviewed by Supreme Court by petition for writ of certiorari. 15 U.S.C. Sec. 45(e)(g).

Interstate Commerce Commission: File complaint in District Court to set aside, annul or enjoin order. 28 U.S.C. Sec. 2321–2325. Request three judge Court. 28 U.S.C. Sec. 1336. Appeal taken direct to Supreme Court. 28 U.S.C. Sec. 1253.

National Labor Relations Board: 29 U.S.C. Sec. 160(e). The Board upon petition for enforcement or any person aggrieved by a final order of Board upon petition filed in the U.S. Court of Appeals in Circuit where the unfair labor practice occurred or of residence of petitioner or in the District of Columbia Circuit may have Board action reviewed. Expeditious hearing of petition is required. Appeal is to Supreme Court by writ of certiorari. *May Dept. Stores v N.L.R.B.,* (1945) 326 U.S. 376.

National Mediation Board: 45 U.S.C. Sec. 151 et seq. Action of this Board is usually not reviewable. However, under APA Sec. 701 and 28 U.S.C. Sec. 1337 District Court will review order to determine if Board can give extra-territorial effect to order to effect foreign air carriers. *Air Line Dispatchers Ass'n. v National Mediation Board,* (D.C., 1951) 189 F2d 685.

Postmaster General: 39 U.S.C. Sec. 4351. File action for declaratory judgment and injunction in District Court. *Dell Publishing Co. v Day,* (D.C., 1961) 198 F. Supp. 843, affirmed in (D.C., Cir., 1962) 303 F2d 766.

Secretary of Agriculture—Agricultural Adjustment Act, 1938: 7 U.S.C. Secs. 1363–1367. File complaint for declaratory and injunctive relief in District Court. 5 U.S.C. Sec. 701 *Freeman v Brown,* (5 Cir., 1965) 342 F2d 205.

Secretary of Health, Education and Welfare—Social Security Act: 42 U.S.C. Sec. 401–405. Where benefits are denied after hearing final order of Secretary may be reviewed by civil action filed in District Court. Appeal is to U.S. Court of Appeals, 42 U.S.C. Sec. 405(g). However, should Secretary refuse to reconsider a case where plaintiff had foregone regular channel for judicial review, District Court has jurisdiction to review to decide if Secretary abused his discretion in denying reconsideration. *Cappadora v Celebrezze,* (2 Cir., 1966) 356 F2d 1.

United States Immigration and Naturalization Service: In case of refusal to parole alien crewman deserting foreign vessel denial of application for parole will be reviewed on complaint filed in District Court. 8 U.S.C. 1253(h); 5 U.S.C. Sec. 701; *Vucinic v United States Immigration & Naturalization Service,* (Or., 1965) 243 F. Supp. 113.

Pertinent Law Review Articles on
Judicial Review of Findings of Administrative Agencies

"Standing Again," Louis L. Jaffe, *Harvard Law Review,* Vol. 84, p. 633 (1971)

"Administrative Summary Judgment," Ernest Gellhorn and William F. Robinson, *Harvard Law Review,* Vol. 84, p. 612 (1971)

"Nonreviewability: A Functional Analysis of 'Committed to Agency Discretion'," Harvey Saferstein, *Harvard Law Review,* Vol. 82, p. 320 (1968)

"Review of Administrative Adjudicatory Action Taken without a Hearing," *Harvard Law Review,* Vol. 70, p. 698 (1957)

"Expansion of Reviewability of Administrative Action," *Harvard Law Review,* Vol. 70, p. 156 (1956)

"Constitutional and Jurisdictional Fact in Judicial Review," Louis L. Jaffe, *Harvard Law Review,* Vol. 70, p. 953 (1957)

"Judicial Review: Questions of Fact," Louis L. Jaffe, *Harvard Law Review,* Vol. 69, p. 1020 (1956)

"Judicial Review: Questions of Law," Louis L. Jaffe, *Harvard Law Review,* Vol. 69, p. 239 (1955)

"Ripeness of Governmental Action for Judicial Review," Kenneth Culp Davis, *Harvard Law Review,* Vol. 68, p. 1122, 1326 (1955)

"The Democratic Character of Judicial Review," Eugene Rostow, *Harvard Law Review,* Vol. 66, p. 193 (1952)

"Trial Examiners Machinery and Achievements under the Administrative Procedure Act," *Harvard Law Review,* Vol. 66, p. 1065 (1953)

Appellate Review of   11
Findings of Fact—
The "Unless Clearly
Erroneous" Rule

We are here concerned with how the eleven U.S. Court of Appeals and the United States Supreme Court handle on review findings of fact made by the District Court.

Article III of the Constitution gave the Supreme Court appellate jurisdiction over both facts and law; however, as an outgrowth of the English common law the Supreme Court had always refused to review facts found in actions at law[1] but would reject findings of fact in suits in equity if found to be clearly erroneous.[2] As to suits in admiralty federal appellate courts traditionally exercised in a restrained manner a *trial de novo* jurisdiction over the facts on appeal. This later free review of maritime facts was restricted to the equitable standard of the "unless clearly erroneous" rule in 1954 by the Supreme Court in *McAllister v United States*, (1954) 348 U.S. 19. Because of the broad scope of Article III of the Constitution the extent to which federal appellate courts will review facts is controlled exclusively by the Supreme Court and conceivably can be modified or changed in the future. As was seen in the previous chapter there are statutory restrictions to judicial review of facts as found by administrative agencies.[3] The next chapter will deal with the Constitutional prohibition against reexamining facts as found by a jury.[4]

---

1 Jessup v United States (1882) 106 U.S. 147
2 Lawson v United States (1907) 207 U.S. 1
3 5 U.S.C. Sec. 706
4 Seventh Amendment, U.S. Constitution

Rule 52(a) Brings Law, Equity and Admiralty Under Same Tent

With considerable wisdom the Supreme Court standardized the scope of review of facts as found by the trial court when it promulgated in 1948 the Federal Rules of Civil Procedure. By enacting Rule 52(a) the Supreme Court pulled up from the depths of no review the findings of fact in actions at law and pulled down from the sky the free review of facts in admiralty cases. It put actions at law and suits in admiralty at a level with suits in equity where traditionally the trial court's findings of fact would be reviewed on appeal but would not be set aside unless found to be clearly erroneous. Rule 52(a) provides that:

> Findings of fact shall not be set aside unless clearly errone-
> ous, and due regard shall be given to the opportunity of the trial
> court to judge of the credibility of the witnesses.

This standardization made sense in 1948 because the Rules provided for only one form of action. It makes even more sense today since 1966 amendments abolished the Admiralty and Equity Rules and brought these kind of cases under the tent of the Federal Rules of Civil Procedure.

The Supreme Court more fully defined Rule 52(a) in *United States v United States Gypsum Co.,* (1948) 333 U.S. 364. In that anti-trust case the District Court, after listening to defendants denying any combination to monopolize the plaster board market through patents and licensing agreements and reviewing the various written agreements found that the defendants were not combining to restrain trade. The Supreme Court reversed. It struck down the District Court's finding that there was no combination in restraint of trade as being clearly erroneous. In doing so it stated at page 395:

> Since judicial review of findings of trial courts does not have
> the statutory or constitutional limitations of judicial review of
> findings by administrative agencies or by a jury this Court may
> reverse findings of fact by a trial court where "clearly errone-
> ous." The practice in equity prior to the present Rules of Civil
> Procedure was that the findings of the trial court, when depend-
> ent upon oral testimony where the candor and credibility of the
> witnesses would best be judged, had great weight with the
> appellate court. The findings were never conclusive, however.

> *A finding is "clearly erroneous" when although there is evidence to support it, the reviewing court on the entire evidence is left with the definite and firm conviction that a mistake has been committed.* (emphasis supplied).

Keep in mind that "candor and credibility" of a witness is more than having the trial court listen to and observe the witness while on the witness stand. Credibility apprehends the overall evaluation of the testimony in light of its rationality or internal consistency and the manner in which it hangs together with other evidence. *Jackson v United States* (D.C. Cir., 1965) 353 F2d 862.

More recently the Supreme Court in *Zenith Radio Corp. v Hazeltine Research, Inc.* (1969) 395 U.S. 100 admonished that "clearly erroneous" did not mean fact finding *de novo* when at page 123 it stated:

> In applying the clearly erroneous standard to the finding of a district court sitting without a jury, appellate courts must constantly have in mind that their function is not to decide factual issues *de novo*. The authority of an appellate court, when reviewing the findings of a judge as well as those of a jury, is circumscribed by the deference it must give to decisions of the trier of the fact, who is usually in a superior position to appraise and weigh the evidence. The question for the appellate court under Rule 52(a) is not whether it would have made the finding the trial court did, but whether "on the entire evidence (it) is left with the definite and firm conviction that a mistake has been committed." *United States v United States Gypsum Co.*, 333 U.S. 364, 395 (1948). See also *United States v National Assn. of Real Estate Boards*, 339 U.S. 485, 495–496 (1950); *Commissioner v Duberstein*, 363 U.S. 278, 289–291 (1960).

To be sure, the "unless clearly erroneous" rule is far from precise. It is in the nature of the "substantial evidence" rule which the trial court employs to measure sufficiency of evidence for jury consideration in that here as there the court applies the rule by making a factual judgment. Again, we see the marvel of common sense being injected into the common law as an adhesive to fuse law to facts in order to produce a just result.

Just as a motion for judgment notwithstanding the verdict in the case of insufficient evidence provides an escape hatch through which the court may prevent an unjust judgment, so does the "unless clearly erroneous" rule serve the appellate court for correcting a miscarriage of justice which it finds stemming from a clearly erroneous finding of fact. This limited supervisory power over fact finding is a wholesome feature of our federal judicial system for the reason that it insures due process of law.

It seems appropriate to observe that the "unless clearly erroneous" rule affords a broader scope for federal appellate courts to review facts than is usually accorded state appellate courts by their respective organic laws. For example, the federal power of review is broader than that afforded appellate courts in both California[5] and Oregon.[6] Furthermore, no state law can impinge upon federal courts in their application of the "unless clearly erroneous" rule.[7]

Supreme Court Limits Itself in Applying "Clearly Erroneous"

Most cases reach the Supreme Court after the District Court has made findings of fact and after the Court of Appeals has found those facts not to be clearly erroneous. What does the Supreme Court do about such findings when it is reviewing the case? Generally, it considers that both the courts below concurred in the finding and will not disturb it. In reviewing the denial of a petition for naturalization based on the District Court having found that the petitioner had lied about his Party membership, the Supreme Court stated in *Berenyi v Immigration Director,* (1967) 385 U.S. 630 at 635:

> The petitioner asks us to reject as "clearly erroneous" the factual conclusion about his Party membership reached by the District Judge and accepted by the Court of Appeals. In order to do so, we would be forced to disregard this Court's repeated pronouncements that it "cannot undertake to review concurrent findings of fact by two courts below in the absence of a very obvious and exceptional showing of error."

However, one exception to the "two courts below" rule is where the finding of fact is decisive of a person's Constitutional right, privilege or immunity. In such situation the Supreme Court will make an independent examination of the critical finding and determine for itself

---

[5] Gates v General Casualty Co. of America, (9 Cir., 1941) 120 F2d 925
[6] Constitution of State of Oregon
[7] London v Troitimo Bros., Inc., (4 Cir., 1962) 301 F2d 116

whether it is "clearly erroneous." *Hoffa v United States,* (1966) 385 U.S. 293.

"Ultimate" Findings Appear Excepted from Rigor of Rule 52(a)

No sooner had Rule 52(a) been promulgated in 1948 than the federal appellate courts began to fashion an exception to the "unless clearly erroneous" rule.

The idea was soon advanced that an ultimate finding of fact such as, for example, "negligence," partook not only of fact but also of law in that within such ultimate finding the standard for reaching the conclusion was inextractably concealed. Since the trial court did not objectively instruct itself upon the law for measuring negligence as it would the jury if the jury was trying the facts the appellate court had no means of knowing whether the trial court was clearly erroneous because of fact or because of law. Upon this rationale the Second,[8] Third[9] and Fifth[10] Circuits held that in reviewing ultimate facts where principles of law were hidden these Court of Appeals would review the ultimate finding free of the "unless clearly erroneous" rule. During this same period the Sixth[11] and Ninth[12] Circuits treated ultimate facts like any other findings of fact subject to Rule 52(a). However, the Ninth Circuit might have weakened when it found "good cause" for discharge of an agent to be a conclusion of law free of Rule 52(a).[13]

The Supreme Court in its own way seems to be holding that when an ultimate fact has within it an element of law or when it appears that the trial court erred in making its crucial finding because of a misunderstanding of the law, such ultimate finding of fact will be set aside without regard for the "unless clearly erroneous" rule. When the Supreme Court lectured the bench and bar as to how good findings of fact were to be made in *Dalehite v United States,* (1953) 346 U.S. 15 at 24 it noted that findings of fact:

---

[8] Kane v Branch Motor Express Co. (2 Cir., 1961) 290 F2d 503 (negligence)

[9] Around the World Shoppers Club v United States, (3 Cir., 1962) 309 F2d 324 (conclusion that sale occurred in the United States)

[10] Consolidated Naval Stores Co. v Fahs, (5 Cir., 1955) 227 F2d 923; Galena Oaks Corp. v Scofield, (5 Cir., 1954) 218 F2d 217, 219

[11] C.I.R. v Spermacet Whaling and Shipping Co., (6 Cir., 1960) 281 F2d 646

[12] Shaver Transportation Co. v Alaska Freight Lines, (9 Cir., 1963) 315 F2d 97; Ramos v Matson Navigation Co., (9 Cir., 1963) 316 F2d 128

[13] Kippen v American Automatic Typewriter Co., (9 Cir., 1963) 324 F2d 742

. . . to the extent that they are of law, of course they are not binding on appeal. E.g. *Great Atlantic & Pacific Tea Co. vs Supermarket Equipment Corp.,* 340 U.S. 147, 153–154.

Of recent the Supreme Court has on several occasions set aside ultimate findings of fact in anti-trust cases because it was of the view that such findings partook of standards of law. In *United States v General Motors,* (1966) 384 U.S. 127 the District Court had found that General Motors and certain of its dealers in the Los Angeles area had made no agreements among themselves to restrain trade in violation of Section 1 of the Sherman Act through eliminating sales of new Chevrolets to "discount houses." The Supreme Court rejected such "conclusionary" finding as the evidence showed that a conspiracy to restrain trade had been proved. The District Court, it said, made its erroneous finding because it misunderstood the law, believing that such conspiracy required proof of an agreement when it did not. The first paragraph of Note 16 at page 141 is of particular interest:

> 16. We note that, as in *United States v Parke, Davis & Co.,* 362 U.S. 29, 44–45, the ultimate conclusion by the trial judge, that the defendants' conduct did not constitute a combination or conspiracy in violation of the Sherman Act, is not to be shielded by the "clearly erroneous" test embodied in Rule 52(a) of the Federal Rules of Civil Procedure. That Rule in part provides: "Findings of fact shall not be set aside unless clearly erroneous, and due regard shall be given to the opportunity of the trial court to judge of the credibility of the witnesses." As in *Parke, Davis, supra,* the question here is not one of "fact," but consists rather of the legal standard required to be applied to the undisputed facts of the case. See *United States v Singer Mfg. Co.,* 374 U.S. 174, 194, n. 9; *United States v Mississippi Valley Co.,* 364 U.S. 520, 526, and cases there cited.

This reversal of a finding of fact which involves "intent" or "purpose," if anything, seems to do violence to the "unless clearly erroneous" rule.[14] Whether the Supreme Court limits its expansiveness only to anti-trust actions remains to be seen.

Seeing a question of law hidden in an ultimate finding of fact is no mean trick and always subject to varying points of view.[15] How-

---

[14] United States v Board of Education of Greene County, (5 Cir., 1964) 332 F2d 40

[15] United States v Armature Rewinding Co., (8 Cir., 1942) 124 F2d 589

ever, when it appears that the trial court in arriving at its findings labored under a misapprehension of the pertinent law, reversal is made easier.[16]

A unique approach for setting aside a finding based on conflicting evidence for the reason it was believed the trial court did not evaluate its alternatives in the light of proper legal standards is found in *McGowan v United States,* (5 Cir., 1961) 296 F2d 252. In that case the critical fact question was whether or not the taxpayer had included a transportation tax in the amount he charged his customers for riding his excursion vessel. Taxpayer testified that the tax was not included. Government put an agent on the stand who testified that on a prior occasion the taxpayer had told him it was included. With acquiescence of the trial judge on rebuttal it was stipulated that if the taxpayer took the stand he would deny the agent's testimony concerning the prior statement. The Court of Appeals remanded the case for the trial court to make a new finding, believing the trial judge should have insisted taxpayer take the stand and stand cross examination on such critical issue. The Court stated:

> But because the findings carry such weight, we must be certain that in making credibility choices—particularly of the basic kind in which the question revolves around the selection of one or two divergent statements—the trier of fact has evaluated them in the light of proper legal standards. . . . In this approach we are of the view that the finding ought not to stand. In so holding we do not determine that the District Court, as a matter of law, had to conclude one way or the other, that Taxpayer had or had not sustained the economic burden test.

Kind of Evidence Presented May
Relax Court's Application of Rule 52(a)

The federal appellate courts seem to more readily set aside findings as being clearly erroneous where the evidence does not involve "live witnesses" or where the findings are predicated upon opinions of experts. It is for this reason the character of the record on appeal should be carefully considered in deciding whether you have a fair chance to reverse findings of fact on appeal.

---

[16] Fromberg, Inc. v Thornhill (5 Cir., 1963) 315 F2d 407; Davis v Parkhill-Goodloe Co., (5 Cir., 1962) 302 F2d 489

Fact Review in the "Paper Case": Because Rule 52(a) contains the admonishment that "due regard shall be given to the opportunity of the trial court to judge credibility of the witnesses" it was quickly urged that in the case presented upon written documents, or on depositions or on stipulations of fact that the appellate court is free to set aside findings even if they not be found to be clearly erroneous.

On the one hand, we find what has been called the *Frank* view as expressed by Judge Frank in *Orvis v Higgins,* (2 Cir., 1950) 180 F2d 537 at 539:

> (I)f (the trial judge) decides a fact issue on written evidence alone, we are as able as he to determine credibility, and so we may disregard his findings.

On the other hand, we find the view of Judge Clark, who drafted Rule 52(a) to the effect that "clearly erroneous" in Rule 52(a) is the criteria to be applied to all findings of fact irrespective of the nature of the evidence upon which the finding is predicated.

After itself having gone in both directions on the *Frank* view and the *Clark* view of Rule 52(a), the Court of Appeals for the Ninth Circuit in a thorough opinion adopted the *Clark* view as the most sound in *Lundgren v Freeman,* (9 Cir., 1962) 307 F2d 104. In doing so, it believed that the Supreme Court in *C.I.R. v Duberstein,* (1960) 363 U.S. 278 strongly suggested that the *Clark* view was the more appropriate. It also took the position that the *Clark* view of Rule 52(a) would encourage litigants to limit appeals to cases where they were firmly convinced that the trial court had erred on facts rather than upon the idea in a "paper case" they had a hope that the appellate court might second guess the trial court in their favor.

It is only by limiting an appellate court to setting aside those findings which are found to be clearly erroneous can the traditional province of the trial court to find facts be preserved. Ability to see and appraise "live witnesses" is not the only reason for the rule. Litigation upon undisputed facts only arises because the parties with good reason draw different inferences from the same evidence to arrive at different ultimate conclusions. The trial court's experience with the mainsprings of human conduct is just as sound as that of the appellate court and for that reason should be fully respected.[17]

While the *Clark* view of the "paper case" appears the most sound

---

[17] Zenith Radio Corp. v Hazeltine Research, Inc. (1969) 395 U.S. 100, 123

of the two discussed, it just might happen that ultimately an in-between view will be accepted; that is to say, that while the "paper case" will not be free of the "clearly erroneous" rule it will be relaxed or modified to some unspecified extent. This idea was expressed in *Cardelis v Refineria Panama, S.A.,* (5 Cir., 1967) 384 F2d 589. That a "paper case" should be treated with less reverence than a "live witness" case is suggested in the second paragraph of Note 16 to *United States v General Motors,* (1966) 384 U.S. 127 at 141 where the Supreme Court uses the "paper case" record to justify its holding that certain findings of fact were clearly erroneous:

> Moreover, the trial court's customary opportunity to evaluate the demeanor and thus the credibility of the witnesses, which is the rationale behind Rule 52(a) (see *United States v Oregon State Med. Soc.,* 343 U.S. 326, 331–332), plays only a restricted role here. This was essentially a "paper case." It did not unfold by the testimony of "live" witnesses. Of the 38 witnesses who gave testimony, only three appeared in person. The testimony of the other 35 witnesses was submitted either by affidavit, by deposition, or in the form of an agreed-upon narrative of testimony given in the earlier criminal proceeding before another judge. A vast number of documents were also introduced, and bear on the question for decision.
>
> In any event, we resort to the record not to contradict the trial court's findings of fact, as distinguished from its conclusionary "findings," but to supplement the court's factual findings and to assist us in determining whether they support the court's ultimate legal conclusion that there was no conspiracy.

Setting Aside Findings Based on Expert Opinion: Where a critical finding of fact is based upon the opinion of an expert witness who draws his conclusions from undisputed facts as does perhaps the opposing expert with an opposing view your chances for setting aside the trial court's finding as being "clearly erroneous" greatly improve.

In *Hicks v United States,* (4 Cir., 1966) 368 F2d 626, the issue was whether a treating doctor in a Naval Dispensary at Norfolk, Virginia was negligent in his diagnosis which failed to reveal an intestinal obstruction in the deceased patient. Expert witnesses went in both directions although the view of each was based upon the same set of facts as to how the defendant had carried out his ill-fated diagnosis. The District Court found the defendant doctor not to be negligent.

The Court of Appeals for the Fourth Circuit reversed and in doing so stated:

> . . . But we are dealing here with the testimony of expert witnesses who are not in controversy as to the basic facts; thus, the opportunity of the trial court to observe the witnesses is of limited significance. It has often been held that where the trial court's conclusions are based on undisputed facts, they are not entitled to the finality customarily accorded basic factual finding under Rule 52(a). . . .
>
> The question before us is not one of fact in the usual sense, but rather whether the undisputed facts manifest negligence. Although the absence of a factual dispute does not *always* mean that the conclusion is a question of law, it becomes so *here* since the ultimate conclusion to be drawn from the basic facts, i.e., the existence or absence of negligence, is actually a question of law. For this reason the general rule has been that when a judge sitting without a jury makes a determination of negligence, his conclusion, as distinguished from the evidentiary finding leading to it, is freely reviewable on appeal. *Mamiye Bros. v Backe Steamship Lines, Inc.,* 360 F2d 774, 776 (2 Cir., 1966)

It has also been held that where the trial court's finding is based upon an expert's opinion which in turn is shown to be unsound the trial court's finding is no better than the expert's opinion and both will be rejected as being "clearly erroneous."[18] However, a finding as to the qualifications of an expert witness is subject to the "unless clearly erroneous" rule.[19]

Protective Findings Against Reversal
Because Findings Are Clearly Erroneous

Often in cases where factual issues are in keen controversy and a trial court may with some trepidation be required to base its finding on the testimony of one witness rather than another he may have to decide upon the witness's credibility as much by how he appears and acts as by what he says. In this situation a trial court which makes an explicit finding of fact as to the particular witness's credibility will

---

[18] United States v Certain Interest in Property in Cumberland County, (4 Cir., 1961) 296 F2d 264

[19] Lee Shops, Inc. v Schatten-Cypress Company, (6 Cir., 1965) 350 F2d 12

bulwark its finding based on such testimony to a point where an appellate court will almost dare not to find such finding to be clearly erroneous. The respect accorded such credibility findings which in turn protect the crucial finding is seen from time to time in the decisions.[20] By the same token, where a trial court expressly rejects certain testimony as not being credible, it has been held that the appellate court cannot use such rejected testimony as a basis for holding that the finding is clearly erroneous.[21]

"Mechanical" Rules Employed by Appellate Courts in Reviewing Findings of Fact

It is good to keep in mind some of the rules which the appellate courts use to handle the review of findings of fact. We call these the "Mechanical" rules.

Where the trial court's findings of fact are incomplete[22] or irreconcilable[23] the case will be remanded for better findings. Sometimes, when it appears the trial court misunderstood the evidence on a critical point, the case will be remanded to the trial court so it can reconsider a critical finding. This was what was done in *Tug Port of Bandon,* (9 Cir., 1966) 367 F2d 857 where the trial court had found the master of the shipwrecked tug not negligent because the unusual weather arose at noon, within an hour before he shifted his anchorage, while the evidence showed that the unusual weather was apparent at the break of day.

The appellate court looks at the entire record to determine if a finding is clearly erroneous.[24] Findings as to amount of damages[25] as well as the jurisdictional fact of a party's residence[26] or that one

---

[20] Republic of the United States of Brazil v The Markland, (5 Cir., 1961) 290 F2d (Court specifically pinning his finding to oral testimony of critical witness); *Cardali v A/S Glittre,* (2 Cir., 1966) 360 F2d 271 (Court expressly disbelieving certain witness and believing others with his reasons for doing so); *Smith Scow Corp. v Consol. Iron & Metal Co.,* (2 Cir., 1960) 275 F2d 367 (Court labeled testimony of Captain of barge as being unworthy of belief.)

[21] United States for use of Browne & Bryan Lumber Co. v Mass. Bonding and Ins. Co., (2 Cir., 1962) 303 F2d 823; Lizza & Sons, Inc. v D'Onfro, (1 Cir., 1960) 282 F2d 175

[22] Kruger v Purcell (3 Cir., 1962) 300 F2d 830

[23] Freightways, Inc. v Stafford, (8 Cir., 1955) 217 F2d 831

[24] Commercial Nat. Bank of Shreveport v Parsons, (5 Cir., 1944) 145 F2d 191; Tanzer v Huffines, (3 Cir., 1969) 408 F2d 42

[25] Traylor v United States (6 Cir., 1968) 396 F2d 837

[26] Janzen v Goos (8 Cir., 1962) 302 F2d 421

corporation is the *alter ego* of another[27] are subject to Rule 52(a) like any other findings. Even if a finding of fact is found in a conclusion of law it is still subject to Rule 52(a).[28]

When an appellate court gets an appeal wherein the only issue is whether or not a finding of fact is clearly erroneous, it may render a summary decison without calling for oral arguments.[29] Furthermore, merely because one panel of a Court of Appeals might believe that another panel of the same Court was mistaken in holding a finding of fact to be clearly erroneous such situation does not justify a rehearing *en banc*.[30] Where an appellate court remanded a case to a trial court to make proper findings on reducing wrongful death damages to present worth and the trial court raises the total and then reduces it to arrive at its original award, the appellate court on the second appeal will disregard Rule 52(a) and make its own findings.[31]

The trial court in reviewing findings of fact of a master or referee has more latitude in rejecting such findings than the appellate court on appeal.[32]

Pointing out to an appellate court that the trial court waited over five months after trial to make its finding of facts gets you nowhere in attacking the finding as being clearly erroneous.[33]

In a comparative negligence case where contributory negligence of decedent needs to be found and it has not been found, Court of Appeals will remand for the making of the required finding.[34] Where a longshoreman is injured due to two unseaworthy conditions of the ship; one of which the longshoreman was aware of and the other of which he was not, the case will be remanded to reconsider contributory negligence and mitigation of damages.[35] Where the evidence on a critical point is too inconclusive to support a finding rather than reverse a Court of Appeals will sometimes remand for trial court to determine the appropriate finding.[36]

Where on appeal it is claimed that personal injury damage items

---

[27] National Bond Finance Co. v General Motors Corp. (8 Cir., 1965) 341 F2d 1022

[28] Barryhill v United States, (8 Cir., 1962) 300 F2d 690

[29] Williams v Anderson, (5 Cir., 1969) 407 F2d 348

[30] United States v Page, (9 Cir., 1962) 302 F2d 81

[31] Alexander v Nash-Kelvinator Corp. (2 Cir., 1959) 271 F2d 524

[32] In re Novelty Belts Mfg. Co., (SDNY, 1959) 173 F. Supp. 461

[33] Ciccarello v Graham (5 Cir., 1961) 296 F2d 858

[34] Gill v United States, (5 Cir., 1970) 429 F2d 972

[35] Phipps v SS Santa Maria, (5 Cir., 1969) 418 F2d 615

[36] United States v Smith, (5 Cir., 1969) 418 F2d 589

overlapped in that award included damages for plaintiff's loss of physical capacity as well as loss of earning capacity, the Court of Appeals will remand for trial court to: (1) find factors which it considered in awarding damages for lost wages; and (2) factors which it considered and nature of the injury for "loss of physical capacity other than capacity to earn wages."[37]

In a civil rights case a Court of Appeals even undertook to retain jurisdiction of the appeal and at the same time remand the case to the District Court for it to make findings to support its order issuing a temporary injunction in a civil rights case.[38]

Findings of Fact Which Federal Courts Have Found to Be Clearly Erroneous

The rarity with which federal appellate courts have reversed a case because of having found a finding of fact to be clearly erroneous makes it practical to comment on most if not all of these cases. Seeing what has in fact compelled an appellate court to reverse a finding of fact under the rigor of Rule 52(a) is the best standard we know for you to judge whether you have an appeal worth the Herculean task of securing a reversal. It might be of interest that out of the 701 cases annotated in 28 U.S.C.A. Rule 52(a) Note 44, only 85 or 10.7 percent of them found findings to have been clearly erroneous.

In Admiralty Cases

Finding that tug which was overrun and sunk by a tanker was at fault for not having a stern lookout was clearly erroneous. *Ellis Towing & Transportation Co. v Socony Mobil Oil Co.,* (5 Cir., 1961) 292 F2d 91.

Finding that tug was negligent in not inspecting and watching her houseboat-tow was clearly erroneous as houseboat owner had inspected tow just prior to departure and did not report that vents of houseboat which were not in view were open and tug did have deckhand on stern watching the tow while underway. *Hart v Blakermore,* (5 Cir., 1969) 410 F2d 218.

---

[37] Neill v Diamond M. Drilling Co., (5 Cir., 1970) 426 F2d 487
[38] Heard v Lowe, (5 Cir., 1970) 427 F2d 846

Finding that one of two tug masters was not negligent in case where two tugs were to take un-manned barge through bridge with each master claiming the other to be in charge of the operation was clearly erroneous as no meaningful understanding was ever reached by both masters for handling the job. *Shaver Transportation Co. v Alaska Freight Lines*, (9 Cir., 1963) 315 F2d 97.

In a "paper case" a finding that vessel owner was negligent in not countermanding order of master to beach his vessel following collision with other vessel was clearly erroneous as owner upon radio report neither approved nor disapproved the master's action taken *in extremis*. *United States Steel Corp. v Furhrman*, (6 Cir., 1969) 407 F2d 1143.

Finding that stow of sacks of cement in hold of a ship was head high was clearly erroneous where physical dimensions of the sacks demonstrated the stow could not have been more than waist high. *Bordas & Co. et al v Serrano, et al*, (1 Cir., 1963) 314 F2d 291.

Finding that damage to scow which carried breakwater rock was wholly fault of charterer was clearly erroneous as physical facts showed that a fore and aft bulkhead was damaged only on one side which was inconceivable due to dropping rocks under the circumstances. Damages divided between owner and charterer. *Moran Towing Corp. v M. A. Gammino Const. Co.*, (1 Cir., 1969) 309 F2d 917.

Finding that shipowner had made an affirmative representation that his ship had been "completely Butterworthed" in sense of cleaning the upper areas of the tanks was clearly erroneous. *Sicula Oceanica, S.A. v Wilmar Marine Eng. & Sales Corp.*, (5 Cir., 1969) 413 F2d 1332.

Finding that a shipowner's violation of Safety Regulations promulgated by the United States for safety of longshoremen pertaining to an open man-hole in hold of vessel was not proximate cause of accident was clearly erroneous. *Manning v M/V SEA ROAD* (5 Cir., 1969) 417 F2d 603.

Finding that a fire and resulting catastrophy was precipitated because of use of an unapproved flashlight on a tug was clearly erroneous. *Tug RAVEN v Trexler*, (4 Cir., 1969) 419 F2d 536.

Finding a North Atlantic storm not sufficiently severe to constitute a peril of the sea in a cargo case was clearly erroneous. Appellate court found contrary to trial court that ship's master was not exaggerating his testimony taken by deposition. *J. Gerber & Co. v S.S. SABINE HOWALDT*, (2 Cir., 1971) 437 F2d 580.

Finding that a seaman, who struck another seaman with his fists, had such a vicious disposition as to render the ship unseaworthy was clearly erroneous. *Kirsch v United States,* (9 Cir., 1971) 450 F2d 326.

In Anti-Trust—Business—Labor and Patent Cases

Finding in a Millar Act case that a surety company by its conduct did not induce the insured to delay commencement of litigation until after it became time-barred was clearly erroneous. *United States v Reliance Ins. Co.,* (10 Cir., 1971) 436 F2d 1366.

Finding that corporation and its dealers did not combine to monopolize plaster board industry through patents and licensing agreements was clearly erroneous as oral testimony of denial was inconsistent with the various writings. *United States v United States Gypsum Co.,* (1947) 333 U.S. 364.

Finding that General Motors and certain dealers were not conspiring to restrain trade by not selling to "discount houses" was clearly erroneous. *United States v General Motors,* (1966) 384 U.S. 127.

Finding of order given by customer to stock broker to sell securities at a certain price instead of exercising his discretion as to when to sell was clearly erroneous. *James Wood General Trading Establishment v Coe,* (2 Cir., 1961) 297 F2d 651.

Finding that one company had apparent authority to cash checks of another company was clearly erroneous as bank had to rely upon evidence it knew about in order to establish its reliance upon apparent authority. *Bogue v Cocoanut Grove Bank,* (5 Cir., 1959) 269 F2d 1.

Referee's finding in bankruptcy proceeding that Mexican twine exporters knew or should have known they were dealing with bankrupt instead of another corporation was clearly erroneous. *Potucek v Cordeleria Lourdes,* (10 Cir., 1962) 310 F2d 527.

Finding that an accused device did not infringe upon a patented device was clearly erroneous where its final design was substantially identical to the patented device, *P & D Sales & Mfg. Co. v Winter,* (7 Cir., 1964) 334 F2d 830.

Finding that claimant in a bankruptcy proceeding had reasonable cause to believe debtor was insolvent at time he took oral assignment of debtor's bank account was clearly erroneous as based at best upon suspicion. *Moran Bros. Inc. v Yinger*, (10 Cir., 1963) 323 F2d 699.

Finding that unregistered bonds of church were taken by a builder as his fee was clearly erroneous. *Eastside Church of Christ v National Plan, Inc.*, (5 Cir., 1968) 391 F2d 357.

Finding that cooperative member-workers controlled cooperative enterprise was clearly erroneous where evidence showed that former employer of workers was manager of the cooperative which in turn had its offices at employer's place of business, *Fleming v Palmer*, (1 Cir., 1941) 123 F2d 749.

Finding that former local union president's expulsion from union for misconduct was motivated by his circulation of a letter critical of certain union officials was clearly erroneous. *Barbour v Sheet Metal Workers International*, (6 Cir., 1968) 401 F2d 152.

Finding in patent case that defendant had infringed upon a patent which made no mention of prior art was clearly erroneous as the patented device was invalid because invention was obvious to any mechanic of ordinary skill. *Enterprise Ry. Equip. Co. v Keystone Ry., Equip. Co.*, (7 Cir., 1959) 267 F2d 102.

Finding that officer of acquiring corporation had an unswerving intention to gain control of target corporation was clearly erroneous in an appeal from order granting a limited temporary injunction in a tender offer action. *Electronic Specialty Co. v International Control Corp.*, (2 Cir., 1969) 409 F2d 937.

Finding that company acted in good faith and did not know of its contractor's violation of Section 15(a) of Fair Labor Standards Act was clearly erroneous when company knew that an investigation was being made of such violation and did not check contractor's pay records which it had a right to do. *Wirtz v Lone Star Steel Co.*, (5 Cir., 1968) 405 F2d 668.

Finding that difference between a patented device and prior art was not obvious to a person reasonably skilled in the art was clearly erroneous, *Eisele v St. Amour*, (6 Cir., 1970) 423 F2d 135.

Finding that there was reasonable probability that target corporation in attempted take over through a tender offer would prevail on issue which the acquiring corporation did not disclose in its SEC

Schedule 13D was clearly erroneous. *Susquehanna Corp. v Pan American Sulphur Co.,* (5 Cir., 1970) 423 F2d 1075.

Finding that wage differential between female day workers and night male workers was based on factors other than sex was clearly erroneous, *Schultz v American Can Co.—Dixie Products,* (8 Cir., 1970) 424 F2d 356.

Finding that a creditor lacked reasonable cause to believe that the bankrupt was insolvent was clearly erroneous as creditor had knowledge that bankrupt was three months late in his payments to the trade. *Yorke v Thomas Iseri Produce Co.,* (7 Cir., 1969) 418 F2d 811.

In Contract and Insurance Policy Cases

Where pledgee had use and possession of truck a finding in an insurance policy case that truck had been sold to pledgee so as to terminate coverage was clearly erroneous. *Wright v Southern Farm Bureau Casualty Ins. Co.,* (5 Cir., 1960) 279 F2d 363.

Finding that in a telephone conversation between insured and insurer that liability insurance policy was not agreed to be renewed was clearly erroneous. *Epperson v Connecticut Fire Ins. Co.,* (10 Cir., 1963) 314 F2d 486.

Finding that parties to a written agreement had put a "practical" construction upon their writing so as to permit one to sell a competitive product in spite of agreement was clearly erroneous. *Federal Welding Service, Inc. v Dioguardi,* (2 Cir., 1961) 295 F2d 882.

Finding that under franchise agreement franchisor had "good cause" to discharge franchisee because he was an alcoholic was clearly erroneous as franchisor knew of his alcoholism at time agreement was executed. *Kippen v American Automatic Typewriter Co.,* (9 Cir., 1963) 324 F2d 742.

Finding that mortgagee had taken possession of mortgaged property covered by an unrecorded mortgage was clearly erroneous because documents recited possession to be in mortgagor and mortgagor at trial had represented that mortgagee had threatened to take possession. *In Re Power Engineering Co.,* (7 Cir., 1949) 177 F2d 240.

Finding that flight school had breached its contract with Government when it refused to permit Government inspector to use plane to check out flight student was clearly erroneous where it appeared that on prior occasions Government inspector had demonstrated incompetence and recklessness in flying plane. *Daitz Flying Corp. v United States,* (2 Cir., 1948) 167 F2d 369.

Finding in a land purchase that there was no evidence that option price included amount that seller asked for land plus 5% fee was clearly erroneous. Though direct evidence was lacking on point it was proved that the transaction was handled within procedures and orders by Government for other previous like purchases. *United States v Muschamy,* (8 Cir., 1944) 139 F2d 661.

Finding that where a friend takes car of another to his home to repair and rebuild with no intent to charge except for parts, that he was engaged in business and thus beyond insurance coverage was clearly erroneous, *Cherot v U.S. Fidelity & Guaranty Co.,* (10 Cir., 1959) 264 F2d 767.

Finding that no mention was made of sewer and water connections to land prior to execution of lease was clearly erroneous as evidence showed that "septic tanks" had been discussed. *Homelite v Trywilk,* (4 Cir., 1959) 272 F2d 688.

Finding that a subcontract did not continue in existence where there was no evidence that it had been rescinded was clearly erroneous, *S.S. Silberblatt v Seaboard Surety Co.,* (8 Cir., 1969) 417 F2d 1043, 1055.

Findings in a case involving breach of a complicated contract for erection and construction of a debarker that certain pits were required to be constructed under the contract was clearly erroneous, *Sodehamn Mach. Mfg. Co. v Martin Bros. Con. & T. PR. Corp.,* (9 Cir., 1969) 415 F2d 1058.

In action on an insurance policy a finding that one person had orally sold a truck to another for satisfaction of a debt where the other had permissive use of truck but had refused to accept truck for debt was clearly erroneous. *Wright v Southern Bureau Cas. Ins. Co.,* (5 Cir., 1960) 279 F2d 363.

In All Cases As to Damages, Amount or Value

Finding that three defendants deposited industrial solid waste in river of not less than 81½ percent of all in river between certain points was clearly erroneous because it was based upon speculation. *United States v Republic Steel Corp.,* (7 Cir., 1961) 286 F2d 875.

Finding that an accountant's fee of $45,000 for preparing application for and securing war time emergency certificate was clearly erroneous as not more than $15,000 was reasonable. *Hardt v Heller Bros. Co.,* (3 Cir., 1948) 171 F2d 644.

Finding of Commission to determine valuation of property which fixed value the same as a previous appraisement was clearly erroneous as it appeared Commission was more intent upon supporting its prior appraisal than considering the evidence presented to show a higher value. *Rait v Federal Land Bank of St. Paul,* (8 Cir., 1943) 135 F2d 447.

Where District Court relies upon counsel's statement of the evidence presented before a Commission to fix land value its finding is clearly erroneous and it will be set aside and case remanded so Court can exercise its duty of reviewing Commission's report and supporting evidence. *United States v Certain Lands in City of Statesboro,* (5 Cir., 1965) 341 F2d 742.

Finding of damage award in personal injury case to wife in amount of $165,000 and husband in amount of $47,000 was clearly erroneous as not sufficiently explicit as to whether damages were reduced to present worth. *Alexander v Nash-Kelvinator Corp.,* (2 Cir., 1959) 271 F2d 524.

District Court's award of attorney fees to union member who prosecuted representative case for all union members was clearly erroneous as Court failed to evaluate the contributions for successful outcome of litigation as made by others. *Powell v Pennsylvania R.R. Co.,* (3 Cir., 1959) 267 F2d 241.

Finding of personal injury damages in seaman's action which described severe injury but fixed low monetary amount was clearly erroneous. Plaintiff's attorney had prepared descriptive finding while Court inserted money amount. Case remanded for trial Court to revise and change one or the other. *Farley v United States,* (9 Cir., 1958) 1958 AMC 303.

Finding on value of land in an eminent domain action was clearly erroneous where it appeared that the court did not consider the riparian rights value of the land sought to be condemned. *United States v Birnbach,* (8 Cir., 1968) 400 F2d 378.

Finding of damages in a wrongful death case was clearly erroneous where court refused to reduce future earnings to present worth. *Pierce v New York Central Railroad Co.*, (6 Cir., 1969) 409 F2d 1392.

Finding that plaintiff's attorney was entitled to a $39,000 attorney fee in action against insurance company merely because he had a one third contingency agreement was clearly erroneous. *Travelers Ins. Co. v Davis*, (5 Cir., 1969) 411 F2d 244.

In Negligence Cases

Finding that air controller at airport negligently failed to warn one aircraft of presence of more than one other aircraft and had failed to identify which of two aircraft he was referring to was clearly erroneous. *United States v Schultetus*, (5 Cir., 1960) 277 F2d 322.

Finding that automobile accident was caused by faulty brakes of which used car dealer had knowledge was clearly erroneous as based upon discredited testimony. *Miller v East Georgia Motor, Inc.*, (4 Cir., 1962) 303 F2d 488.

Finding that owner of a river dredge was not negligent in leaving important decision of whether to wear a life vest up to a new deckhand who was an inexperienced untrained farm boy was clearly erroneous. *Davis v Parkhill—Goodloe Co.*, (5 Cir., 1962) 302 F2d 489.

Finding that a sub contractor's employee was not negligent in view that the danger was obvious and recognized by the employee was clearly erroneous. *Gowdy v United States*, (6 Cir., 1969) 412 F2d 525.

Finding of causal connection between decedent's contributory negligence and his failure to use a seat belt was clearly erroneous. *Peterson v Klos*, (5 Cir., 1970) 426 F2d 199.

In Tax Cases

Finding that payments made by taxpayer were for alimony and not property settlement on ex-wife was clearly erroneous. *Riddell v Guggenheim*, (9 Cir., 1960) 281 F2d 836.

Finding that periodic payments to ex-wife by taxpayer were in satisfaction of property settlement and not alimony was clearly erroneous. *Taylor v Campbell,* (5 Cir., 1964) 335 F2d 841.

Finding by Tax Court as to percentage of profit from gross food sales was clearly erroneous as based upon speculation. *Angellino v C.I.R.,* (3 Cir., 1962) 302 F2d 797.

Finding that a family partnership existed to cause a tax consequence was clearly erroneous as documents at most showed only an anticipatory assignment of property to children. *United States v Ramos,* (9 Cir., 1968) 393 F2d 618.

Tax Court finding that bank accumulated profits beyond reasonable needs was clearly erroneous. Two 50% stockholders could not agree what to do with the accumulation so nothing was done. *Casey v C.I.R.,* (2 Cir., 1959) 267 F2d 26.

Finding that defendant bootlegger was not indebted to United States at time of transferring land to his wife to avoid collection of alcohol tax was clearly erroneous. *United States v Kaplan,* (2 Cir., 1959) 267 F2d 114.

Finding that taxpayer's holding of land was not in ordinary course of business was clearly erroneous. *United States v Beard,* (9 Cir., 1958) 260 F2d 81.

Finding that corporation paid to widow of deceased employee a sum equal to a nine-month salary was a gift and not income was clearly erroneous. *Simpson v United States,* (7 Cir., 1958) 261 F2d 497.

Finding by Tax Court that work of employee was temporary so as to justify deducting certain expenses was clearly erroneous. *Peurifoy v C.I.R.,* (1958) 358 U.S. 59.

Finding that trust was not organized to carry on business enterprises was clearly erroneous. *Nee v Main Street Bank,* (8 Cir., 1949) 174 F2d 425.

Finding that Government's assessment of additional cabaret taxes had not been established by the greater weight of the evidence was clearly erroneous. *Mladinich v United States,* (5 Cir., 1969) 417 F2d 700.

In Miscellaneous Cases

In habeas corpus proceeding finding that petitioner was no longer mentally ill was clearly erroneous as both doctors conceded illness but differed only as to degree. *Overholser v Russell,* (D.C. Cir., 1960) 283 F2d 195.

Finding that a returning veteran entitled to his former job was entitled to be employed as an apprentice when he had only been a laborer was clearly erroneous. *Special Service Co. v Delaney,* (5 Cir., 1949) 172 F2d 17.

Finding that a City Liquor Commission denied license to a Negro because of its racial prejudice was clearly erroneous. *Lewis v City of Grand Rapids,* (6 Cir., 1966) 356 U.S. 276.

Finding that plaintiff had voted in a Mexican election based only upon his prior admission and which was later repudiated was clearly erroneous. *Gonzalez-Jassu v Romers,* (D.C., Cir., 1959) 264 F2d 584.

In habeas corpus proceeding it was clearly erroneous for not giving time credit to convict during period he reported to parole officer but was not required by law to do so. *United States ex rel Binion v O'Brien,* (3 Cir., 1959) 273 F2d 495.

Finding that manager of War Assets Administration was a silent partner with a purchaser of Government property contrary to law was clearly erroneous as monetary interest was not established by clear and convincing evidence. *Bishop v United States,* (5 Cir., 1959) 266 F2d 657.

Finding that reasonable inquiry had been made by defendant charged with selling an automobile to a bootlegger was clearly erroneous where evidence showed inquiry was made seven months prior to transaction. *United States v One 1955 Model Ford 2-Door Coach,* (5 Cir., 1958) 261 F2d 125.

Finding that employer who drilled wildcat oil well was engaged in producing oil—commerce and subject to Fair Labor Standards Act was clearly erroneous. *Sealy v Mitchell,* (5 Cir., 1957) 249 F2d 327.

Finding on the domiciliary issue for a homestead claim was clearly erroneous, *Johnston v Cordell Nat. Bank,* (10 Cir., 1970) 421 F2d 1310.

Finding that defendant charged with armed robbery received effective aid and assistance from his Legal Aid attorney was clearly erroneous where it appeared the attorney saw his client only briefly before trial, did not endeavor to impeach prosecuting witness with criminal record and had not taken time to prepare his case. *United States ex rel Washington v Maroney,* (3 Cir., 1970) 428 F2d 10.

In housing discrimination case a finding that landlord always told applicants for the renting of apartments about certain requirements before accepting applications was clearly erroneous. *United States v West Peachtree Tenth Corp.,* (5 Cir., 1971) 437 F2d 221.

Pertinent Law Review Articles on Appellate Review of Findings of Fact

"Rule 52(a): Appellate Review of Findings of Fact Based on Documentary or Undisputed Evidence," G. K. T., Jr., *Virginia Law Review,* Vol. 49, p. 506 (1963)

"Federal Rules 52(a) and 60(b)—A Chinese Puzzle," T. Neal Combs, *Southwestern Law Journal,* Vol. 21, p. 339 (1967)

"Reviewing the Evidence on Appeal," Earl Klein, *Los Angeles Bar Bulletin,* Vol. 44, p. 159 (1969)

"Appellate Review of Facts in Louisiana Civil Cases," David W. Robertson, *Louisiana Law Review,* Vol. 21, p. 402 (1961)

"Further Observations on Appellate Review of Facts in Louisiana Civil Cases," Judge Albert Tate, Jr., Court of Appeals, Third Circuit, State of Louisiana, *Louisiana Law Review,* Vol. 22, p. 605 (1962)

The Seventh Amendment— A Constitutional "No-No"

12

As we have seen, the federal appellate courts have reserved for themselves the power to re-examine and set aside court-made findings of fact when deemed to be clearly erroneous. Not so with jury made findings of fact. The bastion of the Seventh Amendment to the United States Constitution forbids any court from tampering with facts as found by a jury. The Seventh Amendment reads:[1]

> . . . the right of trial by jury shall be preserved, and no fact tried by a jury shall be otherwise reexamined in any Court of the United States, than according to the rules of the common law.

In Seventeenth Century the People Feared Losing Right to Jury Trial

The vigilance of the Supreme Court in seeing that lower federal courts scrupulously observe the mandate of the Seventh Amendment is better appreciated by understanding that which prompted its enactment. The original Constitution which came out of the Constitutional

---

[1] Do not be surprised to see the Seventh Amendment as the Ninth of the original Bill of Rights resting under glass in the National Archives, Washington, D.C. as the original Bill contained 12 amendments of which the first two failed to be ratified.

Convention of 1787 was silent on whether the right to trial by jury in civil cases was to be preserved in the proposed federal judicial system. The statesmen who drafted the Constitution were not insensible to the value of preserving a jury trial in civil cases but because of the diversity of practices in the several states at that time it proved too difficult to draft an acceptable provision. Rather than run the risk of not getting any Constitution which could gain ratification this facet of jury trials in civil cases was side stepped.

However, Article III of the proposed Constitution gave the Supreme Court "appellate Jurisdiction, both as to Law and Fact." While it was understood that this broad appellate authority was intended to give review of facts only to equity and admiralty cases and restricted review of common law cases strictly to issues of law the provision was far from reassuring. Many were skeptical that a broader scope of appellate review would develop in the future. If facts could be set aside in common law cases, the right to trial by jury in civil cases could very well be nullified.[2] On top of this, many of those who occupied our shores came from England with fresh memories of how thoroughly unpopular was the English practice of men being required to stand trial without a jury in the admiralty courts.[3]

Thus, it was not surprising that when the first session of Congress in 1789 proposed the Bill of Rights amendments to the Constitution, that there was included the Seventh Amendment. Likewise, it is not surprising that the required States ratified the Bill of Rights containing the Seventh Amendment in 1791.

In What Cases Is the Right to Trial by Jury Preserved?

In appraising the facts in order to best select your client's remedy, a determination of whether your client is better off with or without a jury is inescapable. If the case appears "thin" on the facts, you might do well to look ahead and decide if you later might need Seventh Amendment protection from an appellate court reexamining the facts should your client be fortunate enough to win on the facts in the court below. It is for this reason it becomes relevant to consider to what kind of cases the Seventh Amendment attaches.

---

[2] Storey, Commentaries on the Constitution of the United States, Vol. 2, p. 540, ##1763–1769.

[3] Reid v Covert, (1957) 354 U.S. 1, 29

The problem of identifying jury issues is not always easy. The Federal Rules of Civil Procedure which allow informal pleading, commingling of law and equity, claims and cross claims and joinder or impleading of many parties does not make the task any easier. But the task must be done as Congress, in authorizing the Supreme Court to promulgate these rules, provided that they should not abridge, enlarge or modify substantive rights and particularly the right to jury trial as guaranteed by the Seventh Amendment.[4]

Whether your client shall sue at law or in equity ceases to remain academic as soon as one party demands trial by jury. A good illustration of how perplexing the segregation of jury issues can become is found in the five-to-three decision of the Supreme Court in *Beacon Theatres v Westover*, (1959) 359 U.S. 500. In that case when a Beacon Theatre threatened a Fox Theatre with a treble damage action because Fox's exclusive-right contract for first run motion pictures violated the anti-trust laws, Fox beat Beacon to the first punch by filing in a District Court a complaint seeking a declaratory judgment declaring its contract not to be in violation of anti-trust laws and an injunction to forbid Beacon from threatening or filing a treble damage anti-trust action. Thereupon, Beacon came in with the second punch—a counterclaim for treble damages because Fox's contract violated anti-trust laws and because Fox was conspiring with its distributor to monopolize first run pictures to Beacon's damage.

The complication developed when Beacon demanded trial by jury. The District Court was of the view that the issues in Fox's complaint including the question of competition between the two theatres were equitable and so it ordered those issues to be tried first to the Court and thereafter the issues of Beacon's counterclaim to the jury. At this juncture Beacon saw the handwriting on the wall. Its treble damage action was becoming fragmented with part of the fact issues to be decided by the Court and part by the jury. Beacon had to use a remedy of last resort. It petitioned the Court of Appeals for the Ninth Circuit for a writ of mandamus to compel the District Court to give it the full jury trial to which it was entitled. The Court of Appeals denied the writ. On certiorari to the Supreme Court the writ of mandamus was granted.

Mr. Justice Black, speaking for the Court, stated that certiorari was granted because:

---

[4] 28 USC #2072

> Maintenance of the jury as a fact-finding body is of such importance and occupies so firm a place in our history and jurisprudence that any seeming curtailment of the right to a jury trial should be scrutinized with the utmost care.

The Court then held that Beacon had a right to try all fact issues of its treble damage action to a jury and that its right could not be taken away merely because Fox took advantage of the availability of declaratory relief to sue Beacon first. Furthermore, the Court held that while the District Court under Rule 42(b) FRCP had discretion to separate trials and segregate issues it could not use such discretion to deprive Beacon of a full jury trial on its counterclaim.

Three years later the Supreme Court again spoke of how equity practice and principles were not to be allowed to frustrate a person's right to trial by jury as guaranteed by the Seventh Amendment. In *Dairy Queen, Inc. v Wood, District Judge,* (1962) 369 U.S. 469, the owner of a trademark commingled equitable and legal relief for breach of a contract. The Court held that a prayer for money unquestionably marks the claim as one at law for which defendant is entitled to a trial by jury. The jury trial cannot be circumvented by couching the money demand in allegations paying for an accounting or contending that the money relief sought is but incidental to the equitable relief sought. Where a shareholder brings a derivative suit against directors of a corporation for gross abuse of trust, he is entitled to trial by jury on the same issues the corporation would be entitled to if it were suing, *Ross v Bernhard,* (1970) 396 U.S. 531.

Strictly construed, the Seventh Amendment only preserves right to trial by jury in those cases where the common law of England as it existed in 1791 gave right to trial by jury. In those days neither equitable nor admiralty cases carried a right to trial by jury. So it appears that the Seventh Amendment can be circumvented by either suing in a court of equity or admiralty or showing that the case at law is of modern statutory origin and not known of in 1791. Therefore, it is not wholly correct to assert that an action seeking money is always one at law in which a party has a right to trial by jury. This is seen in recent Supreme Court decisions.

When an employee is entitled to severance pay by reason of a labor agreement which provides that all disputes be arbitrated, he cannot sue his employer in court for the severance pay without first arbitrating.[5] The same is true where the employee is entitled to extra

---

[5] Republic Steel v Maddox (1964) 379 U.S. 650

pay by reason of a labor agreement of which the National Railroad Adjustment Board has exclusive primary jurisdiction over the matter.[6]

Nor does the Seventh Amendment command a jury trial in an action where the Secretary of Labor sues to restrain an employer from violating the Labor Fair Standards Act and in connection therewith seeks an order requiring the employer to reimburse employees with back pay who were found to have been unlawfully discharged.[7] Nor, does the Seventh Amendment have any application of its own force to any case where one sues the United States for a money judgment.[8]

A word about admiralty. It is only when the District Court is sitting in admiralty that a jury trial cannot be demanded. When an action involving any maritime matter is brought *in personam,* i.e. against the owner of a vessel and not *in rem* against the vessel and on the law side of the District Court, any party is entitled to a jury trial upon a timely demand. Furthermore, any reexamination of the facts as found by the jury is forbidden by the Seventh Amendment.[9] Likewise, when the admiralty claim for maintenance and cure is joined with a Jones Act claim for personal injury on the law side of the Court, both claims must go to the jury.[10]

Other types of cases to which trial by jury is not preserved by the Seventh Amendment include: (1) An action for the condemnation of land.[11] (2) Where a bankruptcy court summarily adjudicates a creditor's preference.[12] (3) An action under the Federal Tort Claim Act.[13] (4) Probably an original action in the Supreme Court between a State and the United States.[14] (5) In a proceeding involving criminal contempt.[15] (6) In an unfair employment practice case (42 USC #2000e)[16] (7) A stockholder's derivative action until *Ross v Bernhard,* (1970) 396 U.S. 531.[17] (8) Or a Miller Act action based upon equitable rights.[18]

---

[6] Pennsylvania R. Co. v Day, (1959) 360 U.S. 548

[7] Mitchell v De Mario Jewelry Co., (1960) 361 U.S. 288, 296

[8] Galloway v United States, (1942) 319 U.S. 372, 388

[9] Atlantic & Gulf Stevedores v Ellerman Lines, (1962) 369 U.S. 355

[10] Fitzgerald v United States Lines, (1963) 374 U.S. 16, 20

[11] United States v Reynolds, (1970) 397 U.S. 14, 18

[12] Katchen v Landy, (1965) 382 U.S. 323, 336

[13] United States v Yellow Cab Co., (1951) 340 U.S. 543

[14] United States v Louisiana (1950) 339 U.S. 699

[15] United States v Barnett, (1964) 376 U.S. 681, 725

[16] Culpepper v Reynolds Metals Co., (Ga., 1969) 296 F. Supp. 1232

[17] Ross v Bernhard (2 Cir., 1968) 403 F2d 909

[18] Great American Insurance Co. v United States, (Ct. Cl., 1968) 397 F2d 289

"Any Court of the United States" Means Just That

The Seventh Amendment is aimed only at federal courts—the District Court, the United States Court of Appeal and the Supreme Court of the United States. The prohibition against reexamining facts goes to federal courts, not federal juries. Consequently, when a case tried in a state court with a state jury comes to the Supreme Court of the United States on appeal from the highest court of the state, the Supreme Court of the United States is forbidden to reexamine the facts found by the state court jury even though the highest court of the state might be free to do so.[19] Furthermore, the command of the Seventh Amendment is not made applicable to state courts through the due process clause of the Fourteenth Amendment.[20]

We know that in *Erie R. Co. v Tomkins,* (1938) 304 U.S. 64, the Supreme Court reversed a trend by holding that henceforth in all cases in the District Courts, whose jurisdiction is founded upon diversity of citizenship that the federal courts will embrace as much as possible state substantive law so that as far as legal principles are involved, the result will be reached in the District Court the same as it would be reached in the state court. This shift in judicial policy did not disturb the Seventh Amendment.

In *Byrd v Blue Ridge Cooperative,* (1957) 356 U.S. 525, 537 a personal injured plaintiff sued in the District Court gaining jurisdiction by reason of diversity of citizenship. The defendant raised the affirmative defense that he was immune from the action by reason of plaintiff being his employee within the meaning of the Louisiana Workmen's Compensation Act. Under Louisiana's law, the fact of employment was to be decided by the court and not jury. The trial court denied the affirmative defense after listening to defendant's evidence and not that of plaintiff. The Court of Appeals for the Fifth Circuit reversed. The Supreme Court affirmed the reversal and in so doing held that in spite of policy laid down in *Erie v Tompkins,* supra, there was no compelling reason to deny right of defendant to have the fact of employment decided by the jury. It assumed without deciding that the Seventh Amendment compelled trial by jury.

However, in *Bernhardt v Polygraphic Co.* (1956) 350 U.S. 198

---

[19] Chicago & Burlington & Quincy R. Co. v Chicago, (1897) 166 U.S. 226; Dillingham v Hawk, (5 Cir., 1894) 60 F 494

[20] Fay v New York, (1947) 332 U.S. 261

the Supreme Court embraced state law to give plaintiff right to trial by jury. In that case plaintiff sued his employer in a Vermont District Court for past wages and demanded jury. Jurisdiction was based on diversity of citizenship. Action was based upon an employment contract which required arbitration under New York law. Defendant pleaded failure to arbitrate as bar. Under Vermont law, unlike New York law, agreements to arbitrate were unenforceable until arbitration became final. Supreme Court held that in Vermont plaintiff could avoid arbitration and go to trial before a jury.

". . . According to the Rules of the Common Law" Means the Law of England in 1791

The Supreme Court has held that the federal courts cannot reexamine fact found by a jury except to the limited extent permitted by the common law of England as it existed in 1791. It was not to be measured by common law as it may have existed in one of the states.[21] Nor may the principle that common law may be adopted to meet new and varying conditions modify the prohibition of the Seventh Amendment.[22] So what do we have?

New Trial: In 1791 the common law of England permitted the court to reexamine a verdict by granting a new trial if the court was of the view that the weight of the evidence was against the verdict as returned.[23] If the trial court granted a new trial because the verdict was considered excessive, such could not be assigned as error on appeal.[24] Of course, only the trial court can set aside the verdict and grant a new trial. A Court of Appeals can review the granting or denial of a new trial but it cannot direct a verdict unless a proper foundation is laid in the trial court.[25] Where action of trial court in granting or denying a new trial is reviewed on appeal, it is reviewed as a question of law as to whether trial court abused its discretion.[26]

---

[21] American Refrigerator Transit Co. v Hall, (1899) 174 U.S. 70; Glazer v Glazer, (La., 1968) 278 F. Supp. 476

[22] Dimick v Schiedt, (1935) 293, U.S. 474

[23] Parsons v Bedford, (1830) 28 U.S. 433; Marsh v Illinois Central RR Co., (Miss., 1949) 175 F2d 498

[24] Atlantic Greyhound Corp. v Lyon, (Va., 1939) 107 F2d 157

[25] Young v Central R. Co., (1914) 232 U.S. 602

[26] Whiteman v Pitrie, (5 Cir., 1955) 220 F2d 914

Directed Verdict: The only other way in which the trial court under the English common law could disturb a jury verdict was for it to direct a verdict before submitting the case to the jury or granting a judgment notwithstanding the verdict afterwards. This could only be done where there was not sufficient evidence to support the verdict.[27] The power to grant a directed verdict is indeed very narrow. Only if the court finds that all reasonable men must find the evidence to be insufficient can it direct a verdict.[28]

Where after verdict a plaintiff moves for a new trial, but not a directed verdict, the Court of Appeals has power to reverse the lower court's denial of motion for a new trial, but it cannot on its own direct a verdict to the plaintiff.[29] Likewise, should the defendant in the trial court move for a directed verdict and not follow it up with a motion for judgment notwithstanding the verdict, the Court of Appeals under Rule 50(b) FRCP cannot enter a judgment n.o.v.[30]

Practices Within Ambit of the Seventh Amendment

What the Supreme Court finds to have been the practice of the English common law in 1791 determines what jury trial practices are permitted within the proscription of the Seventh Amendment. Prior to 1970 it was understood that the Seventh Amendment required a twelve man jury. Since the Supreme Court in *Williams v Florida,* (1970) 399 U.S. 78 found that it was only a historical accident that twelve men were selected for a jury in old England, a jury today of a lesser number than twelve is constitutionally permissible. However, whatever the number of persons comprising the jury, any verdict returned must be unanimous.[31] The Seventh Amendment only affects federal courts. Thus, even if a case based upon federal law is tried in a state court, it is the law of the state that controls both the size of the jury and the number required to return a verdict.[32]

---

[27] Galloway v United States, (1943) 319 U.S. 372; Helene Curtis v Pruitt, (5 Cir., 1958) 385 F2d 841

[28] Peterson v Exum, (9 Cir., 1960) 283 F2d 499

[29] Aetna Insurance Co. v Kennedy, (1937) 301 U.S. 389; Indemnity Ins. Co. of N. A. v Levering, (9 Cir., 1932) 59 F2d 719

[30] Johnson v N.Y.N.H.R. Co., (1952) 344 U.S. 48, 51

[31] Andres v United States, (1948) 333 U.S. 740, 748; Maxwell v Dow, (1900) 176 U.S. 581

[32] Chicago R. Co. v Ward, (1920) 252 U.S. 18

Inasmuch as English common law courts in 1791 were permitted to comment upon the evidence when charging the jury the District Court can likewise do so without colliding with the Seventh Amendment.[33] Likewise, the idea of remittitur was no novelty in old England, so a District Court may condition denial of defendant's motion for a new trial conditioned upon plaintiff remitting a part of the jury verdict which the court regarded to be excessive.[34] *Arkansas Valley Land Co. v Mann,* (1889) 130 U.S. 72.

Because the Seventh Amendment concerns itself with substance rather than form, it does not forbid special interrogatories to be submitted to the jury.[35] However, what the Seventh Amendment does not regard as a formality is the court rejecting as the verdict the special interrogatories which the court considers inconsistent if they can in any way be found consistent with the evidence.[36] An appellate court should give weight to the trial court's view of the sufficiency of evidence where it has denied motions for new trial or judgment n.o.v.[37]

When remanding a case, an appellate court may either grant a new trial or limit the issues to be tried in the next trial without violating the Seventh Amendment.[38]

The granting of a summary judgment on basis of there being no genuine issue of fact does not deprive a person of right to trial by jury as there is no fact issue for a jury.[39]

Trial Court Review of the
Excessive Verdict or Inadequate Award

It has become well established that the trial judge sitting in the District Court may on motion for new trial grant a new trial if he regards the verdict excessive. In fact, from the very early days the District Courts assumed they had such power and could exercise it without offending the command of the Seventh Amendment. Further-

---

[33] Quercia v United States, (1933) 289 U.S. 466, 469

[34] Arkansas Valley Land Co. v Mann, (1889) 130 U.S. 72

[35] Walker v New Mexico and Southern Pacific R. Co., (1897) 165 U.S. 598

[36] Gutierrez v Waterman S. S. Corp., (1963) 373 U.S. 206; Machado v States Marine-Isthmian Agency, Inc., (5 Cir., 1969) 411 F2d 584

[37] Cone v West Virginia Pulp & Paper Co., (1947) 330 U.S. 212

[38] Gasoline Products Co. v Champlin Refining Co., (1930) 282 U.S. 824; Thompson v Camp, (6 Cir., 1948) 167 F2d 733

[39] United States v Stangland, (7 Cir., 1957) 242 F2d 841

more, when Mr. Justice Storey, sitting on circuit as a trial judge, authorized a remittitur in *Blunt v Little,* (1822) Fed. Case No. 1, 578, 3 Mason 102, the District Courts were quick to include remittitur in their bag of judicial tools. A remittitur is simply an order of the District Court telling the plaintiff to agree to entry of judgment for a specified sum less than the amount of the verdict or that a new trial will be granted. This power of the District Court grew like Topsy and today the Supreme Court has no objection to this power.

What standard does the trial court use in determining whether or not a jury award in a personal injury case is excessive? The standard in the Court of Appeals for the Fifth Circuit is that the trial court's judgment should be based upon the maximum amount it believes the jury could award without being excessive; not what the trial court would have awarded and not the minimum amount it believes the jury could give within the zone of reasonableness. *Gorsalitz v Olin Mathiesen Chemical Corp.,* (5 Cir., 1970) 429 F2d 1033.

As to the matter of a District Court awarding a new trial in the case of a grossly inadequate jury award, this practice was also approved in the case of *Dimick v Schiedt,* (1935) 293 U.S. 474. In that case, however, the Supreme Court emphatically struck down the power of any federal court to order an additur as a condition to not granting the plaintiff a new trial because of a grossly inadequate award. An additur is the reverse of a remittitur. It is an order to the defendant that the District Court will grant a new trial to the plaintiff unless the defendant agrees to the entry of a judgment against him in a specified amount higher than the inadequate award in the verdict. In the *Dimick* case the jury awarded the plaintiff, who was injured in an automobile collision, $500. The District Court regarded the amount inadequate and ordered defendant to pay $1,500 or be required to retry the case. The defendant paid the $1,500 and then appealed to the Court of Appeals which reversed the District Court because it found additur to be repugnant to the Seventh Amendment. The Supreme Court agreed with the Court of Appeals. It had the following to say about "additur" (p. 485):

> . . . the power to conditionally increase the verdict of a jury does not follow as a necessary corollary from the power to conditionally decrease it. As the court below correctly pointed out, in the case of a conditional remittitur "a jury has already

awarded a sum in excess of that fixed by the court as the basis for the remittitur, which at least finds some support in the early English practice; while in the second case, no jury has ever passed on the increased amount, and the practice has no precedent according to the rules of the common law."

The right of trial by jury is of ancient origin, characterized by Blackstone as "the glory of the English law" and "the most transcended privilege which any subject can enjoy" (BK. 3 p. 379).

To so hold is obviously to compel the plaintiff to forego his constitutional right to the verdict of a jury and accept an assessment partly made by a jury which has acted improperly, and partly by a tribunal which has no power to act.

Appellate Court Review of the
Excessive Verdict or Inadequate Award

There has long been controversy over the power of the Court of Appeals to review decisions of the trial court on motions for a new trial based on the excessiveness of a jury award. As yet the Supreme Court has not met the question.[40]

In the meantime, the Court of Appeals in the various Circuits have been going in both directions at various times.[40] At one time the notion prevailed that a Court of Appeals should not undertake to "second guess" a District Court's estimation of excessiveness.[41] Later, and perhaps with one eye on the Seventh Amendment, the Court of Appeals took the view that when a jury award is so high as to shock the judicial conscience, the review of a trial judge's denial of motion for new trial transformed itself from one of fact to one of law.[42] Now it seems that Court of Appeals in all Circuits have assumed the power to review excessive verdicts and grant remittiturs in appropriate cases.[43]

In one of the most thoroughly considered decisions of all times the Court of Appeals for the Second Circuit, in opinion by Circuit

---

[40] Dagnello v Long Island Railroad Co., (2 Cir., 1961) 289 F2d 797 at 800

[41] Fairmount Glass Works v Cub Fork Coal Co., (1933) 287 U.S. 474; Stevenson v Hearst Consolidated Publications, (2 Cir., 1954) 214 F2d 902 and other Second Circuit decisions reported in the Dagnello case, 289 F2d 797 at 805

[42] Sunray Oil Corp. v Allbritton, (5 Cir., 1951) 188 F2d 751

[43] Footnote in Grunenthal v Long Island Railroad, (1968) 393 U.S. 156 at 157

Judge Medina, ruled precisely on this power question in *Dagnello v Long Island Railroad Co.*, (1961) 289 F2d 797. In that case a jury awarded a railroad worker $130,000 for an amputated left leg. The District Court denied motion for new trial based upon contention that $97,000 included in the award for pain and suffering was excessive. The Court of Appeals considered its power to review the District Court's denial of motion for new trial and to grant remittitur and then affirmed the District Court on its denial of motion for new trial. In doing so it held:

> ... it is our view and we hold there is no constitutional obstacle to the exercise by a federal Court of Appeals of the power to review the exercise of discretion by the trial judge in refusing to set aside a verdict for excessiveness, and to resort to remittitur in proper cases, because: (1) if, as concededly is the case, a trial judge may set aside a verdict for excessiveness, or direct remittitur, even though he did not have the power to do so at common law, without infringing the Seventh Amendment, it should follow that an abuse of discretion in failing to take such action can be reviewed on appeal without doing violence to the Amendment; (2) there is English precedent prior to 1791 for appellate review of the amount of the verdict, in respect of excessiveness; and (3) adopting the views of Stone, Hughes, Brandeis and Cardozo, the exercise of this appellate power of review will "preserve the essentials of the jury trial as it was known to the common law before the adoption of the Constitution," and will not "curtail the function of the jury to decide questions of fact as it did before the adoption of the Amendment."

As to the standard for the Court of Appeals to measure excessiveness the Court ruled that as appellate judges they should decide from the evidence whether the amount is so high that it would be a "denial of justice"[44] to permit it to stand; not whether they would have set the verdict aside if they were sitting as a trial judge. Every benefit of doubt should be given to the judgment of the trial judge. However, there is an upper limit to a money award and when that is reached, ruled the Court, the abuse of the trial judges' discretion becomes a question of law.

Observe that the power of review in the Court of Appeals exists only when the excess is a "whopper"—so much as to amount

---

[44] What the Second Circuit did was apply a common adjective of "denial of justice" in lieu of the several such as "grossly excessive" or "inordinate" or "shocking to the judicial conscience" or "outrageously excessive," etc.

to a denial of justice. On the other hand, the District Court's standard is more practical—excess when amount of verdict is against the weight of the evidence. This is as it should be because the trial judge always has the "feel" of the case which a Court of Appeals can never acquire.

Because of *Dagnello* the Supreme Court granted certiorari and decided *Grunenthal v Long Island Railroad,* (1968) 393 U.S. 156. In that case a jury had awarded $305,000 to a railroad worker who sustained a severe foot injury. The District Court denied motion for new trial as made by defendant on contention that the verdict was excessive. The Court of Appeals for the Second Circuit, acting upon its *Dagnello* decision granted defendant a new trial and ordered plaintiff to remit all but $105,000. The Supreme Court dodged. It held that irrespective of what issues the litigants might raise, it would follow its traditional practice of not ruling upon Constitutional issues if the case can be otherwise decided. This is exactly what the Supreme Court did in the comparable case of *Neese, Admx. v Southern R. Co.,* (1955) 350 U.S. 77 prior to *Dagnello.* Having avoided approving or disapproving *Dagnello,* the Supreme Court then proceeded to examine the evidence of damages for itself and determined that the District Court was right in not granting a new trial and that the Court of Appeals was wrong. In fact, the Supreme Court chided the Court of Appeals for not making as thorough an analysis of the facts as did the District Court.

What about the inadequate verdict and "additur"? Since the Seventh Amendment applies to all federal courts, it seems that the Supreme Court, in striking down "additur" in *Dimick v Schiedt,* (1935) 293 U.S. 474, has put additur in its grave. In that case, however, the Supreme Court seemed not to object to the District Court granting a new trial without additur.

One could rationalize that the Supreme Court would sanction at least the granting of a new trial without additur in the Court of Appeals except for its holding in *Fairmount Glass Works v Coal Co.,* (1933) 287 U.S. 474. In that case, where a jury returned only nominal damages of $1.00 and the District Court refused to grant a new trial, the Court of Appeals reversed. However, the Supreme Court reversed the Court of Appeals, telling it that it should not review a trial court's denial of a new trial because of an inadequate award. But it muddied the waters more than ever by also stating it was not ruling upon the Court of Appeals' power but rather its practices.

When the Supreme Court is required to address itself to the power question it will be required to deny "additur" to the Court of Appeals unless it reverses itself in *Dimick v Schiedt,* supra. As to power of the Court of Appeals to grant a new trial without additur, the Supreme Court kept its options open in *Fairmount Glass Works v Coal Co.,* supra and could recognize such power without difficulty. The dissent in *Dimick v Schiedt,* supra of Mr. Justice Stone, concurred in by Chief Justice Hughes, Mr. Justice Brandeis and Mr. Justice Cardozo on intent of the Seventh Amendment greatly impressed the Court of Appeals for the Second Circuit in *Dagnello,* supra. It could well be that in time the Supreme Court will find a way to recognize that the Court of Appeals has the same power in respect to the inadequate award as it appears to have with respect to the excessive award.

How the Supreme Court Has Enforced the Seventh Amendment

The moment that one raises on appeal to the Supreme Court that a court below has reexamined facts contrary to the admonishment of the Seventh Amendment, there is of necessity raised the burdensome task of reviewing the pertinent evidence to see if this is so.

The late Mr. Justice Black expressed the view in *Curtis Publishing Co. v Butts,* (1966) 388 U.S. 130 at 171, that every time the Court reviewed a writing to determine if it was libelous at the Constitutional level, it was in flat violation of the Seventh Amendment. Mr. Justice Black warned:

> It strikes me that the Court is getting itself in the same quagmire in the field of libel in which it is now struggling in the field of obscenity.

The contention of a Seventh Amendment violation also brings into issue a delicate balance of judgment upon facts. Is the evidence insufficient for jury consideration so that a court does not violate the Seventh Amendment? It is not surprising that as litigants climb the judicial ladder that each court has a different appraisal of the facts. What the mythical "reasonable person" might conclude is indeed a fine question of fact and not law. To further complicate the problem some believe the Supreme Court is applying the "scintilla" rule to FELA and Jones Act cases while the "substantial evidence" rule to other kinds of cases. However, the Supreme Court has never expressed itself on this point. See: *Boeing Company v Shipman,* (5 Cir., 1968) 389 F2d 507.

For these various reasons we merely list Supreme Court decisions ruling upon whether a court violated the Seventh Amendment, some of them being summary reversals. Also, we list denials of petitions for writ of certiorari where justices have dissented in the denials because of a Seventh Amendment question.

Cases Reversed by Supreme Court Because
Lower Court Reexamined Verdicts

Adickes v Kress & Co., (1970) 398 U.S. 144, 176. (Existence of conspiracy is a fact question for jury. Summary judgment in civil rights action under 42 U.S.C. #1983 reversed).

International Co. v Nederl Amerik, (1968) 393 U.S. 74 (stevedore negligence in an indemnity action).

Atlantic and Gulf Stevedores v Ellerman Lines, (1962) 369 U.S. 355 (stevedore's performance of workmanlike service)

Continental Ore Co. v Union Carbide, (1962) 370 U.S. 690 (cause of damage in anti-trust case)

Dick v New York Life Insurance Co., (1959) 359 U.S. 437 (cause of death—life insurance policy)

Dice v Akron C & Y R Co., (1952) 342 U.S. 359 (unfairness in taking release of claim in FELA case)

Harris v Pennsylvania R. Co., (1959) 361 U.S. 15 reversing the Supreme Court of Ohio in 156 NE2d 822 (a FELA case)

Schultz v Pennsylvania R. Co., (1956) 350 U.S. 523 (a wrongful death Jones Act case)

Stone v New York Central & St. L. R. Co., (1953) 344 U.S. 407 (FELA case)

Carter v Atlantic & St. A. B. R. Co., (1949) 338 U.S. 430 (FELA case)

Wilkenson v McCarthy, (1949) 336 U.S. 53 (FELA case)

Anderson v Atchison T & S. F. R. Co., (1948) 333 U.S. 821 (FELA case)

Lillie v Thompson, (1947) 332 U.S. 459 (FELA case)

Myers v Reading Co., (1947) 331 U.S. 477 (FELA case)

Ellis v Union Pacific Railroad Co., (1947) 329 U.S. 649 (FELA case)

Jesionowski v Boston & M. R. Co., (1947) 329 U.S. 452 (wrongful death FELA case)

Lavender v Kurn, (1946) 327 U.S. 645 (wrongful death FELA case)

Keeton v Thompson, (1945) 326 U.S. 689 reversing the Arkansas Supreme Court in 183 SW2d 505 (wrongful death FELA case)

Blair v Baltimore & O. R. Co., (1945) 323 U.S. 600 (FELA case)

Tiller v Atlantic Coast Line R. Co., (1945) 323 U.S. 574 (FELA case)

Tennant v Peoria & P. U. R. Co., (1944) 321 U.S. 29 (FELA case)

Bailey v Central Vt. R. Co., (1943) 319 U.S. 350 (FELA case)

Tiller v Atlantic Coast Line R. Co., (1943) 318 U.S. 54 (FELA) case)

Seago v New York Central R. Co., (1942) 315 U.S. 781, reversing the Missouri Supreme Court in 155 SW2d 126 (FELA case)

Jenkins v Kurn, (1941) 313 U.S. 256 (FELA case)

Johnson v Union Pacific Railroad Co., (1957) 352 U.S. 957 summarily reversing the Court of Appeals for Ninth Circuit in 233 F2d 427 (a negligence case involving the supply of electricity)

Gibson v Phillips Petroleum Corp., (1956) 352 U.S. 874 summarily reversing the Court of Appeals for the Fifth Circuit in 232 F2d 13 (negligence case—welding on gasoline drum)

Union Trust Co. v Eastern Air Lines, Inc., (1955) 350 U.S. 907 summarily reversing Court of Appeals for the District of Columbia in 221 F2d 62 (negligence case—following orders of air controller)

Swafford v Atlantic Coast Line RR Co., (1955) 350 U.S. 807 summarily reversing the Court of Appeals for the Fifth Circuit in 220 F2d 901 (negligence case—railroad crossing collision)

Williams v Carolina Life Insurance Co., (1954) 348 U.S. 802 summarily reversing the Court of Appeals for the Fifth Circuit in 210 F2d 477 (death in life insurance policy case)

Denial of Certiorari with Dissent
Because of Seventh Amendment

Warner v Kewahee Machinery & Conveyor Co., (1970) 398 U.S. 906 to Court of Appeals for the Sixth Circuit in 411 F2d 1060. (Farm boy injured in a conveyor belt)

Detenber, Admx. v American Universal Ins. Co., (1967) 389 U.S. 987 to Court of Appeals for the Sixth Circuit in 372 F2d 50 (bad faith defense—action for excess of insurance policy)

Southern Railway Co. v Jackson, (1963) 375 U.S. 837 to Court of Appeals for the Fifth Circuit.

North Carolina Natural Gas Corp. v McJunkin Corp., (1962) 371 U.S. 830 to Court of Appeals for Fourth Circuit in 300 F2d 794 (case involved implied in fact covenant to written purchase order)

Gunderson Bros. Engineering Corp. v Merritt Chapman and Scott Corp., (1962) 371 U.S. 935 to Court of Appeals for Ninth Circuit in 305 F2d 659 (Implied in fact acceptance of written offer)

Pierce Ford Sales, Inc. v Ford Motor Co., (1962) 371 U.S. 829 to Court of Appeals for Second Circuit in 299 F2d 425 (action for intentional interference in another's business negotiations)

Mathiasen Tanker Industries, Inc. v Mason, (1962) 371 U.S. 828 to Court of Appeals for the Fourth Circuit in 298 F2d 28 (Jones Act case)

Du Bois v Mossey, (1952) 344 U.S. 869. Facts in 195 F2d 56

Cases Where Supreme Court Found
No Seventh Amendment Violation

Moore v Chesapeake & O. R. Co., (1951) 340 U.S. 573

Eckenrode v Pennsylvania R. Co., (1948) 335 U.S. 329

Brady v Southern R. Co., (1943) 320 U.S. 476

**Pertinent Law Review Articles
on the Seventh Amendment**

"From *Beacon Theatre* to *Dairy Queen* to *Ross:* The Seventh Amendment, the Federal Rules, and a Receding Law-Equity Dichotomy," John G. Gibbons, *Journal of Urban Law,* Vol. 48, p. 459 (1971)

"The Background of the Seventh Amendment," Edith Guild Henderson, *Harvard Law Review,* Vol. 80, p. 289 (1966)

"Right to Jury Trial in a Stockholders Derivation Action," *Southwestern Law Journal,* Vol. 24, p. 860 (1970)

"Remedies for Excessiveness or Inadequacy of Verdicts: Remittitur and Additur," Fleming James, Jr., *Duquesne Law Review,* Vol. 1, p. 143 (1963)

"Remittitur of Jury Verdicts in Iowa," *Iowa Law Review,* Vol. 48, p. 649 (1963)

"Remittitur and Additur in Personal Injury and Wrongful Death Cases," Francis X. Busch, *Defense Law Journal,* Vol. 12, p. 521 (1963)

"Inadequate Damages in P. I. Actions: Trends in Appellate Decisions," Owen T. Palmer, Jr., *Cleveland-Marshal Law Review,* Vol. 17, p. 413 (1968)

Index

A

Abandonment of property, 40
Aberdeen and Rockfish Co. v United States, 162
Abuse of discretion, 164
Accidents, unusual, 89
Account, 23
Account stated, 23
Accounting, 23
Additur, 208–209, 211, 212
Admiralty cases, 143, 187–189, 202, 203
Admiralty Rule 46-½, 143, 144
Adverse possession, 23
Advisory jury, 144
Age, 40
Agricultural Adjustment Act, 171
Air Line Dispatchers Ass'n v National Mediation Board, 171
Airplane pilot, 33, 47
Alimony, 44
Anti-trust:
 boycotts, 23
 division of markets and territory, 24
 insufficient evidence, 139
 monopoly, 24
 price fixing, 23, 76, 78
 tying arrangements, 24
 "unless clearly erroneous" rule, 176, 180, 189
 use of patents to coerce, 24
"APA," 158, 160–162, 164–169
"Arbitrary," 161, 162
Arkansas Valley Land Co. v Mann, 207
Arrow Transportation Co. v Northwest Grocery Co., 87–88
Ashworth Transfer Inc. v United States, 130

Assumpsit, 23
Atewooftakewd v Udall, 164
Attaint, 60–61
Attorney fees, 25
Automobile, leaving road, 95

B

"Badges of fraud," 79
Banking Act, 170
Baumann v Maloney Concrete Co., 56
Baumgartner v United States, 147
Beacon Theatres v Westover, 201–202
Berenyi v Immigration Director, 178
Bernhardt v Polygraphic Co., 204
Bill of Sale, 43
Bills, 24, 46
Blunt v Little, 208
"Boeing Company" rule, 66–68
Boeing Company v Shipman, 66, 213
Bonica v Olesen, 166
Broker, 24
Brown Paper Co. v Irvin, 152
Business cases, 41–42, 137–138, 189–190
Byrd v Blue Ridge Cooperative, 204

C

California Western State Life Ins. Co. v Vaughan, 111
"Candor and credibility" of witness, 176–177
Cappadora v Celebrezze, 172
"Capricious," 161, 162
Cardelis v Refineria Panama, S.A., 183
Causation, 134–135
Cause, 40

Certiorari, writs, 63–64, 65, 67, 201, 213, 215
Charles L. D., 150
Chattel mortgage, 43
Child, 44
C.I.R. v Duberstein, 182
Circumstantial evidence:
  collective impact, 72–74, 76–80
    "badges of fraud," 79
    circumstances when taken together, 73
    definition, 73
    fraudulent transfers of property, 79
    most evident in fraudulent schemes or conspiracy, 73
    recent successful application, 77–78
    validity first recognized, 73–74
  conspiracy, 74–80
    anti-trust laws in a price fixing case, 76, 78
    corporation and its employees or its officers and directors, 76
    equivocal circumstantial evidence, 76
    inferred participation, 74
    insufficient circumstantial evidence, 74–76
    knowledge and scienter, 76
    knowledge of purpose, 74
    law review articles pertinent, 80–81
    sufficient circumstantial evidence, 74–79
    two or more persons, 74, 76
  fraudulent scheme, 74, 76, 79
  fraudulent scheme—conspiracy case, 77–78
  illustration, 71–72
  implied consent, 97–98
  implied-in-fact contracts, 99–108
  (*see also* Implied-in-fact contracts)
  "more probable than not" rule, 83–89
    Arrow Transportation Co. v Northwest Grocery Co., 87–88
    Coburn v Utah Home Fire Ins. Co., 86
    collisions, head-on, 87
    Conger v Dant and Russell, Inc., 86
    Kaufman v Fisher, 85, 88
    mostly evident in negligence cases, 83
    not beyond criticism, 88
    not everything put to jury, 86–89
    one of most articulate expressions, 85
    Southern Pacific Co. v Campbell McLean, Inc., 86
    test of preponderating probabilities, 85, 88
    testing worth, 87

not inferior to direct, 71
pertinent law review articles, 96
pyramiding of inference upon inference, 95–96
  basic inference not too remote or conjectural, 96
  conspiracy, 95–96
res ipsa loquitur, 89–95
  defendant had control of event, 91–92
  defendant knows cause of injury, 94
  definition, 89–90
  FELA and Jones Act cases, 95
  inclusive within "more probable than not" rule, 89
  injured passenger, 92
  Lux Art Van Service, Inc. v Pollard, 91
  meaning in English, 89
  negligence without the unusual, 91
  not applicable in *Otis Elevator Co. v Robinson,* 93
  plaintiff knows cause of injury, 94
  policy considerations, 93–94
  product liability case, 92
  single vehicle inexplicably leaving highway, 95
  ultra-hazardous products under defendant's control, 93–94
  unusual accidents, 89
  unusual which suggests negligence, 90, 92
  Weeks v Latter Day Saints Hospital, 91
  Zenty v Coca Cola Bottling Co. of Fresno, 89–90
  reserving rulings on motion to strike, 79–80
Citizenship:
  diversity, 22, 58, 66, 67, 68, 69, 204
  residence and, 41
Civil Aeronautics Board or Administrator, 170
Civil rights, 25, 187
Civil Service Commission, 169
Coburn v Utah Home Fire Ins. Co., 86
Coleman v United States, 163
Collateral estopple, 142, 147
Collective impact, 72–74, 76–80
  (*see also* Circumstantial evidence)
Collision:
  head-on, 87
  marine, 34–35, 185
Commissioner of Internal Revenue, 169–170
Commissioner v Duberstein, 177
Comparative negligence concept, 106, 186
Competition, unfair, 41

Comptroller of Currency-Banking Act, 170
Conclusion, 144–145
Conger v Dant and Russell, Inc., 86
Consent, implied, 97–98
Consolo v Federal Maritime Commission, 170
Conspiracy, circumstantial evidence, 74–80
  (*see also* Circumstantial evidence)
  "unless clearly erroneous" rule, 180
  question of fact, 40
Constitutional right, privilege or immunity, 178
Contempt, 40, 203
Contract:
  abandonment, 25–26
  breach, 26, 27, 33, 44
  cases, 42–44, 135–137, 191–192
  express, defined, 99
  implied-in-fact, 99–108
  (*see also* Implied-in-fact contracts)
  maritime, vessel, 35
  "quasi," 99, 105
  rescission for breach, 26
  rescission, induced by fraud, 26
  reformation, 25
  specific performance, 26–27
Credibility, witness, 1761–177
Cruelty, extreme, 44
Curtis Publishing Co. v Butts, 212
Custom and usage, 40

D

Dagnello v Long Island Railroad Co., 210, 211, 212
Dairy Queen, Inc. v Wood, District Judge, 202
Dalehite v United States, 145, 179
Damages:
  amount and kind, 40, 192–194
  breach of contract, 27
  cargo, vessel, 34
  civil rights, 25
  destruction or loss of property, 27
  fire, 44, 47
  insufficient evidence, 135
  lightning, 45, 46
  liquidated, 43
  punitive, 27
  "unless clearly erroneous" rule, 185–187, 192–194
  wrongful death, pecuniary loss, 27–28
Death:
  by other than use of liquor, 44
  except as result of internal disease, 44

high seas, wrongful act, 32
  seaman, from unseaworthiness, 31–32
  wrongful, 27–28, 32
Debt, acknowledging, 104
Declaratory judgment, 28
Dedication to public, 40
Deed, delivery, 40
Defense Production Act of 1950, 169
Delivery, deed, 40
Dell Publishing Co. v Day, 171
Demurrer to evidence, 61
Denver and R.G.W.R. Co. v Union Pacific R. Co., 166
Description, land, 47
Dimick v Schiedt, 208, 211, 212
Directed verdict, motion:
  after opening statement, before evidence, 54
  before end of proof, 55
  burden of persuasion, 57
  carry over from common law, 53
  challenging all evidence, 56
  close of plaintiff's case in chief, 54
  decision on merits, 55
  doubt about deciding, 58–59
  effect, 52
  granted at intermediate stage, 54
  mistrial or "hung jury," 58
  motion for new trial, 59
  moving party not having burden of proof, 55
  plaintiff carrying burden of proof, 55–56
  preclude re-filing new action, 55
  required before motion for judgment notwithstanding verdict, 57–58
  Seventh Amendment, 206
  state specific grounds, 54
  when made, 51–52
  written requested instruction as equivalent, 58
Disability, total, 45
Discretion, abuse of, 164
Di Silvestre v United States, 159
Diversity case, 22, 58, 66, 67, 68, 69, 204
Divorce cases, 44
Domiciliary issue for homestead claim, 196
Drowning, 46
Duress, 40
Dutchess County Aviation Adm. v Federal Aviation Agency, 170

E

Ejectment, 28

Elliot v Federal Home Loan Bank Board, 170
Equity practice and principles, 202
Erie R. Co. v Tomkins, 204
Errion v Connell, 77–78, 150
Estopple:
  collateral, 142, 147
  in pais, 28
  waiver and, 41
Evergreens v Nunan, 147
Evidence:
  circumstantial, 71–108
  (*see also* Circumstantial evidence)
  conflicting, 181
  demurrer, 61
  insufficient, 129–139
    anti-trust cases, 139
    Ashworth Transfer Inc. v United States, 130
    business transactions, 137–138
    causation, 134–135
    damages, 135
    double talk, 129–130
    insurance policy or contract cases, 135–137
    negligence, 131–133
    NLRB unfair labor charge, 138
    promissory notes, 139
    tax cases, 137
  sufficiency, challenging, 51–69
  (*see also* Directed verdict, motion; judgment notwithstanding verdict, motion)
    common law cases tried before a jury, 66
    diversity case, 58, 66, 67
    federal courts, federal law, 58
    measuring stick, 60–68
    motion to strike particular allegation, 56
    motion to withdraw specific issue, 56
    naming standard applied, 64
    pertinent law review articles, 68
    rehearing *en banc,* 66
    relaxed view of Supreme Court, 64
    requesting peremptory instruction to jury, 56
    substantial evidence, 60–68
    (*see also* Substantial evidence)
Evidentiary findings, 145, 146
Excessive verdict, 207–212
Express contract, 99

F

Fair Labor Standards Act, 196, 203
Fairmount Glass Works v Coal Co., 211, 212

Farley v United States, 149
Federal Administration Procedure Act, 158, 160–162, 164–169
Federal Aviation Agency, 170
Federal Communication Commission, 170
Federal Home Loan Bank Board or Federal Savings and Loan Ins. Corp., 170
Federal Maritime Commission—Shipping Act, 170
Federal Power Commission—Natural Gas Act, 171
Federal Tort Claim Act, 203
Federal Trade Commission, 171
FELA and Jones Act cases:
  comparative negligence features, 64
  injury to railroad employee, 31
  relaxed view of Supreme Court, 64
  res ipsa loquitur, 95
  reversing *per curiam,* 65
  "scintilla," 64, 212
  "substantial evidence" not measuring stick, 66
  writs of certiorari, 63–64, 65, 67
  wrongful death, 32
Findings of fact:
  after notice of appeal is filed, 156
  appellate review, 175–197
  collateral estopple, 146
  concise but meaningful, 145
  conclusions, 144–145
  court-fashioned versus attorney-fashioned, 148–150
    Charles L. D., 150
    commingling fact and law, 150
    common sense on case to case basis, 149
    complex technical case, 149
    every case different, 148–149
    Farley v United States, 149
    ideal, 148
    not mere recital of evidence, 150, 152
    Polarusoil-Sandefjord, 149
  Dalehite v United States, 145
  damages sustained for repair of vessel, 150
  de novo, 177
  distinguished from "conclusion of fact," 155
  Evergreens v Nunan, 146
  Great Atlantic and Pacific Tea Co. vs Supermarket Equipment Corp., 145
  Hartford-Empire Co. v Shawkee Mfg. Co., 142
  inadequate, 152–155, 164–166
    Brown Paper Co. v Irvin, 152
    crucial fact, 154

failing to find "stepping stone" finding, 154
failing to include finding on essential fact, 154
no co-tenancy existed between plaintiff and defendant, 155
no findings of fact, 153
overlooking essential finding not in dispute, 153
plaintiff "has sustained burden of proof," 155
setting aside agency action, 164–166
Tug Port of Bandon, 154
Zack Metal Co. v S. S. Birmingham City, 152
judicial review, 157–172
(*see also* Judicial review of agency findings)
Kelly vs Everglades Drainage District, 145
kinds, 145–147
  evidentiary, 145, 146
  general, 145, 146
  special, 145, 146
  subsidiary, "mediate" or "stepping stone," 145, 146, 147
  ultimate, 145, 146, 147
most vital step to judgment, 141–142
personal injury case, 150
pertinent law review articles, 156
quality varies, 147–148
  Baumgartner v United States, 147
  findings based on writings, 148
  "negligence" finding, 148
  revocation of citizen's naturalization certificate, 147
  Schneiderman vs United States, 148
  staying power of finding on review, 147
  "unless clearly erroneous," 147–148
Ramos v Matson Navigation Co., 145
res adjudica, 147
Rule 52, 142–144
(*see also* Rule 52)
securities fraud, *Errion v Connell,* 150
settling, 150–151
significant purposes, 141–142
"unless clearly erroneous" rule, 175–197
(*see also* "Unless clearly erroneous" rule)
what they are not, 155–156
Fire damage, 44, 47
First National Bank of Smithfield, North Carolina v Saxon, 170
Florida v United States, 166
Food, Drug and Cosmetic Act, 28
Fourteenth Amendment, 204

Fraud:
  common law, 28
  purchase or sale of securities, 28–30
Fraudulent scheme, 74, 76, 79
Fraudulent transfer, 30
Freeman v Brown, 171

G

General findings, 145, 146
Good faith, 40
Gorsalitz v Olin Mathiesen Chemical Corp., 208
Grace Lines, Inc. v Motley, 58
Grace Lines v Federal Maritime Board, 163
Great Atlantic and Pacific Tea Co. vs Supermarket Equipment Corp., 145
Grunenthal v Long Island Railroad, 211

H

Habeas corpus proceedings, 196
Halcyon Lines v Haenn Ship Ceiling and Refitting Corp., 106, 107
Hanley v Hedler, 56
Hartford-Empire Co. v Shawkee Mfg. Co., 142
Hazardous products, 93–94
Hicks v United States, 183
Hill v Waxberg, 100
Hoffa v United States, 179
Hoffman v C.I.R., 119
Homestead claim, domiciliary issue, 196
Hospital bills, 46
Housing discrimination, 197

I

Ideas, furnishing for boss, 102–103
Identity, 40
Implied consent, 97–98
Implied-in-fact contracts:
  agreement to later agree-not contract, 99–100
  called "quasi," 99
  defined, 99
  furnishing ideas for the boss, 102–103
  furnishing things or services, 100–102
  Hill v Waxberg, 100
  implied covenants to express contracts, 103–104
    customs and usages of particular trade, 104
    general principle, 103

Implied-in-fact contracts (*cont.*)
   two situations, 104
   where party acknowledges debt, 104
   Wood v Lucy, Lady Duff-Gordon,
     103–104
  maritime indemnity, 105–107
   comparative negligence concept, 106
   eternal triangle, 106
   Halcyon Lines v Haenn Ship Ceiling
     and Refitting Corp., 106, 107
   Jones Act, 105
   Longshoremen's and Harbor Workers
     Act, 105
   McLaughlin v Trelleborgs Angfar-
     tygs, 107
   Ryan Stevedoring Co. v Pan-Atlantic
     SS. Corp., 105, 106, 107
   Seas Shipping Co. v Sieracki, 105,
     106, 107
  Merritt-Chapman and Scott Corp. v
     Gunderson Bros. Eng. Corp., 100
  Milone and Tucci, Inc. v Bonafide
     Builders, Inc., 100
  Western Asphalt Co. v Valle, 100
Implied covenants to express contracts,
   103–104
  (*see also* Implied-in-fact contracts)
Imprisonment, false, 28
Improvement Co. v Munson, 62
Inadequate award, 207–212
Indemnity, 35, 105–107
Indirect evidence
(*see* Circumstantial evidence)
Influences:
  distinguished from presumptions, 109–
   111
  pyramiding, 95–96
Influence, undue, 41
Injury:
  facts necessary to be found, 31
  passenger, 92
  permanent, 41
  personal, 186–187, 203, 208
Insufficient evidence, 129–139
(*see also* Evidence)
Insurance policy cases, 30, 44–45, 191–
  192
Intent, 40, 180
Interpleader, 30–31
Interstate Commerce Commission, 171
Invention, 41

J

Jackson v United States, 177
Jenkins v Macy, 169
Jones Act, 105, 203, 212

(*see also* FELA and Jones Act cases)
Judgement notwithstanding verdict, motion:
  conditional rulings on grant, 52–53, 59
  denial, 53
  entered or re-entered, 60
  mistrial or "hung jury," 58
  motion for directed verdict required,
   57–58
  motion for new trial, 52, 59
  motion to strike evidence or pleadings,
   57
  when made, 52, 57
  written requested instruction for directed verdict, 58
Judicial notice:
  facts of common knowledge, 122–123
  facts of which federal courts have taken,
   123–126
  pertinent law review articles, 126–127
Judicial review of agency findings:
  abuse of discretion, 164
  actions not subject to review, 159–160
  arbitrary or capricious, 162–163
  contrary to constitutional right, power,
   privilege or immunity, 168
  excess of statutory jurisdiction, 168
  Federal Administration Procedure Act
   ("APA"), 158, 160–162, 164–169
  how and where to get, 169–172
  inadequate findings, 164–166
  lack of substantial evidence, 166–167
  pertinent law review articles, 172–173
  requirements, 158–159
   Rasmussen v United States, 158
   relevancy of aggrievement, 158–159
   truly being aggrieved, 158
  ripeness for review, 160
  scope limited, 161
  "unwarranted by facts" where review
   subject to trial *de novo,* 168–169
  without observance of procedure required by law, 168
Justification, 41

K

Kaufman v Fisher, 85, 88
Kelly v Everglades Drainage District, 145

L

Labor:
  damages against union for breach of
   contract, 33

recover unpaid wages below minimum, 32–33
"unless clearly erroneous," 189–190
unpaid minimum wages, air pilot, 33
Land:
  abandonment, 40
  adverse possession, 40
  condemnation, 203
  description, 47
  fraudulent transfer, 79
Legal Aid attorney, 197
Liability:
  vessel, limitation, 35
  product, 92
Life insurance, 30
Lightning, 45, 46
Liquidation, corporation, 163
Longshoremen's and Harbor Workers Act, 105
Louisiana Workmen's Compensation Act, 204
Louisville and N. R. Co. v United States, 163
Lundgren v Freeman, 182
Lux Art Van Service, Inc. v Pollard, 91

M

Malicious prosecution, 48
Malpractice, 84, 94
Mamiye Bros. v Backe Steamship Lines, Inc., 184
Maritime implied-in-fact indemnity contract, 105–107
May Dept. Stores v N.L.R.B., 171
Mayfield Casualty Co. v Williams, 113
McAllister v United States, 175
McFarland v Gregory, 114
McGowan v United States, 181
McLaughlin v Trilleborgs Angfartygs, 107
"Mechanical" rules, 185–187
"Mediate" findings (subsidiary), 145, 146, 147
Mental capacity, 41
Merritt-Chapman and Scott Corp. v Gunderson Bros. Eng. Corp., 100
Miller Act, 203
Miller v United States, 74–75
Milone and Tucci, Inc. v Bonafide Builders, Inc., 100
Mississippi River Fuel Corp. v Federal Power Comm., 163
Mitchell Bros. Truck Lines v United States, 165
Mixed question, 38
Morrison v California, 122

N

National Enforcement Commission, 169–170
National Labor Relations Board, 33, 138, 171
National Mediation Board, 171
National Trailer Convoy, Inc. v United States, 162
Natural Gas Act, 171
Naturalization:
  certificate, 147
  petition, 178
Neely v Martin K. Elby Construction Co., 59
Neese, Admx. v Southern R. Co., 211
Negligence, 31, 45–47, 64, 106, 131–133, 145, 148, 179, 183–184, 185, 186, 194
  (*see also* Circumstantial evidence)
New trial, 59, 205
NLRB unfair labor charge, 138
Non-tort claim, U.S., 33–34
Notes, 24, 139
Nuisance, 41

O

Oak Mfg. Co. v United States, 170
Orvis v Higgins, 182
Otis Elevator Co. v Robinson, 93

P

"Paper case," 182–183
Partnership, 42
Passenger, injured, 92
Patent cases, 189–190
Payment, voluntary, 41
Pedestrians, 46
Personal injury, 186–187, 203, 208
Pilot, plane, 33, 47
Planters Manufacturing Co. v Protection Mut. Ins. Co., 66
Polarusoil—Sandefjord, 149
Possession, adverse, 23
Postmaster General, 171
Pre Fab Transit Co. v United States, 163
"Preponderating probability" concept, 85, 88
Presumptions:
  arise simultaneously with inferences, 111
  California Western State Life Ins. Co. v Vaughan, 111
  conclusive, 120–122

Presumptions *(cont.)*
  constitutionality, 121–122
  deduction law directs made from particular facts, 110
  distinguished from inferences, 109–111
  examined for rationality to support inference, 111
  indirect evidence, 109
  Morrison v California, 122
  pertinent law review articles, 127
  procedural effects, 110
  rebuttable, 113–120
    codified inferences, 113
    continuity, inference of backward relation, 114–115
    founded upon public policy as well as reason, 115–117
    Hoffman v C.I.R., 119
    in aid of business transactions, 117–119
    McFarland v Gregory, 114
    ordinary course of nature, ordinary habits of life, 115
    useful in carrying burden of persuasion, 119–120
  Rehm v United States, 110
  rule of law requiring inference, 111
  state created, in federal courts, 112–113
    Mayfield Casualty Co. v Williams, 113
    Rule 43(a) of Federal Rules of Civil Procedure, 112
    Weber v Continental Casualty Co., 112–113
  United States v Bowen, 121
Price fixing, 23, 76, 78
Price v Udall, 163
Principal and agent cases, 48–49
Principal, non-disclosed or partially disclosed, 24
Product:
  hazardous, 93–94
  liability case, 92
Promissory notes, 139
Property *(see* Land)
"Purpose," 180

Q

"Quasi" contract, 99, 105
Questions of fact:
  business transaction cases, 41–42
  contract cases, 42–44
  different from mixed question, 38
  distinguished from question of law, 38–39
  divorce cases, 44

few reserved for court, not jury, 39
general cases, 40–41
insurance policy cases, 44–45
malicious prosecution and slander cases, 48
negligence cases, 45–47
principal and agent cases, 48–49
real property cases, 49
tax cases, 49–50
Questions of law, 38–39

R

Racial prejudice, 196
Railroad, 33
Railroad workers, 31, 66, 95
Ramos v Matson Navigation Co., 145
Rasmussen v United States, 158
Real property cases, 49
Reasonableness, 41
Rebuttable presumptions, 113–120
(see also Presumptions)
Recission, 42
Rehearing *en banc,* 66
Rehm v United States, 110
Remittur, 208
Res ipsa loquitur, 89–95
(see also Circumstantial evidence)
Res judicata, 142, 147
Residence and citizenship, 41
Reynolds v Penn R. R. Co., 54
Richardson v City of Boston, 61
Right by prescription, 23
Rogers v Missouri Pacific Railroad Co., 63, 64, 65
Ross v Bernhard, 202
Rule 10B-5, Securities and Exchange Commission, 28, 29, 151
Rule 42(b) FRCP, 202
Rule 43(a) of Federal Rules of Civil Procedure, 112
Rule 46-½, 143, 144
Rule 50:
  constitutional, 53
  doesn't violate Seventh Amendment, 53
  elimination of waiver traps, 53–54
  motion for new trial, 59
  reads, 52–53
Rule 52 *(see also* "Unless clearly erroneous" rule):
  amendment, 144
  application, 144
  effect, 143–144
  law, equity and admiralty cases, 143
Rule 70, 144
Ryan Stevedoring Co. v Pan-Atlantic SS. Corp., 105, 106, 107

S

Safeway Stores v Fannon, 55
Schneiderman v United States, 148
"Scintilla" rule, 61–65, 67–68, 212
S. D. Warren Co. v N.L.R.B., 163
Seaman, 31, 66, 95
Seas Shipping Co. v Sieracki, 105, 106, 107
Seaworthiness, 31–32, 105, 106, 107, 145
Secretary of Agriculture—Agricultural Adjustment Act, 171
Secretary of Health, Education and Welfare—Social Security Act, 171–172
Securities:
  application for registration, 42
  fraud, 28–29, 150
Securities Act of 1933, 29
Securities and Exchange Act of 1934, 29–30
Senkler v Missouri Pacific Railroad, 65
Servant, 43
Seventh Amendment:
  according to rules of the common law, 205–206
  action under Federal Tort Claim Act, 203
  additur, 208–209, 211, 212
  admiralty cases, 202, 203
  "any court of the United States," 204–205
  Arkansas Valley Land Co. v Mann, 207
  bankruptcy court summarily adjudicates creditor's preference, 203
  Beacon Theatres v Westover, 201–202
  Bernhardt v Polygraphic Co., 204–205
  Blunt v Little, 208
  Boeing Company v Shipman, 213
  Byrd v Blue Ridge Cooperative, 204
  cases reversed by Supreme Court, 213–215
  found no violation, 215
  condemnation of land, 203
  criminal contempt, 203
  Curtis Publishing Co. v Butts, 212
  Dagnello v Long Island Railroad Co., 210, 211, 212
  Dairy Queen Inc. v Wood, District Judge, 202
  denial of certiorari with dissent, 215
  Dimick v Schiedt, 208, 211, 212
  directed verdict, 206
  diversity of citizenship, 204
  due process clause of Fourteenth Amendment, 204
  equity practice and principles, 202
  Erie R. Co. v Tomkins, 204

excessive verdict or inadequate award, 207–212
  appellate court review, 209–212
  trial court review, 207–209
  Fairmount Glass Works v Coal Co., 211, 212
  Gorsalitz v Olin Mathiesen Chemical Corp., 208
  Grunenthal v Long Island Railroad, 211
  how Supreme Court has enforced, 212–213
  Jones Act claim for personal injury, 203
  Miller Act action based upon equitable rights, 203
  Neese, Admx. v Southern R. Co., 211
  new trial, 205
  original action in Supreme court between State and U.S., 203
  practices within ambit, 206–207
  remittur, 208
  right to trial by jury preserved, 200–203
  Ross v Bernhard, 202
  segregation of jury issues, 201–202
  seventeenth century, 199–200
  severance pay, 202–203
  stated, 199
  stockholder's derivative action, 203
  sue U.S. for money judgment, 203
  trial by jury not preserved, 202–203
  unfair employment practice case, 203
  Williams v Florida, 206
Severance pay, 202–203
Ship collision, 185
Shipping Act, 1916, 170
Sindicato Puertorriqueno de Trabajadores v Hodgson, 166
Slander cases, 48
Slavers (Reindeer), 73–74
Social Security Act, 171
Soucie v Trautwein Brothers, 56
Southern Pacific Co. v Campbell McLean, Inc., 86
Special findings, 145, 146
Stairs, 46
State of North Carolina v United States, 166
"Stepping stone" findings (subsidiary), 145, 146, 147
Stevedore, 35, 105–107
Subsidiary findings, 145, 146, 147
"Substantial evidence":
  "Boering Company" rule, 66–68
  current struggle, 63–68
  diversity, 67
  FELA and Jones Act, 63–68

"Substantial evidence" (*cont.*)
  (*see also* FELA and Jones Act cases)
  history, 60–63
    demurrer to evidence, 61
    judges to decide law, 61
    jurors to decide fact, 61
    court supervision over jury verdict, 61
    "scintilla" rule, 61–65, 67–68
    liberal, 62
    rule, definition, 62
    setting aside verdict, granting new trial, 62–63
    verdict against weight of all evidence, 62

T

Tallman v Udall, 163
Tax cases, 49–50, 137, 194–195
Tort claim, U.S., 34
Tug Port of Bandon, 154, 185
"Two courts below" rule, 178–179

U

Ultimate findings, 145, 146, 147, 179–181
Undue influence, 41
Unfair competition, 41
United States:
  non-tort claim, 33–34
  tort-claim, 34
United States Immigration and Naturalization Service, 172
United States v Baltimore and O. R. Co., 166
United States v Bowen, 121
United States v General Motors, 180, 183
United States v Mississippi Valley Co., 180
United States v National Assn. of Real Estate Boards, 177
United States v Oregon State Medical Society, 183
United States v Parke, Davis and Co., 180
United States v Singer Mfg. Co., 180
United States v United States Gypsum Co., 176, 177
"Unless clearly erroneous" rule:
  admiralty cases, 187–189
  anti-trust case, 176, 180, 189
  appellate court lets down bars, 147–148
  application relaxed, 181–184
  assistance from Legal Aid attorney, 197

Berenyi v Immigration Director, 178
business, labor and patent cases, 189–190
"candor and credibility" of witness, 176–177
Cardelis v Refineria Panama, S.A., 183
cases reversed by federal courts, 187–197
character of record on appeal, 181
C.I.R. v Duberstein, 182
commerce, Fair Labor Standards Act, 196
Commissioner v Duberstein, 177
comparative negligence case, 186
conflicting evidence, 181
conspiracy, 180
Constitutional right, privilege or immunity, 178
contract and insurance policy cases, 191–192
Dalehite v United States, 179
damages, 185–187, 192–194
domiciliary issue for homestead claim, 196
evidence misunderstood on critical point, 185
expert opinion, 183–184
fact finding *de novo,* 177
Great Atlantic and Pacific Tea Co. v Supermarket Equipment Corp., 180
habeas corpus proceedings, 196
Hicks v United States, 183
Hoffa v United States, 179
housing discrimination, 197
"intent" or "purpose," 180
Jackson v United States, 177
law, equity, admiralty, 176–178
"live witnesses," 181
Lundgren v Freeman, 182
Mamiye Bros. v Backe Steamship Lines, Inc., 184
McAllister v United States, 175
McGowan v United States, 181
"Mechanical" rules, 185–187
monetary interest not established, 196
negligence, 179, 183–184, 185, 186, 194
Orvis v Higgins, 182
"paper case," fact review, 182–183
personal injury, 186–187
petition for naturalization, 178
protective findings against reversa', 184–185
racial prejudice, 196
reasonable inquiry, 196
returning veteran, former job, 196
ship collision, 185
stated, 176

Supreme Court limits application, 178
tax cases, 194–195
temporary injunction in civil rights case, 187
time credit to convict, 196
Tug Port of Bandon, 185
"two courts below" rule, 178–179
ultimate findings excepted, 179–181
United States v General Motors, 180, 183
United States v Mississippi Valley Co., 180
United States v National Assn. of Real Estate Boards, 177
United States v Oregon State Med. Soc., 183
United States v Parke, Davis and Co., 180
United States v Singer Mfg. Co., 180
United States v United States Gypsum Co., 176, 177
voting in election, 196
Zenith Radio Corp. v Hazeltine Research, Inc., 177
Unseaworthiness, 31–32, 105, 106

V

Vehicle, inexplicably leaving highway, 95
Vessel:
indemnity by owner against stevedore, 35
limitation of liability, 35
loss or damage to cargo, 34
marine collision, 34–35
maritime contract, 35

non-statutory maritime lien against, 34
statutory maritime lean against, 34
Veteran, job, 196
Voluntary payment, 41
Vucinic v United States Immigration and Naturalization Service, 172

W

Waiver and estopple, 41
Warranty, 42
Water carrier, 36
Weber v Continental Casualty Co., 112–113
Weeks v Latter Day Saints Hospital, 9↳
Western Asphalt Co. v Valle, 100
Wheatley v Adler, 162
Will, execution, 41
Williams v Florida, 206
Williams v Slade, 55
Wood v Lucy, Lady Duff-Gordon, 103–104
Writs of certiorari, 63–64, 65, 67, 201, 213, 215
Writs of mandamus, 201

Z

Zack Metal Co. v S. S. Birmingham City, 152
Zenith Radio Corp. v Hazeltine Research, Inc., 177
Zentz v Coca Cola Bottling Co. of Fresno, 89–90